INTERNET ON THE OUTSTATION

THE DIGITAL DIVIDE AND REMOTE ABORIGINAL COMMUNITIES

ELLIE RENNIE,
ELEANOR HOGAN,
ROBIN GREGORY,
ANDREW CROUCH,
ALYSON WRIGHT &
JULIAN THOMAS

Theory on Demand #19

Internet on the Outstation:
The Digital Divide and Remote Aboriginal Communities

Authors: Ellie Rennie, Eleanor Hogan, Robin Gregory, Andrew Crouch, Alyson Wright, Julian Thomas
Editorial support: Miriam Rasch

Cover design: Katja van Stiphout
DTP: Léna Robin
EPUB development: Léna Robin

Printer: Print on Demand
Publisher: Institute of Network Cultures, Amsterdam, 2016
ISBN: 978-94-92302-07-6

Contact
Institute of Network Cultures
Phone: +31 20 5951865
Email: info@networkcultures.org
Web: http://www.networkcultures.org

This publication is available through various print on demand services.
EPUB and PDF editions of this publication are freely downloadable from
our website, http://www.networkcultures.org/publications/#tods

Institute of
network cultures

Contents

ACKNOWLEDGEMENTS

We are indebted to the residents of Imangara, Kwale Kwale and Mungalawurru communities in the Northern Territory for sharing their time and knowledge with us, and for their active involvement in what they referred to as 'the computer project'.

Internet on the Outstation is the result of a multi-year collaboration between the Swinburne Institute for Social Research, the Centre for Appropriate Technology (CAT), the Central Land Council (CLC), and the Australian Communications Consumer Action Network (ACCAN). Ellie Rennie, Eleanor Hogan and Julian Thomas were all based at Swinburne when the research and writing for this book occurred. Andrew Crouch and Robin Gregory were working at CAT, and Alyson Wright was working for the CLC.

CAT is an Aboriginal not-for-profit organization that works towards sustainable livelihoods for those living in remote communities, and conducts research into, and development of, appropriate technologies. CAT was formed in the 1980s when the outstation movement was gaining momentum, and much of its work today is still focused on small remote communities, known as 'outstations'. In CAT's definition, appropriate technologies meet the economic, cultural, environmental and social needs of the people, and design and development occurs through consultation and collaboration with communities. In his history of CAT, Alan Mayne writes that CAT's 'appropriate technologies', 'together with the research and design process that produces them, their regular servicing and the training and education programmes that inform their use, are making a difference in communities throughout remote Australia'.[1]

The CLC is a statutory body set up under the Aboriginal Land Rights Act (NT). The CLC's history is deeply imbued with Aboriginal justice, recognition and the fight for land rights. The primary functions of the CLC are to help traditional landowners in the management of their country in the southern half of the Northern Territory. Through advocacy and policy work, the ninety-member Council also represents the interests, rights and concerns of Aboriginal people across regions.

The CLC believes that the provision of access to communications technologies is an essential service in remote communities. The focus of much of their work in this area has been on addressing disadvantages in service and access levels for remote residents, affordability issues, rights to service and increasing the choice of communication options for remote communities. The CLC remains concerned about the future of small remote communities in Central Australia because of a lack of funding commitment from both levels of government, and an increasing move to prioritize larger communities when

---

1   A. Mayne, *Alternative Interventions: Aboriginal homelands, outback Australia and the Centre for Appropriate Technology*, Adelaide: Wakefield Press, 2014, p. 136.

allocating funding. This is despite a robust determination of traditional owners to remain living on or near their country.

ACCAN is Australia's peak body for consumer representation in communications, spanning residential consumers and small businesses, including not-for profit organizations, insofar as they are consumers. ACCAN assists people to make good choices about products and services, and makes representations to policy makers and industry on behalf of its broad and diverse membership.

The Swinburne Institute for Social Research is located within Swinburne University of Technology in Melbourne. A core group of researchers within the Institute is looking at digital transformations, and how they are impacting on Australia's economy, social inclusion, cultural policy, health and wellbeing. The Institute is also a node of the ARC Centre of Excellence for Creative Industries and Innovation (CCI), led by Stuart Cunningham, and our research in Central Australia was conducted as part of CCI's wider research program on the social, economic and cultural dimensions of broadband services.

A number of people from each of these organizations provided additional assistance during the project. Thanks are due to Ruth Elvin for her encouragement and advice during her time at CAT; Julian Cleary and Peter Donohoe from CLC for stepping in during Alyson's maternity leave; Robin McNaughton, Michael Charlton, Teresa Corbin, Una Lawrence and Ryan Sengara from ACCAN for their contributions; and Jake Goldenfein from Swinburne for assisting us during the Papunya research fieldwork, and for collaborating on research into the Northern Territory Emergency Response (NTER; known as 'the Intervention').

The research was funded in three phases. ACCAN's Grants Scheme funded the first phase of the project (the 'baseline study') in 2010. As the peak consumer representation body in communications, ACCAN awards grants each year for research and advocacy projects that align with its goal of available, accessible and affordable communications for all Australians. We are very grateful to ACCAN for kickstarting this research, and for continuing on the project after that grant concluded. CCI's support, especially in the early stages of the work, was also critical.

The Aboriginals Benefit Account funded the hardware, maintenance and training components of the project. As described in the book, CAT led the technical and training aspects of the work, and undertook regular visits to the communities to provide them with assistance.

The data collection for the social research (2011-2014) was funded through an Australian Research Council (ARC) Linkage Project grant. In addition to the ARC funding, each organization contributed substantial in-kind time. In particular, CAT provided Andrew's time, CLC provided Alyson's time (and car), and Swinburne contributed Ellie and Julian's time. The Swinburne research team also received a grant from Google Australia, which enabled us to do additional work on the NTER legislation and its implications for funded computers.

During the course of the project, we conducted research in two larger communities. We would like to thank the people of Ali Curung and Papunya for allowing us to carry out this work. In particular, we thank Jessie Simpson and Roseanne Holmes, who worked with Ellie and Alyson to administer the Ali Curung survey, and provided invaluable cultural advice regarding questions to be included. Derek Walker assisted Peter Donohoe with the 'men's side' of the Ali Curung survey. We are grateful to both of them for helping rectify the gender imbalance in our original survey results. We also thank Sammy Butcher at Papunya for his support of the study; Ashton Kealy, Mary McMullen, Rebecca Smith and Ryan Raggatt for their assistance in the computer room; and Jenny and Blair McFarland at the Central Australian Youth Link Up Service (CAYLUS) for providing ongoing information about Information and Communications Technology (ICT) arrangements in the MacDonnell region.

We wish also to thank the members of the Project Reference Group for their advice and guidance. Membership of the Reference Group shifted over time, and included representatives of the Australian government Department of Broadband, Communications and the Digital Economy; the Indigenous Remote Communications Association; the ARC Centre of Excellence for Creative Industries and Innovation; and senior officers of the sponsoring organizations.

Broadband for the Bush (B4B) emerged as a key forum for us to discuss our findings over the course of the project, and to make connections with other organizations working on similar issues. We thank the members of B4B for their committed advocacy and policy development work, and for bringing the communication needs of Indigenous people living in remote areas to the attention of policymakers and telcos.

Finally, the genesis of this work was a conversation between two old friends in 2009: Julian Thomas, Director of the Swinburne Institute for Social Research, and the late Peter Taylor when he was CEO of CAT. Ellie Rennie (who was living in Alice Springs and working for the Swinburne Institute) was introduced to CAT through that connection, and began to explore the issue of the digital divide with Andrew Crouch in 2009. The project would not have happened if it were not for Peter's passion for communications and his deep knowledge of the circumstances of remote communities. His sudden death in 2013 was a great loss for central Australia.

Sections of this book have been adapted from our own prior publications: the opening anecdote comes from an *Inside Story* article.[2] Part of the cyber safety discussion in

2   E. Rennie, 'Internet on the Outstation', *Inside Story*, 9 May 2011, http://insidestory.org.au/internet-on-the-outstation.

Chapter 5 was also published in *Inside Story*.[3] The discussion of gender in Chapter 7 appears in *Australian Aboriginal Studies*.[4] We published the findings from the baseline study in *Telecommunications Policy*, and the findings from the 2009 computer center survey (discussed in Chapter 1) in *Communication Politics and Culture*.[5]

---

3   E. Hogan, 'Behind the Mulga Curtain', 11 July, 2014, *Inside Story*, http://insidestory.org.au/behind-the-mulga-curtain.

4   E. Hogan, 'Gender and ICT Access in Remote Central Australian Aboriginal Contexts', *Australian Aboriginal Studies*, 2016.1 (2016).

5   E. Rennie, A. Crouch, A. Wright and J. Thomas, 'At Home on the Outstation: Barriers to Home Internet in Remote Indigenous Communities', *Communication, Politics and Culture*, 43.1 (2013): 48–69. E. Rennie, A. Crouch, J. Thomas and P. Taylor, 'Beyond Public Access? Reconsidering Broadband for Remote Indigenous Communities', *Communication, Politics and Culture*, 43.1 (2010): 583–593.

NAMES AND PERMISSIONS

The research described in this book was conducted with the informed consent of the communities involved. The individuals concerned gave their approval for the anecdotes to be published. Each individual was given a choice as to whether they wanted their name to appear in the book. Residents from Kwale Kwale and Mungalawurru chose to use their own names, while those at Imangara chose pseudonyms. We also obtained permission from senior residents for the descriptions of the three communities, use of community names, numerous small details, and the overall arguments of the chapters. We presented draft information on Papunya and Ali Curung to senior community members in order to obtain feedback.

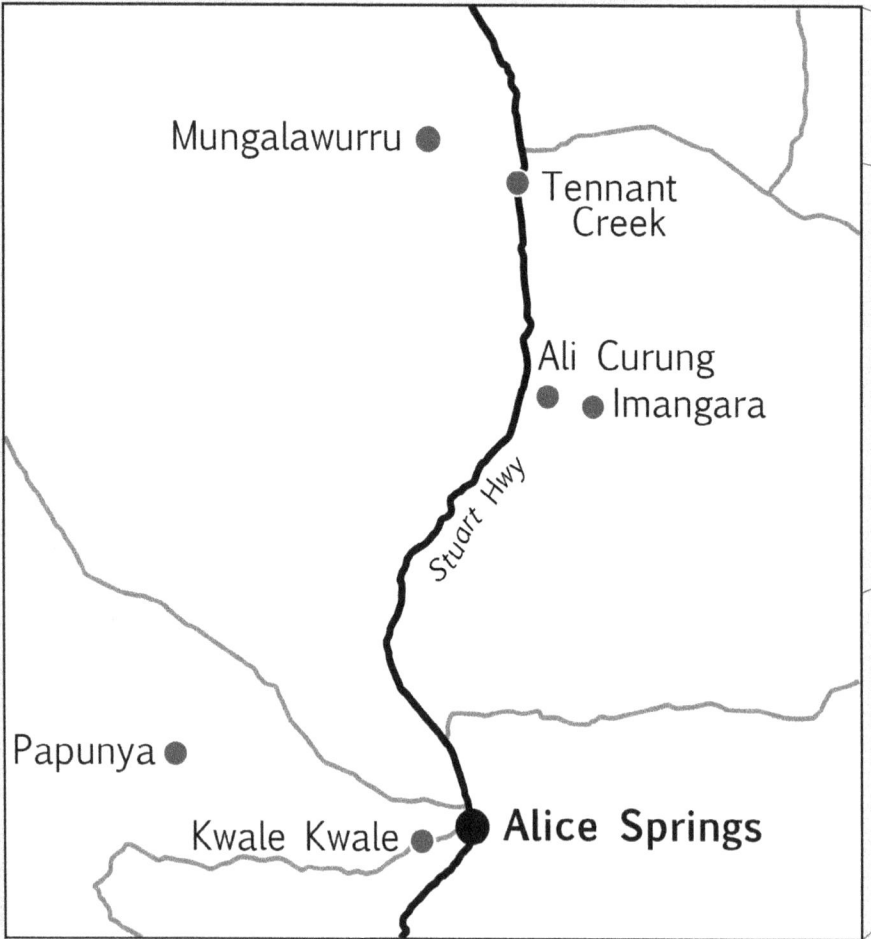

MAP

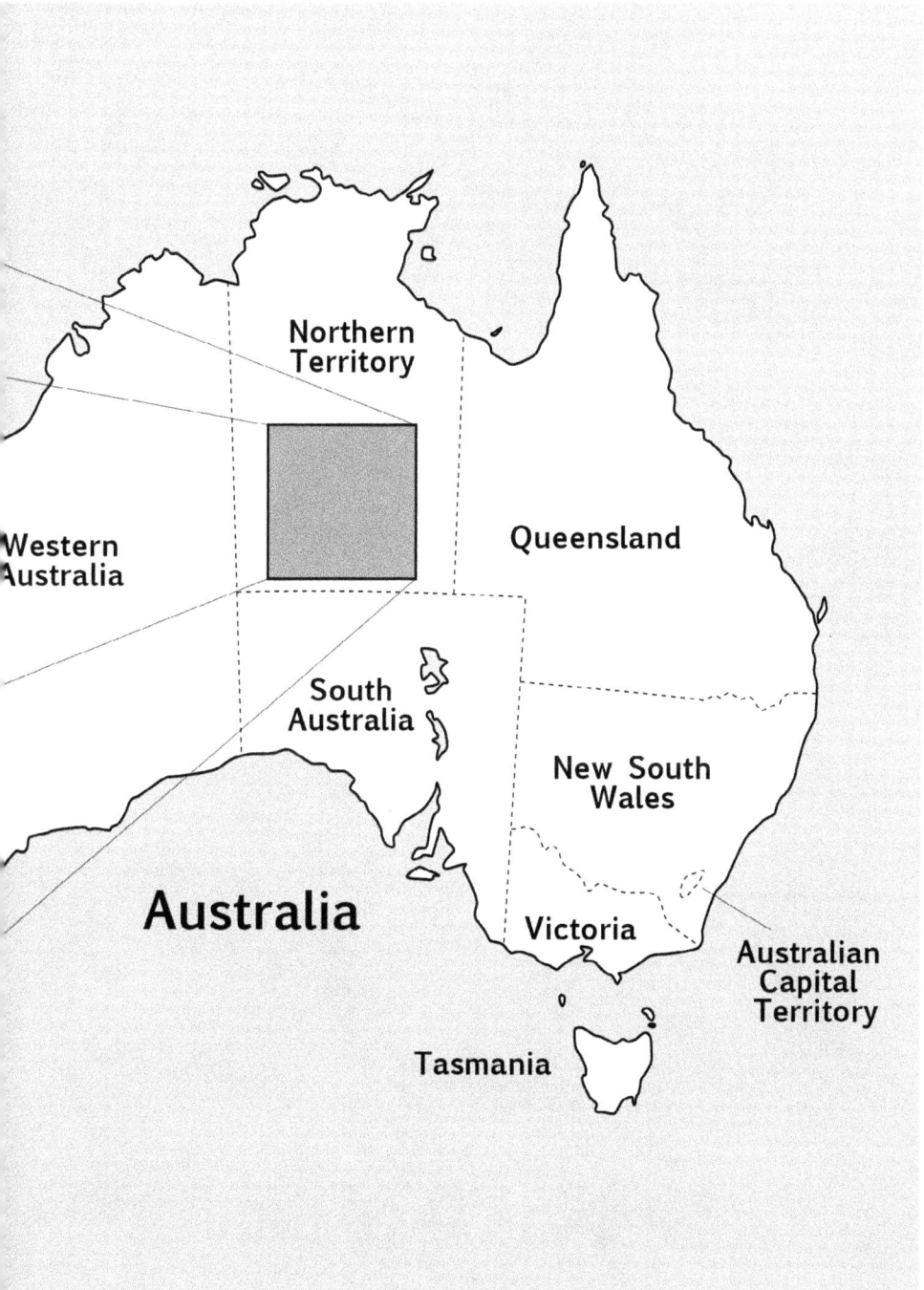

Western
Australia

Northern
Territory

Queensland

South
Australia

New South
Wales

Australia

Victoria

Australian
Capital
Territory

Tasmania

INTRODUCTION

On one of our first visits to Mungalawurru, a small Aboriginal community 80 kilometer northwest of Tennant Creek, a senior man asked if he could use our Toyota Land Cruiser's high-frequency radio. His relative was in hospital and he wanted to know how the man was faring. The extended family gathered around the car as we made contact. The doctor informed everyone that the patient was awake and recovering, but his leg had been amputated.

That day our radio was the only means by which the residents of Mungalawurru could contact the outside world. The one payphone in the community was out of order - a regular occurrence - and there were no home phones. A few people owned mobile phones, but to make the call, they had to drive along an unsealed road halfway back to Tennant Creek to the old Warrego gold mine, where you can pick up a bar or two of reception on some handsets. There was only one laptop among the twenty-two permanent residents of Mungalawurru, but it wasn't connected to the internet.

That visit occurred in 2010, when over 80 per cent of people in Australia over the age of 14 were using the internet.[1] Mungalawurru's somewhat extreme degree of isolation was about to change. We were doing the groundwork for a project that would provide computers and internet access, along with training and maintenance, to households in three small communities. Kwale Kwale, 40 kilometer west of Alice Springs, was the first to be connected, followed by Mungalawurru and then Imangara, which lies between Alice Springs and Tennant Creek, east of the Stuart Highway.

Aside from finding out which households wanted internet access, we hoped to discover why - despite government programs - people didn't have it already and whether they saw potential benefits in being online. We weren't testing new satellite speeds or trying out a new e-health application; we were simply attempting to connect households to the existing, standard satellite broadband, using the most commonly available equipment. The process of doing this, however, revealed the obvious ways in which the broadband market and government policies were failing to serve remote Aboriginal communities.

This book tells the story of what became known in research circles as the Home Internet Project, or 'the computer project' within the communities themselves. The simplicity of those titles belied the bafflingly low rates of internet adoption in these communities. Six in 10 adults in the communities had never used the internet when we made that trip in 2010. A third of those who had used a computer at some point in the past had not used the internet, some having only used computers to play solitaire; others for sharing music. Three-quarters of those who had used the internet were under the age of 30.

---

1   Australian Communications and Media Authority, *The Internet Service Market and Australians in the Online Environment*, Canberra, 2011.

The 2011 census revealed low rates of internet adoption amongst Aboriginal people living in remote areas compared to elsewhere.[2] Fewer than 4 in 10 Indigenous households in remote and very remote Australia had an internet connection at home, compared with over 8 in 10 households of the total Australian population. In some parts of the country the figure was much lower, such as the Barkly region in central Australia (excluding the township of Tennant Creek), where take-up was less than 1 in 10 for Indigenous households. The term 'digital divide' describes those who are accessing the benefits of computers and the internet, and those who are not. In Australia, the divide is widest between Aboriginal people living in remote areas and non-Aboriginal people living in the same area.

The purpose of this book is threefold. Firstly, we examine the reasons for the digital divide, looking at the particular circumstances and ways of life within remote communities that have contributed to low rates of household internet adoption, particularly in small communities. We pay particular attention to the cultural and economic systems (both traditional and contemporary) that influence internet adoption and use. Secondly, we seek to demonstrate the ways in which broadband is changing life in remote communities. What are the consequences of digital exclusion, and to what extent can broadband help overcome the hardship and inconveniences of living in remote settlements? Thirdly, the Home Internet Project was established as a trial (see Chapter 1), in that it set out to implement an alternative to current digital divide strategies in remote Australia. Where the insights of this book relate to policy frameworks and industry behaviours, we have attempted to outline those connections and suggest new approaches.

OUTSTATIONS

The majority of Indigenous Australians live in cities and regional towns along the eastern seaboard. Indigenous Australians, however, are much more highly represented in remote areas, making up 2.4 per cent of the non-remote population and 27.6 per cent of the remote population.[3]

Outstations, also referred to as 'homelands' in some regions of Australia, are small Aboriginal communities located on Aboriginal land. In the Northern Territory, approxi-

---

2   Australian Bureau of Statistics, 'Census of Population and Housing: Counts of Aboriginal and Torres Strait Islander Peoples' (2011), http://www.abs.gov.au/ausstats/abs@.nsf/Lookup/2075.0main+features32011.

3   Australian Bureau of Statistics, 'Australia, Remote and Very Remote (Remoteness Factor), Indigenous Profile, by Household' (2011), www.abs.gov.au/websitedbs/censushome.nsf/home.

mately 10,000 Aboriginal Australians live on outstations.[4] Although outstation residents represent a comparatively small subset of Australia's total Indigenous population, they constitute a significant proportion of total Aboriginal settlements. Of Australia's 1,187 remote communities, 500 are outstations in the Northern Territory, comprising more than 2,400 dwellings. Almost three-quarters of all Aboriginal communities have a population of fewer than fifty people, and only seventeen have a population of more than 1,000 people.[5]

The three communities in this book differ in their size, and in their distance from major towns (Kwale Kwale 40 kilometers; Mungalawurru 80 kilometers; and Imangara 200 kilometers). Between six and eighteen houses were located on each outstation, although not all houses were habitable the entire time. Occupancy fluctuated, dictated by issues including access to services such as schools, incarceration, wasp nests, broken pipes, housing revitalization programs, visitors and family tragedy. Each community also contained additional structures, such as sheds, that were used for a range of activities including clinic visits, as places of worship, and for enterprise (see Chapter 2). The largest community has around one hundred permanent residents, and the smallest only twelve.

It is true to say that outstations are generally very small. However, although defining outstations by size of population is convenient for data collection and bureaucratic processes, it does not adequately convey their purpose or place. Families who choose to live on outstations have a direct ancestral connection to the land. This is distinct from other communities, where people have relocated from different places into administratively identified settlements, either through necessity or coercion. As Jon Altman points out, even this definition tends to create a 'false dichotomy in settlement hierarchies between larger discrete Indigenous townships and smaller outstations', when in fact regular movement between townships and outstations 'is a culturally distinctive feature of the way Aboriginal people live' (see Chapter 2).[6] Our investigation of the internet on outstations works with this more fluid understanding, recognizing both the ties and movements that are typical of outstation life, and which can seem at odds with mainstream conceptions of domestic internet use as a permanent and stable form of connectivity.

Kinship systems and practices carried through from pre colonial times continue to govern life in remote communities to varying degrees, and families in some regions speak one

---

4   Northern Territory Department of Education, 'Enrolment and Attendance Statistics', http://
     www.education.nt.gov.au/students/at-school/enrolment-attendance/enrolment-attendance-
     statistics/2013-enrolment-and-attendance-statistics.

5   Australian Bureau of Statistics, 'Housing and Infrastructure in Aboriginal and Torres Strait Islander
     Communities' (2007), http://www.abs.gov.au/Ausstats/abs@.nsf/Latestproducts/4710.0Main%20
     Features42006?opendocument&tabname=Summary&prodno=4710.0&issue=2006&num=&view=.

6   J. Altman, In Search of an Outstations Policy for Indigenous Australians, Canberra: Centre for
     Aboriginal Economic Policy Research, 2006, p. 1.

or more Aboriginal languages at home. More than five Aboriginal languages were spoken across the three outstations, including Warumungu, Alyawarr and Arrernte. As anthropologists have observed, the contemporary Indigenous sociality of remote communities is an expression of both traditional and Western cultures, including new capabilities 'in language, technology, practical knowledge, ritual, and ways of organizing social, political and economic life'.[7] The communities discussed in this book are still traditional in many respects, while also living within, negotiating and participating in contemporary systems. We were made aware of this regularly during our visits, such as when we attempted to follow up a computer-related request with a resident, only to be told that she had gone 'porcupine' [echidna] hunting. Such practices, a continuation of the oldest living culture in the world, sat alongside media consumption habits not unlike those of mainstream Australian households - including news, video clips, computer games and social networking applications.

Media anthropologist Serper Tenhunen proposes the concept of 'social logistics' as a tool for understanding 'relationships between technology, culture and social structure' of the kind that we are concerned with in this book.[8] Such an approach looks at how communications technologies are taken up and adapted within different cultural settings, showing how the various uses are bent to fit within the particular social organization of a time and place, including cultural and institutional ways of doing. Some scholars have rejected the terms 'adoption' and 'use', as these imply that there exists a uniform and uncomplicated pattern of encountering communications technology, denying that consumption is active and that technologies can be objects of desire for some and disregarded by others.[9] We have chosen to retain the terms adoption and use, partly to emphasize that choices also occur within particular regimes - the retail offerings, infrastructures and programs developed and offered by agencies and businesses that are often separate from, and external to, life in remote communities. The level to which these structures are adaptable or inflexible, and the strategies people develop in order to work around, or away from, such regimes, are important for understanding the digital divide. The various attempts to resolve communication infrastructure in remote Australia also reveal the aspirations and assumptions about how remote communities should exist in relation to the so-called outside world. These mutations of the policy apparatus have been surprisingly disconnected from other attempts to construct, remedy or intervene in the welfare of the Territory's remote communities (see Chapter 1). This book therefore

---

7   D. Austin-Broos, *A Different Inequality: The Politics of Debate About Remote Aboriginal Australia* [Kindle Dx Version], Crows Nest: Allen & Unwin, 2011, Chapter 1, Section 2, Paragraph 6.

8   S. Tenhunen, 'Mobile Technology in the Village: ICTs, Culture, and Social Logistics in India', *Journal of the Royal Anthropological Institute* 14.3 (2008): 517.

9   N. Selwyn, S. Gorard and J. Furlong, 'Whose Internet Is It Anyway? Exploring Adults' (Non) Use of the Internet in Everyday Life', *European Journal of Communication* 20.1 (2005): 5-26.

sits within a media studies tradition of policy analysis, grounded in the observable daily use of information and communications technology (ICT).

Our investigations into internet use revealed a social setting that was embedded within traditional structures, but where those ways of organizing and understanding the world blended into everyday, non-traditional activities. For instance, when we asked about his online contacts, one man told us, 'I don't have friends, only family', referring to a possibly extensive kinship network rather than social isolation. Although we were not privy to the depth of such relationships from our limited position as researchers investigating media, we were given some insights into how communications technologies (internet and mobile phones) are creating new social configurations and placing pressure on customs. Chapter 5 discusses these issues in relation to cyber-safety concerns that arose in the township of Tennant Creek during the course of our work.

The residents' everyday concerns included shopping and transactions as well as interests that were intensely local, such as responsibilities to land councils, ensuring young people are aware of their obligations to others, and negotiating with outsiders, including us. While policy commentators often notice that cultural meetings and funeral business take people away from their outstation base, we observed that rodeos and local show days had the same outcome. To us, such movements between communities and towns were interesting, because they have consequences for how people stay connected, and for their preferences in terms of retail offerings and devices, as discussed in Chapters 8 and 9.

INTERNET ACCESS AND TELECOMMUNICATIONS

The detailed longitudinal data on which much of this book is based concerns one particular regime of access: home internet, meaning internet accessed within the domestic setting and managed by the householders. Our intention in looking at home internet was to test some cultural assumptions that were influencing policy decisions at the time we commenced the study. However, we have also endeavored to describe other systems of internet access (see Chapters 8 and 9) in order to explore the dynamics of other regimes.

From the start, our interest in home internet was more explorative than developmental. We provided households in the three communities with access to a computer and an internet connection in order to understand why such a common means of internet access was not being taken up by residents. Although we were curious to know whether internet would transform life in the communities, we did not set out to achieve transformation, in the way that 'ICT for development' seeks to do (see Chapter 2). Rather, our interest was in how the infrastructures of the internet - including the technologies, public policy programs and retail mechanisms - were serving or failing this particular population. If the residents gave up on their home internet, or decided to do things differently, that would be as revealing as if they embraced the technology outright.

When we commenced the project, we had various hypotheses as to why these outstations had not sought out internet services. One hypothesis was that it was simply a matter of affordability, given the very low income of the households. We also considered practical matters to do with housing, such as living arrangements, the condition of the houses, and being home long enough to want a permanent connection to the internet. We were well aware of the physical challenges to infrastructure, with one of our partners, the Centre for Appropriate Technology (CAT), having conducted various surveys and infrastructure projects in the region over the years. However, we did not know how long computers and related electronics could withstand the heat, dust and vermin.

A great deal occurred during those four years, both within the communities and externally. As described in Chapter 2, we provided free internet connections and maintained computers for two and a half years. Our presence and purpose in the communities changed the dynamics of what home internet meant to these households. CAT dealt with the installers, and replaced and repaired equipment on a regular basis. We all attempted to help residents, showing them how to do certain things, listening to their concerns, and repeatedly explaining how they could maintain a connection of their own in the future. All these efforts meant that when the choice came to take out an internet connection of their own, many households chose to do so.

Beyond these communities, the communications landscape was constantly changing. During our various travels beyond the outstations (comparative work on the project, as well as interactions between the two Indigenous organizations on the project team), we observed that different groups were accessing the internet in different ways. For instance, some were conducting online transactions intermittently at internet kiosks located in caravan parks and council offices. Others were playing computer games while in prison or rehabilitation facilities. Where there were remote media centers or schools, these provided important (although monitored) forms of access. As the years went by, we witnessed more people using mobile phones and tablets when in town, in what seemed to be a sudden spike in mobile device use in the region. We concluded that remote Aboriginal communities have vastly different levels and means of internet access depending on community size, proximity to larger towns or tourist sites, and the agencies and businesses that interact with them. We have incorporated examples of the various regimes of access, and compared and contrasted these where possible (Chapter 8).

BROADBAND POLICY

The assorted and irregular nature of internet use in remote Australia needs to be seen within the historical trajectory of telecommunications in Australia. As we discuss in Chapter 1, remote regions were last to receive telecommunications, and only then through government programs, including payphones, subsidies to offset costs, price controls such as untimed local calls for landlines within certain areas, and community infrastructure programs.[10] By 2007, 77 per cent of all remote communities had some form of telecommunications service, but for many this consisted of one public telephone; only 20 per cent of the population in remote communities had a fixed telephone line, and only 26 per cent of communities had mobile telephone coverage.[11] Since then, various public-private initiatives have extended mobile coverage to more communities, but the cost of mobile telephone infrastructure remains prohibitive for many communities, as well as being economically unviable for providers. By 2015, a total of seventeen locations in the lower half of the Northern Territory had mobile coverage – twelve of which include residential dwellings – making mobile broadband at home available to approximately 50 per cent of the Aboriginal population of the region.[12] Larger communities tend to be better serviced: across the entire Northern Territory (including the Top End), seventy-four remote communities had a population greater than one hundred in 2015 (home to approximately 45,000 people). Of these, thirty communities had ADSL, and mobile telephony was available in forty-four communities.[13]

In addition, various publicly funded social development initiatives have attempted to provide some level of internet access, such as computer rooms and training provided through the Northern Territory Libraries network and remote media organizations. Such programs have been designed to assist Aboriginal people to discover and learn about communications technology within community settings. As outstations are generally too small to be eligible for such infrastructure, the communities we worked with had not experienced the benefits of such projects.

The wide disparities in internet access between different communities sits uncomfortably with Australia's national broadband agenda. In recent years, debates around inequities in broadband performance have centered on the National Broadband Network (NBN),

---

10   S. McElhinney, 'Telecommunications Liberalisation and the Quest for Universal Service in Australia', *Telecommunications Policy* 25.4 (2001): 233-248.

11   Australian Communications and Media Authority, 'Telecommunications in Remote Indigenous Communications', http://www.acma.gov.au/theACMA/telecommunications-in-remote-indigenous-communities.

12   According to Telstra coverage maps (https://www.telstra.com.au/coverage-networks/our-coverage): Granites mine; Barkly homestead Wayside Inn; Ali Curung (Indigenous pop. 486); Barrow Creek; Ampilawatja (Indigenous pop. 350); Urapuntja power station; Arlpara (Utopia homelands, Indigenous pop. 90); Ti Tree (Indigenous pop. 61); Yuendumu (Indigenous pop. 585); Papunya (Indigenous pop. 376); Hermannsburg/Ellery Creek (Indigenous pop. 537); Erldunda Road House; Uluru/Mutitjulu (Indigenous pop. 250); Santa Teresa (Indigenous pop. 502); Lajamanu (Indigenous pop. 586); Elliot (Indigenous pop. 287); Newcastle Waters (Indigenous pop. 61).

13   Northern Territory Government Department of Corporate and Information Services, 'Submission to the Regional Telecommunications Independent Review Committee, 2015', https://www.communications.gov.au/sites/g/files/net301/f/Northern%20Territory%20Government%20-%20Public%20Submission%20RTIRC%202015.pdf.

with a particular focus on regional versus capital city infrastructure and speeds. The NBN is a government-funded wholesale-only broadband network that sells to retail service providers, who in turn sell services to the public. The initial rationale for the NBN was to provide a nation-building infrastructure that could provide fast broadband services to all Australians. A number of aspects of the plan were based on this objective, and satellite internet was incorporated into the NBN, as satellite connections can be received anywhere via domestic satellite receivers. As discussed in Chapter 1, the NBN was also designed with regional parity in mind, insofar as under-serviced areas were the first to receive the infrastructure. The model of a national wholesale infrastructure provider was intended to serve those outside the mainstream areas by providing a wholesale price base that would be consistent as far as possible across the country, rather than being strictly costed at the local level. Pricing was designed to ensure that entry-level prices remain at pre-NBN levels for low-income consumers, providing faster and more reliable service at the same price as ADSL.[14]

We discuss the NBN particularly in relation to the 'last 3 per cent' – those households where satellite internet was considered the only economically viable option at the time the NBN plans were conceived, and still is at the time of writing. As the NBN is a wholesale model, residents in remote communities deal with the retail service providers, rather than with NBN Co. These interactions constituted a significant aspect of our research towards the latter part of the project, as residents began to enter into contracts to receive NBN services (via retail service providers) under the Interim Satellite Service. We began to see clearly the reasons why many households in remote communities are not acquiring satellite broadband, and prefer pre paid mobile in areas where mobile reception is available. Our findings suggest that faster speeds alone, although desirable for services and business in remote Australia, will not encourage residents of remote communities to adopt broadband. We question whether household satellite internet – the government's response to internet access in remote areas – will meet the needs of remote communities under current policy and consumer arrangements.

Australia's telecommunications dilemma is commonly discussed as a story of market failure, where services to those within the country's vast interior are necessarily subsidized by city customers and government programs. The outstation experience, however, reveals a more complex picture. Communications technologies are not necessarily adopted in the way that providers expect they will be. Moreover, what on the surface seems like an individual choice (adoption) can occur as a group dynamic, informed by social factors that may seem far removed from communications policy. When the movement of people within and across communities is taken into account, as well as their economic priorities, social obligations, and capacities within a particular locality, it seems unlikely

---

14   R. Morsillo, 'Affordable Broadband for All Australians', *Telecommunications Journal of Australia* 62.5 (2012): 78.1-78.16.

that the problem of broadband adoption will be resolved through infrastructure alone. However, changes to the way that internet is sold and supported could make a significant difference.

THE DIGITAL DIVIDE AND ACCESS TO SERVICES

When we commenced, only a few studies had looked in depth at the issue of internet adoption in remote communities. Scholars identified that there were differences in the levels and means of access, and some argued that online participation would provide a means for Aboriginal people to maintain their cultural heritage and engage young people.[15] Internet access had also been acknowledged in government policy and funding programs as an area of need, although such programs were limited, as discussed in Chapter 1.[16]

At the same time, the digital divide was not a national emergency. In 2010, remote Aboriginal communities in the Northern Territory were subject to an increased level of state intervention (from 2007), intended to overcome generational social disadvantage and dysfunction. Going without the internet was towards the bottom of a long list of policy concerns, all of which could be characterized as deprivations in policy terms. Indeed, describing low rates of internet adoption as a 'divide' seems something of an overstatement against the Commonwealth government's comparatively modest-sounding Closing the Gap agenda, which includes targets such as improving education outcomes (halve the gap in reading, writing and numeracy achievements by 2018), life expectancy (parity by 2031), and workforce participation (halve the gap by 2018).

As described throughout the following chapters, the elders invited us onto their lands and into their houses, interested in our proposal of measured introduction of computers. However, our research also brought us into contact with another, more skeptical, group

---

15   A.E. Daly, *Bridging the Digital Divide: The Role of Community Online Access Centres in Indigenous Communities*, Canberra: ANU Centre for Aboriginal Economic Policy Research (2005); C. Nobbs, 'Ara Irititja: Protecting the Past, Accessing the Future: Indigenous Memories in a Digital Age', *Artlink* 24.1 (2004): 50-51; H. Verran and M. Christie, 'Postcolonial Databasing? Subverting Old Appropriations, Developing New Associations', in J. Leach and L. Wilson (eds) *Subversion, Conversion, Development: Diversity and the Adoption and Use of Information and Communication Technologies*, Cambridge: M.I.T. Press, 2014, pp. 57-76; S. Thorner, 'Imagining an Indigital Interface: Ara Irititja Indigenizes the Technologies of Knowledge Management', *Collections* 6.3 (2010): 125-146; I. Kral, *Plugged In: Remote Australian Indigenous Youth and Digital Culture*, Canberra: ANU Centre for Aboriginal Economic Policy Research, 2010; I. Kral, 'Youth Media as Cultural Practice: Remote Indigenous Youth Speaking out Loud', *Australian Aboriginal Studies*, 1 (2011): 4-16.

16   Telecommunications Action Plan for Remote Indigenous Communities (TAPRIC), *Report on the Strategic Study for Improving Telecommunications in Remote Indigenous Communities*, Canberra: Department of Communications and Arts, 2002.

of stakeholders. To reach the communities, we travelled alongside a cavalry of remote community workers, taking the 'ideal combination of safety and speed' that 'only white-fella take'.[17] On our visits out to the two northern communities, we talked with various shire officers, government bureaucrats, arts workers, schoolteachers, health workers and television satellite dish installers. To some, our interest in broadband connectivity must have seemed a curious, perhaps trivial, concern to justify regular visits, each comprising a 1,500-kilometer round trip from Alice Springs.

Even if it was not always apparent to those we encountered on the road, our interest in the digital divide was partly aligned with the concerns of the service agencies. The dispersed and remote nature of these communities means that residents face substantial difficulties conducting even simple transactions. In a pre-election document (2013), the Coalition parties stated that while not all government services can be delivered more efficiently online, the majority can be. It commended the US and UK governments on their 'aggressive' commitment to online service delivery.[18] Accessing online services can reduce the need for travel, and provide individuals and families with a level of autonomy over their personal affairs (for instance, reducing the need for phone messages, bank balances and information to be delivered through third parties such as a store keeper or government administrator). Online service delivery could also lower the costs to service agencies, such as the Centrelink officers we met, who had made the journey to check that people's welfare payment information was up to date. For the Central Land Coun-cil (CLC) and CAT – Indigenous organizations themselves facing logistical difficulties providing services and staying in touch with outstation residents – this was a legitimate concern worth exploring.

There are good reasons why the potential benefits of the internet need to be considered at this point in time. As the NBN brings with it new services and applications, those who are not connected now will fall further behind as the benefits for others increase. How-ever, while recognizing the rapid transformations that are taking place at various levels of the economy and society as a result of digital technology, we urge caution to those who see broadband as a remedy for remote Australia. Commonly held aspirations for broadband relating to better service delivery, overcoming remoteness and hardship, and cost savings, reflect a set of external priorities. The agendas of government and NGOs are not necessarily aligned with those of people living in remote communities. Moreover, the expectation that ICTs will provide those living in traditional and remote societies with greater connection to the outside world on their own terms imposes an untested assumption that such engagement is desired in the first place. Regardless of the poten-

---

17   Camilla as quoted in Y. Musharbash, '"Only Whitefella Take That Road": Culture Seen Through the Intervention at Yuendumu', in J. Altman and M. Hinkson (eds) *Culture Crisis: Anthropology and Politics in Aboriginal Australia*, Sydney: University of New South Wales Press, 2010, p. 304.

18   Coalition, 'The Coalition's Policy for E-Government and the Digital Economy', Canberra, 2013.

tial good that may or may not come from this, the personal and socially-specific nature of internet use means that it may never eventuate. And just as there is the potential to provide connectivity in the social world within which these communities operate, so there is potential for the internet to allow communities to retreat further from the government and NGO services, and from non-Indigenous workers who serve and assist Indigenous people through face-to-face encounters.

During the years when our research took place, outstations became the subject of intense public debate, as discussed in Chapter 2. Outstations have historically been associated with a politics of self-determination, representing the right and choice of Aboriginal people to live on country. The outstation debate has revolved around government funding for the maintenance of outstations, including basic infrastructure such as water and roads: whether these are entitlements of all Australians regardless of where they live, or whether outstations should be considered private land that residents themselves must maintain. The practical considerations of outstation maintenance have taken place against a backdrop of Indigenous policy change, which some have characterized as a shift away from self-determination towards 'mainstreaming'. The mainstreaming approach posits that relocating residents to larger settlements with services is necessary in order to overcome the poverty and social exclusion experienced in remote communities. In Chapter 1, we outline the history of the outstation movement as well as the particular policy attempts to provide telecommunications services. Although it is the case that broadband may assist Indigenous people to live on their lands by providing access to some services online, without basic infrastructure, such as roads, power and water, the future of outstations is bleak.

THE DIGITAL DIVIDE AND DIGITAL CHOICES

Digital divide debates center on whether the market can create equitable outcomes in an information society, and on what types of infrastructure and programs may help to overcome the divide. Two unresolved questions preoccupy digital divide studies. Firstly, statistical studies have drawn a link between social exclusion and digital exclusion, in that those who are least likely to have access to the internet are also least likely to have access to other resources. Does this mean that social exclusion is the cause of digital exclusion? The second concern is whether resolving digital exclusion can assist in overcoming social exclusion. Does access to digital resources enable activities and opportunities that can transform lives in positive ways?

Our research uncovered interesting and unique dimensions and patterns of internet access, which took us some way towards answering these questions. As mentioned above, not all communities experience low rates of adoption, but there are pockets of significant exclusion. When we look more closely at what is occurring in places of higher adoption and those with lower adoption, this unevenness begins to make sense. As discussed in Chapters 8 and 9, we observed a reasonably high rate (over 70 per cent) of mobile broadband adoption in Ali Curung, which has mobile broadband coverage; however, in Imangara when we arrived, where the only available connection was satellite internet, there was no internet adoption. Both communities had a similar socio-economic profile. We also observed that people fell in and out of internet use, sometimes on a regular basis, particularly those whose lives were more mobile (see Chapter 4). This suggests that internet adoption is not a fixed event or a linear trajectory from non-use to advanced use. For many, internet access is desirable, but only when other factors allow for it.

Events such as visits by relatives, religious interests, car availability and death impacted on how people used computers and informed their decisions to adopt or keep hardware and internet subscriptions. Seemingly straightforward factors such as available infrastructure, maintenance and consumer concerns (retail options, pricing, assistance) became complicated when the pressures and daily rhythms of living in a remote community came into play. From these observations, we offer some explanations as to why a household, or a community, can go from little or no adoption to rapid adoption in a relatively short space of time, while other households and communities remain disconnected.

Media studies scholars have observed that some make a 'digital choice' not to use the internet, and that this can be related to 'cultural factors and the social context of individuals, which influence the development of positive or negative attitudes towards technologies'.[19] In the case of outstations, factors such as billing difficulties (related to the distinct way that money changes hands) and inconvenience in dealing with retail providers (related to language barriers or lack of other infrastructures such as home phones), were informing the digital choices of residents. We argue that the concept of digital choice, while useful, does not entirely describe what is occurring. Digital choice denotes individual decision-making, whereas in this case the social norms of the group were resulting in whole communities choosing not to adopt. Moreover, studies show that people are more likely to adopt technology if others they know are already using it, suggesting that network effects play a significant role.[20] When we first met the residents, people did not know that satellite internet was an option, because no-one else they knew had chosen to subscribe. The 'groupish' (what we call 'demic') networked nature of internet adoption in remote Australia is explored further in Chapter 9.[21]

19   E. Helsper, 'A Corresponding Fields Model for the Links between Social and Digital Exclusion', *Communication Theory* 22.4 (2012): 410.

20   A. Goolsbee and P. Klenow, 'Evidence on Learning and Network Externalities in the Diffusion of Home Computers', *Journal of Law and Economics* 45.2 (2002).

21   J. Hartley and J. Potts, *Cultural Science: A Natural History of Stories, Demes, Knowledge and Innovation*, London: Bloomsbury Publishing, 2014.

Where others have discussed digital choices, we go further to examine exactly what kinds of choices are being enacted in remote communities. The choice, in this instance, is one where the choosers set targets for particular characteristics and eliminate products that don't meet those targets completely (a 'deal-breaker' scenario). Many make a decision to use computers and the internet regardless of their socio-economic status, as long as the conditions of internet access suit them. Our trial – providing assistance and maintenance for home internet – changed the dynamics and conditions of satellite internet to the extent that many households chose to move to NBN satellite plans at the conclusion of the project. When available under the right conditions, home internet is entirely possible. In Chapters 8 and 9, we offer suggestions as to how small communities can be better served.

SOLVING DISADVANTAGE?

The second concern of digital divide studies is whether digital inclusion can help overcome other exclusions; for instance, whether it enables people to overcome barriers in education, employment and health. In this book we have attempted to provide an answer, with caveats. We looked at what people used the internet for, and concluded that the internet can enable a level of personal autonomy that is significant for residents of outstations, but that this does not necessarily signify a solution to social disadvantage. However, the applications and services that might assist the particular and extreme disadvantages present in remote communities did not exist in 2010–2014. Therefore, the possibility that broadband might enable a better level of service provision remained untested. Moreover, the elaborate uses required for activities such as enterprise development would require a level of training and assistance beyond the capacity of our project (see discussion on training, Chapter 6).

Anderson and Tracey speculated in 2001 that 'applications and services delivered via the internet are not changing the way people live their lives in a simple, straightforward manner, but are supporting and enhancing their existing lifestyles, whatever those lifestyles may be'.[22] As we discuss in Chapter 5, residents' use of computers and the internet was confined to a fairly narrow set of activities: entertainment (downloading music, watching videos), social networking, games, storing photos, shopping, and personal administration, including banking and managing welfare payments. Only a few people used email, and generally to receive notices of meetings or visits from external providers (including us). The uses that we observed were clearly a continuation of everyday activities, such as downloading gospel music in one community where interest in Christianity was high,

---

22   B. Anderson and K. Tracey, 'Digital Living: The Impact (or Otherwise) of the Internet on Everday British Life' in C. Haythornthwaite and B. Wellman (eds) *The Internet in Everyday Life*, Malden, MA, USA: Blackwell Publishers Ltd, 2002, p. 141.

checking welfare payments before making the journey into town, and browsing shopping sites for cars that were being sold cheaper interstate.

Although individuals displayed varying degrees of interest in computers and digital literacy levels, their uses reflected community norms and a particular sociality of place. What then is the hope that digital technologies might help to overcome disadvantage? With respect to activities such as banking and managing welfare payments, internet transactions reduce an individual's need to interact with outside agencies, as well as with intermediaries such as store managers. However, the social and cultural systems that have thwarted government attempts to overcome disadvantage can themselves persist in this scenario.

When the internet arrived in these communities, it became ordinary for them in the way it is for most people. A great deal of Indigenous media studies work begins from a curiosity about whether Aboriginal people living in remote regions are enthusiastic or fearful of the advent of new communications technologies. Scholars have set out with the explicit intention of discovering whether people of traditional cultures deal with technology in unique ways (for instance, the work of Eric Michaels).[23] Although we touch on the question of cultural destruction in our discussion of cyber-safety concerns (Chapter 5), it is worth stating from the outset that the internet rapidly became just another part of life – a mundane asset tied into routines and habits that brought with it some advantages, as well as some newfound frustrations. As we describe in Chapter 5, internet use is a media practice tied in with typical quests for entertainment, to connect with a friend, or for a quick fix for personal administration. The priorities, joys, boredoms and obligations of life in these communities did not shift fundamentally. In Heather Horst's words, what we observed was 'humanity's remarkable capacity to reimpose normativity just as quickly as digital technologies create conditions for change'.[24]

The idea that internet access can resolve the larger problem of government failure in addressing disadvantage is therefore problematic. We can say, however, that the internet brings a level of banal administration which, due to distance, remote communities have not previously had the benefit of, and which otherwise requires arduous strategies such as extended travel, going without, or waiting for service providers to make contact.[25] How

23   E. Michaels, *The Aboriginal Invention of Television in Central Australia, 1982-1986: Report of the Fellowship to Assess the Impact of Television in Remote Aboriginal Communities*, Canberra: Australian Institute of Aboriginal Studies, 1986; E. Michaels, *Bad Aboriginal Art and Other Essays: Tradition, Media, and Technological Horizons*, Vol. 3, University of Minnesota Press, 1994.

24   D. Miller and H.A. Horst, 'The Digital and the Human: A Prospectus for Digital Anthropology' in H.A. Horst and D. Miller (eds) *Digital Anthropology*, London: Bloomsbury Publishing, 2013, pp. 3-35.

25   J. Hartley and E. Rennie, 'Show Business for Ugly People? Media Politics and E-Democracy', Australian Electronic Governance Conference, Melbourne, 14-15 April 2004.

these small instances of autonomy and efficiency - basic activities that reduce otherwise complicated means of making do - can change that critical relationship between a people and the outside world is yet to be seen.

Understanding these dynamics took four years of regular engagement with three small communities, using the least invasive strategies we could manage. This book is as much about our own efforts to assist the residents to access the internet under current constraints as it is about the insights the residents of these communities shared with us. At times it was a complicated endeavor, technically and interpersonally. We went to great lengths and great expense along the way. The message of this book, however, is that the digital divide should not be seen as an intractable problem, and that costly solutions may not always be the right approach. Rather, addressing the digital divide requires understanding people's choices and the capacities and conditions that inform those choices.

This book is divided into three parts. Part I provides the backstory to Australia's digital divide, spanning the communications and Indigenous policy arenas (Chapter 1). We also describe the residents' experiences of the internet before we arrived, and the methods we employed to shed light on the dynamics of internet adoption (Chapter 2). Part II discusses the residents' encounters with the internet and specific issues, including ownership of devices (Chapter 3); people's mobility and travel (Chapter 4); gender dynamics (Chapter 7); training needs (Chapter 6); as well as what people used the internet for (Chapter 5). Part III looks at other scenarios of ICT infrastructure and access in central Australia, including the shared facilities approach that has evolved out of various programs and policies, and mobile internet (Chapter 8). We conclude the book by considering digital choices in relation to the digital divide, as well as the implications for broadband policy (Chapter 9 and Conclusion).

PART I

Chapter 1: Policy

On our way to the Barkly communities, we travelled on the road named after the first European explorer to make the journey from Australia's south to north coasts, John McDouall Stuart, for which he was paid a commission associated with the establishment of a telegraph line. We passed two heritage telegraph repeater stations, one at our starting point in Alice Springs and the other 280 kilometers north at Barrow Creek. Now tourist destinations, the small stone buildings once housed the equipment and operators that connected Adelaide to Darwin and Great Britain. On one particular trip, we asked the bar-tender at the Barrow Creek roadhouse how long he had been living there. He simply pointed to graffiti on the wall, where he, or someone before him, had scrawled the words 'long enough'.

Some months after that trip, in 2014, Barrow Creek received mobile phone coverage as part of a public-private partnership blackspots program to extend mobile coverage and internet access to remote communities. Telstra, the private partner, issued a statement saying that the site was chosen partly for its proximity to fiber optic cable. The Northern Territory government stated that the tower was to serve highway and wayside coverage, rather than to service nearby Aboriginal communities and a school, which remained outside of the coverage area.[1]

The Barrow Creek mobile story illustrates the complexities of communications infrastructure provision in remote areas: the cost imperative (in this instance related to the use of existing infrastructure), and the different needs of various population groups, which include the 'grey nomad' campervan tourists who travel the Stuart Highway, service providers, and Aboriginal communities. The ABC quoted a resident of Tara, a small community near Barrow Creek, who had purchased a mobile phone in anticipation of being able to ring her daughter in Alice Springs from home: 'I'm sad for us [because] I turned it on and it didn't switch on', said Selma Thompson. 'It was a waste'.[2]

The everyday life of residents of remote Indigenous communities is unlike that of most Australians in very many ways. Remote communities are small, isolated settlements, separated by great distances. While they offer many rich social and cultural benefits for their residents, they have poor transport connections, little infrastructure and scarce resources. But as it does for other Australians, life in remote communities involves communications: with family members in other places, with social networks, and with

---

1   L. Fitzgerald, 'New 3G Network Falls Short for Stations and Communities Near Barrow Creek, Northern Territory', http://www.abc.net.au/news/2014-08-25/barrow-creek-3g-network-lacking/5693386.

2   Fitzgerald, 'New 3G Network Falls Short for Stations and Communities Near Barrow Creek, Northern Territory'.

governments, organizations, and businesses. Reliable communications for the people who live and work in remote Australia are all the more essential on account of their isolation, and unlike urban Australians, they have never taken these for granted. Despite many positive developments, adequate communications are still not the reality for most Indigenous communities, and the problem of securing them has been a challenging and defining issue from the beginning.

This chapter discusses the policy contexts of the problem. Policy matters because governments have defined, regulated and largely funded the communications sector in remote Australia, and because governments continue to play a paternalistic role, albeit a contested one, in Indigenous citizens' lives. But these two policy registers – communications and Indigenous affairs – have very different histories, institutional settings and policy languages. Communications has been a core Commonwealth responsibility, and a reasonably important agency, under different guises, since Federation. Despite many large changes in structure and policy, this is a field where the Commonwealth has long been certain of its role. Indigenous affairs, by contrast, is a much more difficult, arduous and wicked problem, which has involved continuing inter governmental skirmishes as to the division of responsibilities. Unlike with communications, the Commonwealth's work in Indigenous affairs has failed to find any ongoing institutional location, with successive shifts from a dedicated department to the Indigenous-elected Aboriginal and Torres Strait Islander Commission (ATSIC), an element within social services, and most recently an anomalous, operational wing of the Prime Minister's department. Far from heralding the progress of Indigenous affairs to the center of national public administration, these migrations signal a volatile history of reversals and revisions, where a lack of governmental confidence is reflected above all in the scant regard paid to domain expertise, experience or memory.[3]

It should not be surprising that these different administrative channels have tangled relations, producing outcomes that occasionally connect but generally bear little relation to one another. We must therefore make an artificial distinction between the communication activities that interest us, and the social settings in which they occur – not because such a distinction is useful, but because the prism of public policy frequently separates these elements, and treats them differently. We start by considering communications, and then move to the Indigenous policy domain.

ISSUES AND IMPERATIVES FOR REMOTE COMMUNICATIONS

If Australian governments have struggled to comprehend the needs and circumstances of remote Australians, this is despite the fact that the geography and social reach of

---

3   See L. Tingle, *Political Amnesia: How We Forgot How to Govern*, Quarterly Essay, Melbourne: Black Inc., 2015, p. 32.

communications has been a common thread in policy and politics since Federation. And if Australia's distinctive human and physical geographies did not themselves make debates about subsidizing rural and regional services an inevitable feature of policy argument, the political economy of the settlements struck between the new Australian states ensured it would be so. A national government required, in effect, a single market for communications, whether these were postal services, telegraphy, or phone calls. In the case of central Australia, governments, rather than the market, have directly shaped communications from the early colonial period. For our purposes, the key developments are recent. Remote communications assumed a new and urgent shape as a problem of contemporary public policy in the first decade of the millennium, at the same time as broadband communications and the mobile internet were becoming embedded in the everyday lives of mainstream, urban Australians.

Understanding how that happened – and the outcomes for remote communities – involves recognizing two connected processes of policy change that were well under way at this time. First, there was a process of digital transformation, driven not only by technical advances in infrastructure, devices and applications, but also, most importantly, by how governments and others responded to new communications technologies. From the 1980s onwards, new communications had undermined confidence in the longstanding model of a government-owned monopoly provider. Then, as mobile and the internet took off, social services, health and community services, education, entertainment, work and commerce began to be redesigned on the assumption that national populations would have access to the necessary infrastructure at an affordable price, and would have the skills and motivations to make use of it. This dynamic had many benefits, while presenting a critical problem, but also an opportunity, for those not online. One effect was to emphasize the increasing relative disadvantage of those Australians without broadband or reliable mobile coverage. While steadily increasing numbers of Australians went online, the question of how to assist and support those without good communications did not diminish in corresponding fashion; instead it grew in importance as a matter for policy and politics.

The second formative change under way over this period was the liberalization of the telecommunications industry, framed by a new, competitive, regulatory model, the incremental sale of Telstra from 1997 onwards, and the subsequent planning and establishment of the National Broadband Network (NBN). This is not the place for a full review of this history, but we should briefly focus on two turn-of-the-century policy imperatives: the Telstra sale, and the creation of a competitive market for telecommunications. In micro-economic terms, there was no simple relation between these. Paul Keating's Labor government had been more concerned with fostering competition, particularly through the entry into the market of Optus as a second carrier. The Coalition government led by John Howard prioritized the sale; as it transpired, the effect of that was not more competition, but the consolidation of Telstra's position as a dominant market player combining control of the infrastructure with a pre-eminent position in retail. This market problem was a key factor in the later development of the NBN. At a political and social level, the sale required the support of regionally based politicians, both within the National Party and outside it. These politicians and their constituencies were motivated by a strong sense of rural and regional disadvantage, and were not naturally inclined to support the disposal of a public enterprise.

On the strength of objections from rural and regional interests, legislation to complete the full sale of Telstra failed in the Senate in 1998. A staged approach, a series of regular reviews, funded programs and accommodations were then necessary for the government to proceed with further public offerings of Telstra shares. The sale was therefore a gradual process, but it represented a slow-motion conclusion to a long period of public control over Australia's chief communications networks, and the commencement of an ongoing and unstable period of regulation, review and subsidy. A proliferation of large and small publicly funded schemes, generally short-term, were devised to meet the needs of those users who could not be provided for by market forces alone. It is important to note that the question of communications services for Indigenous communities came into focus through this particular optic: the perspective of a larger population of telecommunications users, including consumers, businesses, and public entities, who were captured under the rubric of rural, remote and regional Australia. This positioning gave Indigenous organizations – increasingly capable as sources of policy innovation over this period – a voice and a place at the communications policy table, where the 'adequacy' and 'equitable' distribution of services was at issue.

The mobilization of diverse interests in 'regional telecommunications' did not always translate into well-directed initiatives: the term has always struggled to cohere the wide range of experiences, problems and situations of all those excluded from mainstream urban infrastructure. From the first regional telecommunications inquiry in 2000 to the present, Indigenous voices have had to emphasize the particularity of circumstances in their societies. Submissions consistently argue the need to design and implement programs with community involvement, and with on-the-ground knowledge of the conditions and circumstances. As this book argues, basic categories that have passed largely unconsidered in mainstream communications, such as the role of communities, or the continuity of the household as a stable organization for the consumption of services, have generally demanded far more careful thought when placed in an Indigenous context.

Nevertheless, a patchwork of major and minor initiatives followed from 1997 onwards, many of them in direct response to the now-regular cycle of regional communications reviews. While most estimates in this period considered around 2 per cent of Australians to be living in locations where commercial communications services were not viable, a considerable amount of public funding supported services beyond that roughly defined group. Several different approaches were at work. For instance, general purpose grants were offered by Networking the Nation (1997-2004), which used $250 million in proceeds from the sale of Telstra to support improved telecommunications for regional, rural and remote communities. Customer subsidies, intended to offset the greater cost of services outside the cities, were offered through Broadband Connect (2005), a $900 million four-year program then replaced by the Australian Broadband Guarantee (2007–2011), which funded internet service providers to offer a basic broadband service for remote users.

More targeted programs have focused on remote Indigenous community needs. The Telecommunications Action Plan for Remote Indigenous Communities (TAPRIC) (2002), Backing Indigenous Ability (2007–2010) and the successor Indigenous Communications Program (ICP) funded community projects. Much of the funding in these programs was dedicated to the provision of public payphones. According to the 2005–2006 Budget, TAPRIC's initiatives sought 'to overcome a number of complex logistical and social factors affecting the provision of basic telephone services in remote Indigenous communities'.[4] TAPRIC funded the Community Phones Program, which rolled out public phones designed by the Centre for Appropriate Technology (CAT) for the specific needs of remote communities. It also involved a stocktake of the existing infrastructure in remote communities, drawing on Australian Bureau of Statistics (ABS) survey data.

Alongside these specific-purpose programs, a number of longer-term responses to regional disadvantage in a liberalized system were enacted, with lasting consequences. Concerns about consumer safeguards were addressed through a service guarantee, designed to ensure that telecommunications providers repaired faults and dealt with problems in a timely manner. Telstra, as the dominant network operator, has been funded to provide, among other public interest services such as payphones, a standard telephone service (STS) under a Universal Service Obligation (USO).

The USO has been an ongoing topic of debate in Australia, particularly in regard to its impact on competition, what should be included in the USO, and its susceptibility to political interests.[5] In theory, a USO is a market design mechanism that works to transfer some of the consumer surplus from one group as an implicit subsidy to another group by effectively forcing a monopoly provider to treat them all as a single market, and by prohibiting price discrimination. A core rationale for the USO in Australia is to provide access to telecommunications for those residing outside cities. The result should be that everyone receives the same supply and pays the same price: the USO thus imposes a kind of transfer from urban to remote consumers via a single provider. However, this has not been the reality.

---

4   Commonwealth of Australia, 'Budget: Indigenous Partnerships', http://www.budget.gov.au/2005-06/ministerial/html/dotars-12.htm.

5   H. Raiche, 'Universal Communications in a Broadband World: Working Paper', Inaugural Australian Communications Consumer Action Network (ACCAN) Conference, Melbourne, 2010; McElhinney, 'Telecommunications Liberalisation and the Quest for Universal Service in Australia'.

The policy problems of the USO have emerged gradually, but are now manifold and prominent. First, Telstra has not seen the USO as extending to remote services, especially for smaller communities, thereby creating the need for a succession of gap-filling programs. Consumers in remote Australia are generally not able to access landlines (the STS) as the cost of cables and trenches is still borne by the consumer (and is prohibitive).

Second, the STS is conceived in terms of specific technologies and services, which are of diminishing relevance everywhere, and especially in remote Australia.[6] It cannot then reflect the evolving needs of communications users, which now extend well beyond basic telephony, or the rollout of new broadband networks that do not rely on Telstra's copper infrastructure. Voice services are increasingly used through internet applications that are more flexible, and cheaper than the STS, with support for video, messaging and other functions. But internet access is not part of the USO. Mobile cellular services are vital for network access, but neither are these the focus of the USO. Indeed, the failure of the USO model brings into focus one of the central arguments of this book: the need for a more flexible policy framework that ensures continuing funding for uneconomic services, and which that can respond to local community circumstances and preferences.

The election of the Rudd Labor government in 2007 marked a shift away from the cycle of end-user subsidy schemes towards a more ambitious rethinking of Australia's communications system. The NBN was conceived as a universally accessible high-speed network that would ensure Australia's place in the future 'digital economy'. It was intended as a general solution to regional and remote disadvantage, through a uniform pricing structure and advanced satellite and fixed wireless services for those households and premises beyond the reach of viable fiber infrastructure. But the network also embodied a micro-economic reform agenda, with NBN's neutral wholesale role taking over from Telstra's compromised position in the market, and a service design that would encourage and enable a more diverse range of large and small retailers.[7]

For remote communities, the rollout of the NBN meant the closure of the Broadband Guarantee scheme – which had not in any case been easy to access (see Chapter 2) – and the introduction of an Interim Satellite Service (ISS), replaced in 2016 by the much

---

6   E. Rennie and J. Potts, 'Auction Subsidies and the Universal Service Obligation: The Case for Remote Indigenous Communities', Submission to the Regional Telecommunications Independent Review (RTIRC), 2015, http://www.rtirc.gov.au/submissions/.

7   Some have speculated that the current twenty-year USO contract between the Commonwealth and Telstra was arrived at to secure Telstra's existing infrastructure for the NBN, exposing the vulnerability of the USO to manipulation (it is awarded by ministerial powers, see P. Fletcher MP, 'Speech to the ACCAN USO Forum', http://paulfletcher.com.au/speeches/portfolio-speeches/item/1316-speech-to-the-accan-uso-forum.html). Telstra's competitors have argued that the USO subsidy would be better directed at extending the NBN and utilizing it to expand mobile services in particular; Vodafone Hutchison Australia, 'Regional Telecommunications Review 2015: Submission by Vodafone Hutchison Australia', 2015, http://www.rtirc.gov.au/submissions/.

greater capacity Long Term Satellite Service (LTSS), using two new satellites. The ISS was rapidly fully subscribed, and attracted considerable criticism in the 2011 and 2015 regional telecommunications reviews. Bodies such as the Flying Doctor Service drew particular attention to the inability of the service to support time-critical applications such as remote medical consultations.[8] While the long-term solution is likely to considerably improve the performance of the satellite-delivered NBN, the 2015 review forecast a rapid growth in use, and recommended a number of measures to improve the service.

While the NBN will provide a more capable source for the internet on the outstation, it has long been clear that there cannot be any single infrastructure 'fix' for the digital divide in remote Australia. The ICP was intended to be a targeted supply and maintenance program for fixed community phones, mobile satellite phones for very small communities (oddly not covered by the USO), and equipment and training for internet access. The program evolved in interesting ways, reflecting the evolution of communications in the bush from basic telephony to the broader range of internet-enabled services, and from simple shared facilities, such as payphones, to a more varied ecology of mobile devices. So while the ICP began with a focus on payphones, over its course we can see this infrastructure being re conceptualized as general-purpose internet access points, offering not only a phone but also a wireless access point which could then be shared, with mobile devices, across a group of users. The development and installation of the phones, managed for the Department of Communications by Australian Private Networks (2014), is a remarkable story of ingenuity, opportunism and resourcefulness. The addition of the WiFi capability to the community phone was first trialed at the Laura Dance Festival on Cape York in June 2011, and proved instantly popular. The festival organizer reported later that she could not have run the festival without the WiFi.

As part of Labor's 'Closing the Gap' strategy to redress Indigenous disadvantage, internet access was also provided through a Commonwealth funding agreement with the states and territories, the Remote Indigenous Public Internet Access (RIPIA) National Partnership Agreement. In the Northern Territory, the RIPIA contract was awarded to Northern Territory Libraries. RIPIA reflected the broader social policy agenda of Closing the Gap, and signaled a more developed and far-reaching set of concerns than the earlier emphasis on 'adequate' communications and 'equitable' access. These new goals appear to reflect the more ambitious aspirations of the early NBN period. Better internet access was understood explicitly in terms of building economic and social capital in communities. The objectives were to reduce barriers to services, increase digital literacy and social inclusion, and economic, social and political participation. It followed from this broad vision of the benefits of the internet that, as well as establishing services, maintenance and training

---

8   Regional Telecommunications Independent Review Committee (RTIRC), *Regional Telecommunications Review 2015: Unlocking the Potential in Regional Australia*, Canberra: Commonwealth of Australia, 2015, p. 21.

would also be supported. This expansive agenda cut in two ways. The social dimensions of internet access were also reflected in a requirement that filtering mechanisms be in place for 'illegal and offensive materials'. These provisions could well have ameliorated community concerns about internet access; they also echoed the more draconian and paternalistic tenor of those restrictions on computer use that had been imposed under the Howard government Northern Territory Emergency Response (NTER; 'the Intervention'). However, the RIPIA project was limited in what it could reasonably achieve. Northern Territory Libraries set out to provide access and training in forty sites (the majority in the Top End, not the central desert region), receiving only $6,000 per annum per site for equipment, and a similar amount for training (Broadband for the Bush Alliance, 2013). The program was therefore not able to cater for small communities during the period we are concerned with. In 2015 the national RIPIA program funding was redirected into the Indigenous Advancement Strategy, amounting to $2.2 million to provide 'essential infrastructure such as computers, printers and internet access points to improve internet literacy and educational outcomes for children and adults in around seventy-five remote communities', and administered through a competitive grants-based process.[9]

What has been the result of these policy and program decisions? One result has been that, for over a decade, the dominant mode of provision was shared facilities, in the form of dedicated computer rooms or shared computers in existing public spaces. Networking the Nation, TAPRIC, the ICP and the RIPIA program have all incorporated this approach to varying degrees.

The resulting facilities do appear to have been an important means for internet access in some communities, at least in the early years. The 2001 census included questions that enabled A.E. Daly to estimate the difference between home internet use and internet use 'generally', which might include access at a community center, library, workplace or home.[10] She found that internet use for Indigenous people living outside the capital cities in South Australia and the Northern Territory was three times higher than home use, which was not the case for the non-Indigenous population. (From 2006 onwards the census has only measured internet access from private dwellings.)

In 2009 we undertook a survey of shared internet facilities in the central Australia region. The research involved phone interviews with supervisors or council workers in the thirty-four large communities in central Australia (with a combined Indigenous population of 9,724, or 72 per cent of the Indigenous population of central Australia outside Alice Springs) and visits to ten of those communities. From this we gathered basic information, including whether centers existed, whether they were in continuous use, the number of

---

9   Commonwealth of Australia, 'Budget Paper No. 2: Expense Measures: A New Remote Indigenous Housing Strategy', http://www.budget.gov.au/2015-16/content/bp2/html/bp2_expense-19.htm.

10   Daly, *Bridging the Digital Divide*.

hours they were open, how the centers were funded, user charges, internet speeds and download quotas, as well as supervision arrangements. We also asked survey respondents to provide anecdotal comment on the level and use of activities that occurred in those sites. We found that while shared facilities have played an important role in establishing communications infrastructure, sustainability was a significant concern in many instances.[11]

We found that less than half of the thirty-four communities had community internet access and, of these, many were only semi-functional. Thirteen communities had at least some working computers for community use as of December 2009. Fourteen were without and four were under development. We were unable to obtain information for three communities. The computers were located in council offices, training centers, Centrelink offices, remote Indigenous broadcasting stations (RIBS) and schools. Many facilities were only semi-active, operating with part-time or no supervision, or waiting on maintenance and upgrades.

In one community, there was a room in the council administration building that had once been allocated and equipped with computers for residents' use, but at the time of survey the computing equipment had been dismantled and the room given over to use as the community housing office. This ICT center had not been operational for the past two years. Another community was faring better with four operational computers of varying ages, sharing satellite internet access with the council in a room provided by the council in its administration building. However, the room was only semi-active at the time of the survey, and there was little in the way of training and mentoring support available to residents. In another, one of the metropolitan universities was sponsoring internet services in a small public computing building with six computers, using volunteer supervisors where these could be recruited to assist and train residents in using applications such as email, music downloading and internet banking. However, maintaining a steady flow of volunteers who were able to devote sufficient time to settling into the community, gaining the confidence of the residents and making a lasting contribution to their computer learning was difficult. A town camp was awaiting four computers for their community building, which would ultimately be connected by mobile internet with the assistance of their council.

As these examples demonstrate, community media centers have encountered major obstacles, and in general have only provided limited access. A report from September 2003 for the then Department of Communications, Information Technology and the Arts, commissioned in response to the 2002 TAPRIC recommendations, warned that Commonwealth and state-funded centers were already at risk and unlikely to be viable

---

11   Rennie et al., 'Beyond Public Access?'.

without government support.[12] The report found that cooperative centers with a range of stakeholders were more likely to succeed, as funding overheads could be shared. Our survey confirmed this observation. Moreover, as discussed below, government policy and funding, including for programs such as RIPIA, has chiefly been directed to Indigenous communities with populations greater than 300 people, the idea being that the residents of smaller settlements will travel to larger towns to access services. We had little evidence of residents of the three outstations making use of shared computer rooms in other communities when we commenced in 2010.

In 2014 in the central Australia region, computer rooms were operating at Papunya, Mt Alan, Laramba, Mt Liebig, Kintore, Harts Range, Lake Nash, Areyonga, Amoonguna, Ikuntji, Docker River, Tjwanpa, Titjikala and Papunya. The Yuendumu Computer Centre was closed, and Ali Curung's computer room was dormant. Although the shared facilities approach has been fraught, there have been some notable successes. As discussed in later chapters, we visited the Papunya Internet and Computer Room on a couple of occasions to gauge how remote community members were using computers and the internet at a known successful shared internet facility. As of late 2015, that center had also closed.

A MULTIPLICITY OF PROGRAMS AND REVIEWS

The field of remote communications is characterized by an episodic sequence of programs and reviews, each with different emphases and developing in different ways. As mentioned above, many of these have funded the establishment of facilities, but not their ongoing operation. This was an issue addressed in the first regional telecommunications review, when Besley argued that the ongoing costs of community facilities could be supported by a proportion of the universal cost attributable to the community.[13] Many have funded access, but not training, or training, but not the development of relevant content and applications. Limited by the legacy of the 'adequacy' problem, they have rarely approached digital engagement from the perspective of users, who must deal with all of these dimensions of the new information and communication services.

While policy reviews have raised the profile of this issue, their frequency has encouraged a degree of policy churn. The reviews play a useful 'monitory' function, holding governments and commercial parties accountable. But they have also created a start-stop dynamic, and fostered an environment where the longer-term research and evaluation

---

12   Peter Farr Consultants Australasia, *Connecting Our Communities: Sustainable Networking Strategies for Australian Remote Indigenous Communities,* Canberra: Department of Communications, Information Technology and the Arts, 2003.

13   Regional Telecommunications Inquiry, *Connecting Regional Australia,* Canberra: Department of Communications, Information Technology and the Arts, 2002.

problems have been put to one side, while increasingly familiar advocacy – from one sector or another – takes its place. Every review notes the need for more research, but surprizingly little has been done. A better approach, as the 2015 Regional Telecommunications Review suggests, would be to develop a more robust set of indicators, especially regarding the spatial distribution of facilities and services, and a more ambitious research program, aiming for a systematic understanding of the patterns and dynamics of take-up and use.[14] With that in hand, frequent reviews should not be needed for us to monitor effectively the performance of our networks, and the benefits they may bring to remote communities.

GOVERNING REMOTE COMMUNITIES

A feature of the governmental landscape around remote communities are the discontinuities within and between different regulatory and policy positions. There has been no ready trade in concepts, ideas or objectives between communications policies on the one hand, and Indigenous affairs on the other. While the NBN promised to provide high-speed internet to Australians everywhere, other elements of government concentrated service delivery into larger towns. While public funds were being invested in encouraging computer skills, broadly framed restrictions were being implemented that controlled the use of computers (in particular, restrictions under the NTER during the 2007–2011 period). At the beginning of this chapter, we spoke of the two registers of policy: a communications approach, framed around 'adequacy' and equity of access to services, and a more paternalistic Indigenous policy approach with an emphasis on welfare and control. This simple contrast certainly overlooks the diverse motivations and practices of government in remote Australia. But it also prepares us for starkly different approaches and orientations from different policy domains.

In terms of access to services, Aboriginal communities have a particular character and plight in comparison with other localities with the same remoteness status, due to the historical circumstances of their formation. The larger Aboriginal communities, and some smaller ones that predated the outstation movement, were not created as self-sustaining towns, but were formed from Christian missions and ration stations under policies to encourage centralization, forced sedentariness and assimilation.

For instance, a senior woman at Imangara spoke to us of growing up at Hatches Creek before the outstation was established. Her memories were prompted by printouts from a website that someone at the Central Land Council (CLC) had given her, which included an oral history by Joan Deans, wife of the policeman who was based at the waterhole

---

14   RTIRC, *Regional Telecommunications Review 2015: Unlocking the Potential in Regional Australia,* Canberra: Commonwealth of Australia, 2015.

near Hatches Creek. From 1913 until sometime in the 1970s, Hatches Creek was a mining settlement, producing wolframite, a mineral used in the manufacture of ammunition for the first and second world wars. She explained to us that Warlpiri camped on one side of the waterhole and Alyawarr on the other. They also worked in the mines, presumably alongside the Chinese indentured workers mentioned on the website, and received rations. In a separate conversation she mentioned that when she was a kid 'everyone was working', and they had to wait in line to receive tea, brown sugar and flour. Hatches Creek shrank to fewer than a dozen people after the mines closed down, while other such communities grew into sizeable townships.

From the 1970s, a fundamentally discriminatory legislative system began to be challenged, and Indigenous Australians were granted citizenship rights. Under the Whitlam government, the era of assimilation gave way to new policies of self-determination, including what has been referred to as the 'outstation movement'.[15] In the words of the Aborigines' Progressive Association in 1968, returning land to Aboriginal people was an 'assuagement to hurt sensibilities' that could restore Aboriginal dignity.[16] Policy papers from the time expressed an expectation that a return to country would help overcome a 'culture of poverty', lead to self-determination and provide Indigenous people with the power to negotiate over use of land (for instance, with mining companies).

Those who returned to their country were able to access grants to build sewerage systems, basic roads, and water and electricity connections from 1972 - infrastructure not intended to meet conventional standards, but to provide assistance that would be supplemented by community efforts, including the development of makeshift shelters or humpies.[17] A landmark development came in 1976 when the Fraser government passed the Aboriginal Land Rights (NT) Act, which provided a legal mechanism for Aboriginal people in the Northern Territory to reclaim their ancestral lands, including direct transfer of missions and reserves to Aboriginal freehold land, and the ability to fight for land that currently wasn't already claimed. Further development of outstations occurred through the Community Development Employment Projects (CDEP), a subsidized community employment program, from the late 1980s. Funding for housing came later, during the late 1980s and in the 1990s through ATSIC when people could prove their willingness to live remotely.

The Aboriginal Land Rights Act returned large areas of lands to the Aboriginal people in

15   C.A. Blanchard, *Return to Country: The Aboriginal Homelands Movement in Australia*, Canberra:
      The House of Representatives Standing Committee on Aboriginal Affairs, 1987.

16   R. McGregor, *Indifferent Inclusion: Aboriginal People and the Australian Nation*, Canberra:
      Aboriginal Studies Press, 2011, p. 171.

17   B. Beadman, '"A Tortuous Trail": Bob Beadman's Short History of Outstations', http://aliceonline.
      com.au/2011/10/17/a-tortuous-trail-bob-beadmans-short-history-of-outstations/.

the Northern Territory, although it only allowed ability to claim unoccupied land. Half of the land mass in the Northern Territory is now owned by Aboriginal people. The majority of outstations are on Aboriginal land, although some are on excisions from pastoral leases (known as Community Living Areas, or CLAs) or in national parks. The outstations on CLAs form a critical part of the outstations, or homelands, footprint, signalling how some groups remained connected to their lands, despite appropriation of land by pastoralists.[18] Two outstations in this story, Mungalawurra and Kwale Kwale, are on Aboriginal land, whereas Imangara is a CLA.

Outstations are thus settlements where the residents have a descent-based affiliation, and recognized ownership over the land. People returned to country in order to maintain traditional sites, to fulfill their cultural obligations to manage land, and in some cases to avoid political marginalization in the larger settlements, where the artificial collocation of diverse groups had resulted in significant stresses for those who were not traditional owners or who were descendants of the minority language group. As time progressed, outstations also had the appeal of being removed from the social problems of larger settlements, such as alcohol and violence.[19]

Today there are approximately 400 occupied outstations in the Northern Territory, with a population of around 10,000 living in 2,400 dwellings (about 25 per cent of the rural Aboriginal population of the Northern Territory).[20] In the public imagination, outstations have come to represent 'extreme living', in the sense that they are isolated, with limited access to services and little infrastructure, and are thus represented as a choice to live apart from the majority in favor of maintaining tradition.[21]

In a submission to a 2003 review of outstation policy, CAT pointed out that outstations have been subject to a coordination problem, falling through the net of available services, with resource agencies struggling to meet the costs of outstation operation, battling to extract user contributions to such costs, and under pressure by the ad hoc nature of

---

18   Amnesty International, *The Land Holds Us: Aboriginal Peoples' Right to Traditional Homelands in the Northern Territory*, Broadway, NSW: Amnesty International, 2011, p. 13.

19   Blanchard, *Return to Country*.

20   Northern Territory Department of Education, 'Enrolment and Attendance Statistics', http://www.education.nt.gov.au/students/at-school/enrolment-attendance/enrolment-attendance-statistics/2013-enrolment-and-attendance-statistics, p. 1.

21   J. Altman, *In Search of an Outstations Policy for Indigenous Australians*, Canberra: Centre for Aboriginal Economic Policy Research, 2006; See also: E. Kowal, 'Is Culture the Problem or the Solution? Outstation Health and the Politics of Remoteness' in J. Altman and M. Hinkson (eds) *Culture Crisis: Anthropology and Politics in Aboriginal Australia*, Sydney: University of New South Wales Press, 2010.

funding programs.[22] Such concerns regarding the coordination and transparency of fund-ing and programs to outstations continue to this day. Some of the problems recounted to us by the communities reflect the ongoing challenge of maintaining outstations.

When our project commenced in 2010, outstations had become the focus of political contention around how best to overcome Indigenous disadvantage. In July 2008, coin-ciding with the NTER and prior to our first consultations, the Commonwealth began divesting itself of funding responsibility for outstations, handing what was available to state and territory governments.[23] Some saw the move as reducing duplications and creating economies of scale to provide services.[24] The Northern Territory government's policy development – designed to coordinate infrastructure and services and 'set a new path for outstations' – received wide criticism. In Pat Dodson's words, outstations were being left to 'wither on the vine'.[25]

There was a growing inclination amongst some right-wing think tanks to regard outsta-tions as entrenching disadvantage and reducing people's opportunities. For instance, the demonization of location was apparent in the Commonwealth Minister for Indigenous Affairs' description of remote communities and outstations as 'cultural museums', and in commentator Helen Hughes' description of the outstations movements as a form of apartheid and a failed 'socialist utopia'.[26] Further, Gary Johns argued that the residents of remote communities and outstations should migrate to towns with greater employ-ment opportunities.[27]

---

22 Indigenous Housing and Infrastructure Branch of the Department of Family and Community Services, *Review of the National Homelands Policy: Stage One*, Centre for Appropriate Technology, 2004, p. iv.

23 While the resourcing of remote communities and services has largely been managed at the state level, outstation funding had remained with the Commonwealth when the Northern Territory government was formed in 1978. The Commonwealth retained responsibility, possibly because of the assumption that the Northern Territory government (CLP at the time) might be hostile to the intentions of land rights.

24 For instance: Beadman, '"A Tortuous Trail"'.

25 P. Mares, 'Homeland Security: NT Indigenous Affairs Minister Outlines Policy', http://www.abc. net.au/radionational/programs/nationalinterest/homeland-security-nt-indigenous-affairs-minister/3147812#transcript; See also: Altman, *In Search of an Outstations Policy for Indigenous Australians*; S. Kerins, *The First-Ever Northern Territory Homelands/Outstations Policy*, CAEPR Topical Issue No. 09/2009, Canberra: ANU Centre for Aboriginal Economic Policy Research, 2009.

26 A. Vanstone, 'Beyond Conspicuous Compassion: Indigenous Australians Deserve More Than Good Intentions', Address to the Australia and New Zealand School of Government, Australian National University, Canberra, 7 December 2005; H. Hughes, *Lands of Shame: Aboriginal and Torres Strait Islander 'Homelands' in Transition*, Sydney: Centre for Independent Studies, 2007.

27 G. Johns, *No Job No House: An Economically Strategic Approach to Remote Aboriginal Housing*, Canberra: The Menzies Research Centre, 2009.

Hughes' and Johns' ideas are likely to have been influential in the policy shift away from supporting outstations and small communities towards a focus on larger Indigenous communities, known as 'priority communities' by the Council of Australian Governments (COAG), or 'Growth Towns' in the Northern Territory. COAG's National Partnership Agreements saw new funding directed to 'priority towns', with both government policies aiming to support a limited number of communities with additional funding resources to the point where facilities would be comparable with those in equivalent-sized regional towns. While the Commonwealth and Northern Territory government groups were not identical, there was a high degree of overlap, with a total of twenty communities targeted in the Northern Territory, all of which had a population upward of 300. The reason not to direct the new funding to smaller communities and outstations was that the transport links between the 'hub' target towns and the smaller communities in their sphere of influence would be upgraded, with a view to encouraging and assisting residents of these smaller communities to utilize the hub services.

New houses were built on the proviso that the prioritized communities signed a lease, ensuring that the Commonwealth had responsibilities for housing in Aboriginal communities. The lease arrangements were part of the government's secure tenure policy, and allowed all community houses to choose to transfer to a public housing model. Meanwhile, other remote Indigenous communities not classified as priority/growth towns or outstations continued to receive funding targeted towards specific services such as local government municipal services (power, water, waste management, roads), health clinics, schools, and police stations. They would also later be asked for a lease, so that their houses could be renovated, upgraded or rebuilt (for houses deemed uninhabitable).[28] Outstations continued to receive general-purpose infrastructure and service funding through a network of outstation resource agencies and shire/regional councils, which were in turn funded by the Northern Territory government. In 2014–15, 423 were funded under the Northern Territory government's homeland programs for housing and municipal and essential services.[29] The Northern Territory government asserted that the funding provided was making a contribution to living in the outstations, recognizing that funding was insufficient to meet all the service and infrastructure needs of residents. There were no new houses for outstations, and the previous ATSIC moratorium on new outstations remains in place.

While the significant increase in funding was welcomed by large communities that were categorized as priority communities, the policy created uncertainty in funding, programs and service delivery arrangements with respect to the great many communities that were

---

28   Imangara's housing was upgraded under this arrangement.

29   The number 423 includes 348 outstations, forty-five town camps and thirty larger communities (who remain on the outstation funding list as legacy from previous funding arrangements by the Commonwealth).

not captured in the priority/growth town policies. There was also evidence within the COAG documents that governments were trying to encourage people into larger settlements, a policy shift that came to be known as 'mainstreaming'. As Moran articulated at the time, such policies of coercing people did not fit well historically as a development policy for remote Indigenous communities.[30]

The policy effectively established a hierarchy of communities in terms of what should be developed and sustained. For some, the issue was one of unequal access to basic services, shelter and support that should be considered an entitlement for all citizens 'that should not be contingent on geographic location, at least in any policy sense'.[31] The mainstreaming approach was also 'premised on utilizing standardized structures and processes for delivering and managing' housing and infrastructure that did not take into account the particular nuances of outstation needs.[32]

Further, Sanders analyzed the populations that would be serviced under the growth towns policy, demonstrating that there was a significant gap for central Australia regions in particular, where at best only 18 per cent of the population were likely to be captured within the 'hub and spoke' of the twenty priority communities.[33] Even with the best transportation options between these large communities and their surrounding smaller communities, there was a significant lack of service coverage for many communities.

We observed at the time that communications policy and Indigenous policy were largely disconnected from each other.[34] The one exception is education, in that schools in Indigenous communities do have internet access, and have been the beneficiaries of various ICT programs in recent decades, as discussed in Chapter 6. At the local level - regardless of policy - communications and other infrastructures, including housing and power, are dependent on each other.

---

30   M. Moran, 'The Viability of "Hub" Settlements', *Dialogue* 29.1 (2010).

31   Kerins, *The First-Ever Northern Territory Homelands/Outstations Policy*, p. 5.

32   R. Grey-Gardner and M. Young, *Utopia Homelands Project: Lessons from Experience*, Centre for Appropriate Technology, Urapuntja Aboriginal Corporation and the Australian Government Department of Prime Minister and Cabinet, 2014, p. 4.

33   W. Sanders. *Working Future: A Critique of Policy by Numbers*, Canberra: ANU Centre for Aboriginal Economic Policy Research, 2010.

34   Rennie et al., *Home Internet for Remote Indigenous Communities*.

HOUSES AND COMMUNITY INFRASTRUCTURE

The average house in a remote Indigenous community will have a lifecycle of four to eight years, will use about a third of the power of a suburban home, will be six times more likely to be overcrowded than other Australian houses, and will have three times more dogs.[35] In 2014, CAT undertook a survey at the Utopia Homelands as part of a $4 million commitment by the Commonwealth government to improve living conditions. In that report, Grey-Gardner and Young observe that residents preferred box air-conditioners over more robust models, because some families lived between three or four houses, taking the air-Mungalawurrucon with them.[36] Such observations are typical in reports by CAT, an organization that takes into account the social life of infrastructure and objects in its development and maintenance projects. The physicality of the outstation house, its occupants and uses, were thus also integral to understanding 'home internet'. We carefully documented the use of computers and internet in relation to household dynamics and other community infrastructures and utilities.

On our second visit to one community, the residents of three separate houses were living under one roof. The taps were not working in one house, and there was no power in the other (perhaps a decision to economize on power bills rather than a power fault). The elderly couple that usually occupied the house on their own told us they were considering moving to a 'humpy or tent' because the house was so crowded. A few months later they had moved into a caravan, given to them by the Church.

As they were inundated with family members, they thought it unwise to have a computer in the house as it would mean people would spend more time indoors. In other instances, we observed that overcrowding was temporary, until another house was repaired. As discussed in Chapter 4, residents moved into different houses over the course of the project.

From the start we were made aware of the issue of power usage, which seemed something of a deterrent for some residents in their decision whether to have a computer. Each community had a different arrangement for utilities. Mungalawurru has solar power with a back-up generator, and water is supplied via a bore on the land trust. The community houses and shed in Kwale Kwale are serviced by mains power and water supply from Power and Water, except for one outlying house in the settlement with solar power. Imangara has a generator for power supply, shared with the pastoral station and school, and water is supplied from a nearby bore on the pastoral station.

---

35   K.W. Seemann, M. Parnell, S. McFallan and S. Tucker, *Housing for Livelihoods: The Lifecycle of Housing and Infrastructure Through a Whole-of-System Approach in Remote Aboriginal Settlements*, Vol. 29, Alice Springs: Desert Knowledge CRC, 2008.

36   R. Grey-Gardner and M. Young, *Utopia Homelands Project: Lessons from Experience*, p. 10.

Power bills for all purposes at Kwale Kwale and Imangara were a significant expense at around $50 a month (higher during winter). To receive power, residents need to purchase a power card from a store and insert it into a meter. They were thus very aware of their power usage, telling us that they were conscious not to use too many appliances. Some were concerned that having a computer would significantly increase their power costs. As it turned out, power became more of an issue when computers were located in shared spaces, as people did not necessarily contribute to purchasing ongoing power cards for these buildings.

We delve further into the dynamics of housing, bills and other infrastructure issues in Part II of this book. These were to become important for understanding household decision-making in relation to the internet, and revealed how the physical circumstances that have marred remote communications from the start continue to manifest at the level of everyday contemporary household routines, inconveniences and capacities. We conclude this chapter with a brief description of each of the communities.

KWALE KWALE

Kwale Kwale is a small family outstation situated on the Iwupataka Aboriginal Land Trust, approximately 40 kilometers west of Alice Springs. The community is nestled near the foot of the MacDonnell Ranges (an area known as Tjoritja to its traditional owners) in rugged and varied desert landscape. Kwale Kwale is one of twelve or so family homelands across the land trust, residents of which descend from four main family groups. Most residents speak Western Arrernte and Luritja. Kwale Kwale has twelve to fifteen permanent residents, with the majority of these descending from one family group. When we first started visiting the outstation, it was also populated by scores of peacocks, kept as pets by the senior women. The free-roaming menagerie had successfully intimidated the local dogs into submission.

The outstation has six houses (not including an old burnt-out house) and a large shed with concrete floors and a veranda, with the indoor space divided into three rooms. One room of the shed was being used as a chapel during this period; the others for various purposes.

Two of the remaining houses stand at a distance from the others, and were occupied by residents not related to the family. One was being used as a youth respite service for troubled youths, run by an older Aboriginal man. The program was taking on youth with law and justice problems, and providing rehabilitation for them away from town. A single Aboriginal man, who was employed in town but enjoyed living remotely, occupied the other house.

IMANGARA

Imangara is 207 kilometers by road south-east of Tennant Creek, 30 kilometers past Ali Curung. The community has a permanent residency of around eighty residents, who are primarily descendants of five main family groups from the region. The residents mostly speak Alyawarr, but also Kaytetye. The community has eleven houses and three sheds, which are permanently occupied by family groups. As discussed below, there are also other community facilities, including a women's center and a school.

Imangara is a CLA located on the Murray Downs pastoral station. When land rights were granted, those whose country was being used by others for agricultural purposes were left out. CLAs were designed to overcome that by excising land from pastoral leases so that the traditional owners might live there. The Imangara excision was granted in 1979 in recognition of the close ties that a number of Alyawarr families have with the surrounding country. The fenced living area is 84.72 hectares, located 2 kilometers east of Murray Downs homestead. Over the years that we visited, Imangara cycled through hard times and good times. Dwellings were abandoned, and then later some old houses were repaired and new ones built. Grasses would grow dangerously high at times, and be susceptible to fires. Personal tragedies gutted what had seemed a cohesive township, followed by what seemed a spike in religious activities such as gospel music and church services.

MUNGALAWURRU

The Mungalawurru community lies approximately 80 kilometers from Tennant Creek on the Karlantijpa North Aboriginal Land Trust (ALT), along with the homelands of Napagunpa, Blue Bush, Kumunu and Kalumpurlpa, which are all to the north of Mungalawurru. The land trust was established in the 1980s. To the south of Mungalawurru is Karlantijpa South ALT, west is Central Desert ALT, and to the east Phillip Creek pastoral station and the old Warrego gold mine site. Mungalawurru lies on a flat plain in spinifex country. A few trees have been planted for shelter at one end of the community, but otherwise the outstation is exposed to high winds and hot sun. At times, blue-green puddles appeared on the road into Mungalawurru, formed from sulfur used to neutralize cyanide from the tailings dam. The road into the community is bitumen for two-thirds of the drive, but the last third regularly became inaccessible in the rain. We were forced to turn back on occasion, and the residents told us of having to walk that 30 kilometers to the bitumen when they got cut off.

The community has close ties with other homelands on this land trust and the land trust to the south, with many family members residing in Tennant Creek, Mungkarta and Ali Curung. The residents primarily speak Warlmanpa, but also Warumungu and Warlpiri. Mungalawurru is officially home to approximately twenty-two permanent residents.

The Mungalawurru community residents have a close association with Phillip Creek pastoral station and Warrego mine, which ceased production in 1989. Many senior residents were students at the Warrego Mine School before the mine closed down. Now the family's school-aged children reside in Tennant Creek.

The community has five occupied houses and twelve tin sheds, some of which are used as houses and others as community facilities, including an art shed and a health clinic.

CONCLUSION

Indigenous social policy and communications policy have particular histories and objectives, and have at times been contradictory in their treatment of remoteness, including the viability of remote living, and government's responsibility to provide infrastructure to all Australians. As the Australian Commonwealth moves towards a 'digital by default' strategy of service provision, the issue of how those living in remote Australia will access services online becomes more critical. In the next chapter, we take a closer look at the notion of the digital divide and discuss the practical aspects of bringing internet to the outstations.

Chapter 2: Infrastructure

When we first visited the three outstations, only one house out of twenty-four had an internet connection. A man at Kwale Kwale who was living on the community with the permission of the traditional owners had figured out that he could receive a tolerable mobile broadband signal 40 kilometers from Alice Springs by taping a 3G stick modem to a pole on his roof, connected to his computer by a long ethernet cable. His house was located a kilometer from the main cluster of houses, and his solution had gone unnoticed by others at Kwale Kwale, as he did not interact much with the family. Four years later, fifteen households in the three communities had home internet connections, received via domestic satellite dishes planted on the roofs of their houses. The residents were paying for the internet through a retail service provider under standard contracts. We had assisted them to sign up for the services, but the decision to acquire the services was entirely their own.

This chapter describes the decisions and steps that led to residents accessing the internet at the outstations, and how these efforts fitted within our research approach. We discuss the reasons for using a trial approach to understanding a digital divide problem, and how the process of providing computers and internet enabled us to test some policy assumptions around the most effective or most culturally appropriate forms of access. Although on the surface our approach resembles previous studies that have occurred in the area of information and communications technology (ICT) for development, we explain how our motivations and actions differed somewhat from that particular field of research. In the second half of the chapter, we provide a plain-language account of some of the technical components of the project.[37] Our interest in, and documentation of, the material aspects of the hardware, as well as our own interactions with the internet service providers, yielded important insights into how infrastructure can frame social relations and influence people's digital choices.

THE DIGITAL DIVIDE

As discussed in the introduction, we set out to examine a digital divide problem, in that we were interested in understanding what benefits, if any, digital resources confer on individuals and groups, and whether those who are *not* making use of them are disadvantaged as a result. The term 'digital divide' has fallen in and out of favor amongst media studies researchers since it first emerged in public discourse during the 1990s. These debates are helpful in understanding the limits of research on internet adoption and use, and informed how we carried out our work.

---

37   For a detailed description, see: A. Crouch, *Home Internet for Remote Indigenous Communities: Technical Report*, Alice Springs: Centre for Appropriate Technology, 2014.

The digital divide was first used as a measure of how the 'Information Society' was progressing within and between nation-states. Countries began to measure computer and internet ownership as an indicator of knowledge economy growth and competitive advantage. These exhaustive statistical studies were based on a tradition of work on telephone penetration, such as that developed by the National Telecommunications and Information Administration (NTIA) in the United States, and the emphasis on hardware and network reach was carried over to the analysis of the social distribution of the internet. The NTIA positioned the digital divide as physical access to computers by measuring the number of households and individuals with a computer and internet connection, and in 2002 declared the divide was largely overcome – 'we are truly a nation online' – with the internet being used at work, schools, and libraries as well as at home by over half of the American population, and rising by two million new users a month.[38]

However, by the early 2000s, a wave of scholarly attention had emerged that refuted simplistic notions of the divide as referring to physical access to computers. The 'either you have access to ICT or you do not, you are either connected or you are not' approach, it was argued, assumed that with enough resources and political will, the divide was easy to close or bridge.[39] Even with computers, some people did not have the necessary skills or motivation to make use of them to the same degree as others.[40] Skills, autonomy of use (including where access occurred), attitudes towards technology (relevance), and types of use therefore became the main themes of digital divide research. The refocused concern for the social dimensions of usage was considered 'a more elaborate and realistic understanding of inequalities in the information age'.[41]

Analyses of data sets drawn from many different countries have revealed strong correlations between socio-economic status and internet adoption. Some theorists have argued that as social disadvantages, such as low income and lack of education, appear to be linked to the digital divide, the divide can only be addressed by tackling those apparent causes – effectively rendering the concept redundant, or at least unexceptional as a

---

38   US Department of Commerce, *A Nation Online: How Americans Are Expanding Their Use of the Internet*, Economics and Statistics Administration and National Telecommunications and Information Administration, 2002, p. 2.

39   N. Selwyn, 'Reconsidering Political and Popular Understandings of the Digital Divide', *New Media & Society* 6.3 (2004): 345.

40   J. Van Dijk and K. Hacker, 'The Digital Divide as a Complex and Dynamic Phenomenon', *The Information Society* 19.4 (2003); P. DiMaggio and E. Hargittai, 'From the "Digital Divide" to "Digital Inequality": Studying Internet Use as Penetration Increases' *Princeton Center for Arts and Cultural Policy Studies* 4.1 (2001): 4-2.

41   Selwyn, 'Reconsidering Political and Popular Understandings of the Digital Divide': 346.

singular policy concern.[42] However, as Helsper notes, 'there remains significant debate around the existence, nature and causality of these links', a question we address directly in Chapter 9.[43]

The most recent research on the digital divide seeks to know whether internet use produces tangible outcomes, and whether unequal distribution in the ways that people use the internet is reinforcing existing inequalities. These studies are asking who benefits most from being online in terms of economic, cultural, social and personal wellbeing, and how this links to skills and online engagement.[44] Researching tangible outcomes requires establishing a hierarchy in the nature or quality of use and mapping the opportunities people choose to take up.[45] For instance, online resources, such as being able to look at job classifieds online, can translate into being able to find a job through access to more opportunities. Studies of how people enact online opportunities tend to support what is known as the *Matthew effect*, whereby the rich get richer, or the *knowledge gap hypothesis*, which posits that those with more resources gain skills and technologies before others, thus reaping advantages sooner and increasing rather than decreasing knowledge gaps in society.[46] Van Deursen and Van Dijk found that in the Netherlands, where internet adoption is near-ubiquitous (96 per cent of the population), capital-enhancing online opportunities are more likely to be taken up by those with higher education and income 'which would accordingly reinforce their already strong positions in society'.[47] However, some groups defy prediction, displaying high levels of digital inclusion despite experiencing other disadvantages.[48] As part of our research in the outstations, we routinely asked

---

42   M. Warschauer, 'Dissecting the "Digital Divide": A Case Study in Egypt', *The Information Society* 194 (2003): 297-304; P. Norris, 'The Worldwide Digital Divide', Annual Meeting of the Political Studies Association of the UK, London School of Economics and Political Science, 2000.

43   E. Helsper, *Digital Inclusion: An Analysis of Social Disadvantage and the Information Society*, London, UK: Department for Communities and Local Government, 2008, p. 8.

44   For a useful overview, see E. Helsper, A. Van Deursen and R. Eynon, *Tangible Outcomes of Internet Use: From Digital Skills to Tangible Outcomes Project Report*, Oxford Internet Institute, University of Twente and London School of Economics and Political Science, 2015.

45   Such as: S. Livingstone and E. Helsper, 'Gradations in Digital Inclusion: Children, Young People and the Digital Divide', *New Media & Society* 9.4 (2007).

46   E.M. Rogers, *Diffusion of Innovations*, 5th edition, New York: Free Press, 2003; K.E. Pearce and R.E. Rice, 'Digital Divides from Access to Activities: Comparing Mobile and Personal Computer Internet Users', *Journal of Communication* 63.4 (2013).

47   A. Van Deursen, J. Van Dijk, and P.M. Ten Klooster, 'Increasing Inequalities in What We Do Online: A Longitudinal Cross Sectional Analysis of Internet Activities Among the Dutch Population (2010 to 2013) over Gender, Age, Education, and Income', *Telematics and Informatics* 32.2 (2015): 259.

48   E. Helsper, 'A Corresponding Fields Model for the Links Between Social and Digital Exclusion', *Communication Theory* 22.4 (2012).

people questions about their internet use, as well as what they would like to learn to do, in order to understand how the residents responded to the opportunities of being online. Determining whether Indigenous Australians living in remote areas were making different choices from other Australians, and why, was one of the central questions we set out to answer.

In attempting to research the digital divide in remote Aboriginal communities, we were presented with some unique challenges. Many people in remote communities had never used the internet when we commenced (including the majority of adults in the three communities). While other studies have moved on from basic questions of use versus non-use, this was clearly still important to our research. Moreover, although most countries possess longitudinal data on internet adoption and use that enable statisticians to draw correlations between internet access and other forms of social inclusion, as explained below, remote Indigenous populations have been left out of many Australian data sets. We also had serious doubts as to whether the questions being asked of other population groups would tell us much about the dynamics of the digital divide in remote Australia, given that unique factors were in play, including cultural norms, extreme environmental conditions, and a different range of opportunities. Therefore, although we undertook a standard line of questioning around people's online engagement, their attitudes towards technologies and their skills, we set out to examine these in relation to daily life in remote communities.

RESEARCHING THE DIGITAL DIVIDE IN REMOTE AUSTRALIA

Digital inclusion research has mostly been conducted through sample surveys, such as the World Internet Project.[49] These studies show that although the digital divide in Australia is narrowing, it is doing so increasingly slowly.[50] However, sample surveys of internet use in Australia have bypassed remote Aboriginal communities due to the obstacles posed by lack of landlines (generally used to administer surveys), as well as language and cultural barriers. There is also no current data on ICT infrastructures in remote communities, which prevented us from providing an in-depth analysis of adoption in relation to different kinds of internet programs and services nationwide (see Chapter 9 for an analysis of mobile adoption in the central Australia region). Although ICT infrastructure

---

49   ARC Centre of Excellence for Creative Industries and Innovation, 'World Internet Project (Australia)', http://www.cci.edu.au/projects/world-internet-project-australia; See also: Australian Communications and Media Authority, *Communications Report 2012-13*, Canberra: Commonwealth of Australia, 2013.

50   R. Morsillo, 'Affordable Broadband for All Australians', *Telecommunications Journal of Australia* 62.5 (2012): 78.1-78.16; S. Ewing and J. Thomas, *The Internet in Australia*, Brisbane: ARC Centre of Excellence for Creative Industries and Innovation, 2010.

was included in the Community Housing and Infrastructure Needs Survey (CHINS), the last CHINS collection occurred in 2006, and the survey has since been discontinued.[51] A key report on internet use in remote communities produced by the Australian Communications and Media Authority (the communications regulator), published in 2008, relied heavily on this data. Telstra's Telecommunications Action Plan for Remote Indigenous Communities (TAPRIC) data (see Chapter 1) is not publicly available.

For this reason, we restricted our analysis of available statistics to the central Australian region, where we were able to determine available infrastructure through our networks. As described in Chapter 9, the census provides a limited amount of information related to the internet. However, we gained insight into variations in adoption by examining how 2011 census data on households' internet connections corresponded to our own knowledge of types of internet available.

As so little research had been conducted on internet adoption and use in central Australia, we were conscious that measures typically used to gauge 'high versus low order' internet use would not necessarily apply. Determining whether the internet was used for job searches, for instance, says little about digital inclusion when there are no jobs nearby (or where employers are not using the internet to promote those jobs that are available). Understanding the tangible outcomes of internet use thus required significant engagement with communities to understand their particular circumstances and priorities, which we undertook across a four-year time-frame. As Correa and Pavez note in their study of first encounters with the internet in remote (non-Indigenous) communities in Chile, 'geographic isolation makes the social context more decisive in any action or decision', and digital inclusion is a process that involves 'multiple dimensions such as technological access, skills, different uses, social contexts and support'.[52]

Tim Rowse has observed that, when used in policy contexts, statistics can create a 'regime of truth' that overrides the lived realities and dynamics of remote communities.[53] Economist Amartya Sen makes a similar point in relation to social exclusion.[54] Exclusion,

---

51   Administered by the former Department of Families, Housing, Community Services and Indigenous Affairs (FaHCSIA).

52   T. Correa and I. Pavez, 'Digital Inclusion in Rural Areas: A Qualitative Exploration of Challenges Faced by People from Isolated Communities', International Communications Association Conference, San Juan, 2015, p. 5.

53   T. Rowse, 'Re-Figuring "Indigenous Culture"' in J. Altman and M. Hinkson (eds) Culture Crisis: Anthropology and Politics in Aboriginal Australia, Sydney: University of New South Wales Press, 2010, p. 157.

54   A. Sen, Social Exclusion: Concept, Application, and Scrutiny, Manila: Asian Development Bank, 2000.

he argues, needs to be understood in terms of the causal process, which requires an understanding of the social context. Sen's capabilities approach is a useful framework for considering the digital divide, as it asks what substantive freedoms people possess given the constraints placed upon them, and about their ability to enact the outcomes that they value.[55] We found that particular deprivations can be difficult to understand when encountering individuals in remote communities when no background information is available. For instance, on an early visit, we asked a man if he was living in the community, and whether he was interested in having the internet in his house. He replied that he did not have a house and was living in the 'windbreak' – a makeshift shelter of branches and found objects in someone else's yard. Whether the man was permanently living an itinerant lifestyle – having fallen through the cracks of welfare and housing – or whether his circumstances were the result of the 'temporary mobility' discussed in Chapter 4, changes the meaning, duration and consequences of what we might consider to be a hardship. Putting up with inadequate shelter because of a willing decision to visit relatives is different to not being able to afford accommodation, or being excluded from a public housing register. As Sen writes, 'The issue, ultimately, is what freedom does a person have – everything considered. It should come as no surprise that a person's deprivation can have diverse origins and may take disparate forms'.[56]

For Rowse, the appropriate unit of analysis is not comparison between statistically identifiable groups, but an understanding of how a group of people in a particular place is 'doing well or doing badly in ways that are specific to region and cultural heritage'.[57] Although we were not able to conduct a nationwide investigation of internet in remote communities, in conducting our qualitative research on the three outstations (complemented by two case study investigations in two larger towns), we were able to understand better what digital exclusion means in relation to the specific circumstances of remote community life and individual agency.

TRIALS AND EXPERIMENTS

Neither can standard statistical approaches tell us about the effectiveness of particular interventions. A different approach to digital divide studies has been to provide ICT infrastructure where there is none, and to measure the outcomes. The benefit of trials

---

55   Sen, *Social Exclusion*; M. Nussbaum, 'Capabilities as Fundamental Entitlements: Sen and Social
     Justice', *Feminist Economics* 9.2-3 (2003); J. Bath and N. Biddle, 'Measures of Indigenous
     Wellbeing and Their Determinants Across the Life Course', CAEPR Lecture Series, The Australian
     National University, 2011.

56   Sen, *Social Exclusion*, p. 29.

57   Rowse, 'Re-Figuring "Indigenous Culture"', p. 156.

is that they can produce insights into how a technology or system fares within a social context. The small-scale intervention that we designed was intended to examine a specific policy position, in that shared internet facilities were presumed to be the most viable and appropriate, and yet there was no evidence to support one form of internet access over another (see Chapter 1). Moreover, only communities with a population of over 300 people were eligible to apply for funding for shared facilities at the time. By implementing our alternative policy approach, we set out to understand whether shared facilities were the most desirable and practical solution, and what might work in their absence. If personal ownership and acquisition were possible, then understanding what level of assistance and maintenance (if any) was necessary could assist Indigenous organizations to develop their own programs.

A small-scale trial of the kind that we embarked upon cannot be used to make reliable predictions, as the results are specific to the time, place and people involved. However, qualitative research of this kind has the advantage of showing *why* a particular approach works, and of providing insight into complex social dynamics. In the field of education technology, some studies have attempted experimental research using randomized controlled trials, whereby the intervention is applied to a statistically significant group, selected randomly, and compared to a non-treatment group.[58] Such approaches seek to show definitively if an intervention works, and can provide strong evidence that can be used to support and justify particular policy responses. Large randomized controlled trials still require qualitative research in order to understand how or why the particular outcome has occurred. While valuable, the experimental approach is not usually practical when working with Indigenous communities, where the processes of consent and consultation can preclude random selection, and where projects need to be adaptive to accommodate community concerns and needs.

The Home Internet Project trial involved three stages. The first involved consultation with the outstations and a baseline study. On our first visits to the communities in 2010, the Central Land Council (CLC) and the Centre for Appropriate Technology (CAT) made initial contact and consulted with community members, at which time the elders agreed to the project. During our early meetings with the communities, we carefully documented their prior use of ICTs, and tried to ascertain what they perceived to be the barriers to ICT uptake, and the opportunities available through having computers and

58   K.L. Kraemer, J. Dedrick and P. Sharma, 'One Laptop Per Child: Vision Vs. Reality', *Communications of the ACM* 52.6 (2009): 66-73; D.W. Grissmer, R.F. Subotnik, and M. Orland, *A Guide to Incorporating Multiple Methods in Randomized Controlled Trials to Assess Intervention Effects*, Washington, DC: American Psychological Association (2009); Abhijit V. Bannerjee, and Esther Duflo, *Poor Economics: A Radical Rethinking of the Way to Fight Global Poverty*, New York: Public Affairs (2011).

internet access (see below).[59] In the second phase, from 2011, we monitored the issues as they unfolded, and carried out research in two larger communities in order to compare home internet with other types of access. CAT provided a total of twenty computers and associated satellite services connecting all computers to the internet in Kwale Kwale (four), Mungalawurru (five) and Imangara (eleven).[60] Aside from the research field trips, CAT researchers also carried out regular ICT training and maintenance support in the communities for two years from the commissioning of the facilities. In the mid-phase of the project, we extracted usage data from a small number of computers (with the owners' permission) to confirm that the computers were in fact being used in the way we were told. We also broke off into teams to conduct case studies in two larger communities, one with a successful shared internet facility (Papunya), and the other with mobile coverage (Ali Curung). The case studies proved important in that they enabled us to compare home satellite internet with other infrastructures. In the third phase, from the end of 2013, we assisted the households to set up internet services (where desired), and documented the transition. Participants were given the choice to maintain internet access by paying for their own plans under a government-subsidized program, the National Broadband Network (NBN) Interim Satellite Service (ISS). We continued to visit the communities in 2014 in order to understand how the households were faring with their own internet services. That final stage of the research, where households decided whether to transition to the NBN and to maintain their own services, was revealing, providing important insights into how the government's solution to providing internet to remote areas was failing this particular group (see Part III).

Much of our time during our research visits was spent traipsing from house to house, checking up on the computers, providing people with fresh paper, inks and accessories, as well as responding to requests for on-the-spot training in ICT skills and applications. We became the technical help – the IT support – performing mundane tasks to remove a frustration and return things to normality. Those of us who were less IT proficient were asked to help set up accounts, but we also learnt to blow the red dust off a circuit board, and check for first principles (cords plugged in, power supply on). These ad hoc house visits were as informative for us as they were for the residents, giving us a snapshot of how different individuals were learning how to use the computer, how they maintained the computer, and what these factors might say about the relative value of ICTs in the outstations.

Our research approach thus involved a degree of ethnographic observation, but accrued through short visits of a day or two's duration every six weeks or so in each community. CAT and the CLC had a great deal of background knowledge of the families and

59   Rennie et al., *Home Internet for Remote Indigenous Communities*.

60   With funding from the Aboriginals Benefits Account (ABA).

communities, and received information through their extensive networks of events that occurred during the trial period. Such information was useful in helping us to avoid intruding on the communities during difficult or inconvenient times, although sometimes our information networks failed us (the worst example being when we showed up the same day a coffin was delivered). The following chapters draw on such information, but this book should not be taken as a full anthropological account of these communities; nor do we think such an approach was necessary. As the project progressed, we became increasingly aware that a less-intrusive approach was sufficient, and perhaps preferable, for understanding the digital divide, partly as it was easiest to discuss computers in our roles as helpers.

ICT FOR DEVELOPMENT

On the surface, our approach resembled what is known as ICT for development (ICT4D), in that we were introducing a technology to a population that was largely going without. Although the findings and critique of ICT4D are useful in considering the dynamics and outcomes of our work, we do not locate our approach in this field of research. Instead, the trial occurred in what we see as a trajectory of media and communications projects initiated in remote communities through Indigenous organizations in collaboration with researchers.

Development communications (or 'communications for development' or 'development for social change') has a long history that we do not have space to recount here.[61] The practice of development communications generally involves an external agency operating within a situation of need, where this role cannot be performed by the community, or by the government agencies charged with serving it. These projects are based on the rationale that communications technology is integral to social and material advancement in order to facilitate the exchange of ideas in a well-functioning society, and to overcome inequities in access to information. Development communications has been widely critiqued for overlooking the inherently social aspects of communications technology, and for assuming that technical and administrative solutions can overcome structural and political inequalities.

ICT4D is a variant on development communication, in that it moves away from development as merely an outside aid program, to something that could be entrepreneurial

---

61 See F. Enghel and K. Wilkins, 'Communication, Media and Development: Problems and Perspectives', *Nordicom Review* 33 (Special Issue) (2012); J. Servaes, 'Introduction' in J. Servaes (ed.) *Communication for Development and Social Change*, New Delhi: Sage, 2008.

and work in harmony with corporate and national economic aspirations.[62] ICT4D has a tendency to assume that ICT is inherently 'meta-enabling technology that will bypass all institutional and infrastructural obstacles', providing unlimited opportunities for social and economic development.[63] Those at the 'bottom of the pyramid' are assisted to improve their circumstances through online engagement and enterprise. Early iterations of ICT4D argued in favor of shared facilities, which were considered to 'take advantage of economies of scope', as they aggregated demand across an entire community, 'thus reducing costs, while increasing traffic and helping to integrate the facility into the social fabric of the community'.[64]

Faye Ginsburg has critiqued the 'neo-developmental' logic of the digital divide framework generally, arguing that Indigenous peoples in particular are often depicted as 'waiting, endlessly, to catch up to the privileged West' on the technological front.[65] Traditional peoples are thus treated as existing in a separate time, not just place, from the mainstream. As Mazzarella points out, the 'insistence that computers come later' perpetuates the assumption that technology should be evaluated in terms of a hierarchy of needs that can be known in advance.[66] He asks, 'What if the power of a medium is as much performative as it is functional – that is to say, what if it brings about its effects as much through the desires people invest in it as through its ability to deliver predefined utilities?'[67]

Mazzarella's question is important. As explored in Chapter 1, overcoming Indigenous disadvantage has been a contentious and highly politicized field in recent years. The digital divide can appear as a minor concern in contrast to pressing disparities in health and education, or housing needs. However, the possibilities and outcomes of communications technologies are less easy to anticipate and to measure.

---

62   P. Chakravartty, 'Rebranding Development Communications in Emergent India', *Nordicom Review* 33 (Special Issue) (2012).

63   T.T. Sreekumar and M. Rivera-Sánchez, 'ICTs and Development: Revisiting the Asian Experience', *Science Technology & Society* 13.2 (2008): 165.

64   M.L. Best and C.M. Maclay, 'Community Internet Access in Rural Areas: Solving the Economic Sustainability Puzzle', in G.S. Kirkman, P.K. Cornelius, J.D. Sachs and K. Schwab (eds) *The Global Information Technology Report: Readiness for the Networked World*, Oxford: Oxford University Press, 2002, p. 83.

65   F. Ginsburg, 'Rethinking the Digital Age' in D. Hesmondhalgh and J. Toynbee, *The Media and Social Theory*, New York: Routledge, 2008, pp. 129-44.

66   W. Mazzarella, 'Beautiful Balloon: The Digital Divide and the Charisma of New Media in India', *American Ethnologist* 37.4 (2010).

67   Mazzarella. 'Beautiful Balloon'.

We did not see our project as an ICT4D project because we were working with and through Indigenous organizations with long track records in service delivery and infrastructure. CAT in particular performs a watchdog function, starting from a research perspective of determining what works and why before providing services. In the years preceding our project, CAT had been directly involved in government community ICT initiatives, including the development and implementation of an alternative community phone project that provided over 250 pay phones to remote communities. The phone operated with pre-paid cards, and was built from the electronic components of readily available domestic Telstra phones to enable cheap and easy replacement, encased in a stainless steel shell that protected it from damage.[68] The CAT phone became known as the 'NED phone' due to its likeness to Ned Kelly's armor.[69] During the period within which the home internet trial took place, other Indigenous organizations, including the Indigenous Remote Communications Association and its member groups, were striving to bring their board members into the NBN debate, and building knowledge and alliances within communities.

Government agencies that serve remote communities are not necessarily incentivized to commit to small-scale initiatives, particularly trials where the outcome is unknown (the Australian Private Networks community phones WiFi project being an exception). The history of communications in remote Indigenous Australia reflects this, whereby many innovations have occurred 'pre-policy' and in an ad hoc fashion through the efforts of the Indigenous sector, including broadcast infrastructure, screen and radio production, high-frequency (two-way) radio networks, satellite television and videoconferencing. Indigenous-owned organizations, together with local leaders, have carried out these experiments, aided (and in some cases generated) by non-Indigenous workers from the education and media sectors. The enterprises and infrastructures of remote media and communications have thus arisen from two cultural traditions operating together within the one settler state.[70] This is not to say that our presence in the communities was unproblematic – for us or the residents – but only to recognize, as Melinda Hinkson writes, that the sometimes-uneasy coming together of two traditions is the ground upon which the Indigenous communications industry has been built.[71]

---

68 See A. Crouch, 'The Community Phone Project: An Overview', DKCRC Working Paper 46, Alice Springs: Desert Knowledge CRC, 2009.

69 The CAT phones project was replaced with the solar and satellite community phones operated by Australian Private Networks from 2009 (see Chapter 9).

70 See P. Batty, *Governing Cultural Difference: The Incorporation of the Aboriginal Subject into the Mechanisms of Government with Reference to the Development of Aboriginal Radio and Television in Central Australia*, Adelaide: University of South Australia, 2003; M. Hinkson, 'What's in a Dedication? On Being a Warlpiri DJ', *The Australian Journal of Anthropology* 15.2 (2004).

71 Hinkson, 'What's in a Dedication?':110.

PRIOR EXPERIENCE WITH THE INTERNET

What was the nature of internet access when we began? There were six computers to be found across the three communities when we started, including the one house with an internet connection mentioned at the opening of this chapter. Not all of the computers belonged to those residing in the communities – at least two were on loan or gifted from people outside of the community. In our early conversations with forty-eight of the residents (about 50 per cent of the adult population of the three communities combined), we learnt that over half had used a computer at some point in the past. However, only two-thirds of those who had used a computer had also used the internet, and three-quarters of internet users were aged 30 or under. Those in the 30-45 age bracket were most likely to have used a computer, but not the internet.

Although none of the communities had mobile coverage, approximately 30 per cent of people we spoke to had purchased mobiles for use in town. Some mobiles had been given to school-aged relatives who were staying in town, so that the children could ring the community payphone when they needed to contact home. A third of mobile owners were aware of, or using, their mobile for internet access – mostly for music downloads and/or chat – which amounted to 10 per cent of everyone we spoke to. One woman had accessed the internet on a mobile phone, but had never accessed the internet from a computer. She was to become one of the most frequent users of the internet.

Approximately one-third of those without a computer said that either they didn't know how to use it, or had never considered getting one. This last group generally had very little knowledge of what a computer could be used for, and some older people asked us to explain what we meant by the words 'computer', 'laptop' and 'internet' – questions that left us stammering for non-technical descriptions. One man had seen Twitter feeds on television programs, and grasped that it enabled people to participate in conversations, but wanted to know how that worked.

As discussed in later chapters, there was significant interest in getting computers, primarily for kids' schooling, entertainment, and some cultural and enterprise activities. However, there were also significant doubts around affordability, the security of the equipment and language barriers.[72] As the few individuals who owned a computer, or had owned one in the past, were conscious of who they allowed to use the computer, these computers were not necessarily available to others. One young man kept his laptop locked away when he was not using it. Having only a small number of computers in a community also created annoyances for owners, mostly from others who wanted 'to put songs on their MP3 players'. A woman who owned a laptop was protective of it, telling us that 'people want to use it but I tell them no because they might spoil it'. These conversations suggested that

---

72   Rennie et al., 'At Home on the Outstation'.

there was not a critical mass of computers in the community for everyone to experience computer use, and those that did exist were coveted possessions. In the following chapter we explore how these dynamics of ownership changed after the computers arrived.

It is important to consider that the residents had been living with inadequate telecommunications, and that this perhaps influenced their attitude to acquiring their own internet services. Out of the three communities, only two homes had active telephone lines, both in the same community (Kwale Kwale), and both in the homes of older people. One of these phones had restrictions on it; they could receive calls but could not make any charged calls, except by using a pre-paid phone card. Both phones were initially installed to enable contact with medical services. Imangara and Mungalawurru both had a single public payphone in an outdoor cabinet. The distance to houses at the other end of the community was up to 400 meters. Three older people in Imangara expressed a desire for a home telephone: '[We] would like telephones. The one here breaks a lot. I need a phone to ring family and friends in other places', an older woman told us. The older residents had limited knowledge of what services they were entitled to, or what was available for purchase. When asked how they would go about getting a telephone, none was able to provide a straightforward answer. One woman said she didn't have a home phone because she 'hadn't been given one'. Others said they would contact the council in the first instance, rather than a telecommunications company. The elders in Imangara said that they would like at least one public phone for each cluster of houses ('camp'), as it was too far to get to the telephone if someone was calling.

The attitude of waiting for external authorities to provide telephones is unsurprising, given the way in which Australia's USO has been delivered, whereby consumers are entitled to services but must cover the cabling costs themselves – costs that are beyond households or even whole communities (see Chapter 1). Satellite internet, however, was heavily subsidized at the time, including installation costs. That households had not sought out satellite internet, despite this being far more affordable than home telephones, seemed peculiar to us – until we began the process of installing satellite internet ourselves.

CONNECTING TO THE INTERNET

Infrastructure is relational, in that different actors can have a very different experience of it, whereby one person's infrastructure is another's obstacle. Sandvig gives the example of a staircase, which is a means of passage for most, but a barrier for someone in a wheelchair.[73] Moreover, infrastructure is not just the hardware and technicalities, but also the rules, pricing and players that determine who gets to use it. Communica-

---

73   C. Sandvig, 'The Internet as an Infrastructure' in W.H. Dutton (ed.) *The Oxford Handbook of Internet Studies*, Oxford: Oxford University Press, 2013, p. 92.

tions infrastructure is thus tied up in human experience, and evolves through planning, regulation, markets and the networks between them. We began to examine closely who was benefiting from communications infrastructure in remote communities, as well as who was left out. The behavior of the infrastructure providers when we began to install internet services was particularly illuminating.

In early 2011, about a year after our initial meetings with the three communities, installation began. During our initial scoping of the project, we made the decision to provide internet in the most cost-effective way, on the principle that whatever system we installed would be the most affordable for the communities should they choose to continue to keep the internet when the funding ran out.[74] Unfortunately, our low-cost model meant that we were providing limited download capacity and speeds, but we felt that this was better than providing the communities with services that would be expensive for them to maintain at the conclusion of the project. The model we implemented thus involved using as few satellite dishes as possible, with point-to-multipoint wireless transceiver links to other houses. Each household that chose to have a computer and internet connection made that decision with the full knowledge that they would be actively participating in the study.

We set up the accounts using the Commonwealth government's now obsolete Australian Broadband Guarantee (ABG) scheme, which provided subsidized internet to households in remote areas (see Chapter 1). CAT acted as facilitator for the households (or, more precisely, the individuals representing them), whose actual names would be on the application and account for the service.

Although the ABG scheme subsidized provision of satellite broadband to remote areas, connecting computers to these services was not straightforward, but involved a long sequence of steps. Customers had to determine via an online map which registered ISPs operated in their area (or call the government department if internet access was not possible – a likely scenario); register their details online; confirm their permanent residency and the permanency of the building itself; contact one or more of the ISPs to obtain and compare service offerings; and forward the signed declaration form and their contract application to apply for the service. For customers in very remote areas, the ISP would then typically apply to the government department for approval for an additional subsidy. Assuming the customer had arranged for a continuous 240-volt power supply, installation could then commence (notwithstanding what could be several changes to the installation schedule due to weather conditions affecting roads). Once the service was installed, normal billing processes would ensue.

---

74   Funding from the Aboriginals Benefit Account.

This series of actions is reasonably straightforward if the customer is readily contactable by phone, has a good grasp of English and has sufficient knowledge about broadband services to be able to make an informed choice of service plan. However, the process can be particularly trying for remote community residents who do not meet all these criteria, and whose only external communications option is a single payphone. Organizing the connections from the relative convenience and comfort of CAT's Alice Springs office took co-author Andrew thirty phone calls. CAT was also quoted $1,100 to have an additional power point installed in a shed already serviced with power. It was little wonder that no households had organized satellite internet services.

The computer equipment supplier visited the communities with CAT to get an idea of their layout and the dimensions and conditions of the buildings, in order to design arrangements for the WiFi directional antenna equipment. A separate company from Mount Isa, a sub-contractor to the ISP, installed the internet satellite facilities the following month with CAT's assistance. Each installation only took several hours; the sub-contractor's visits to Mungalawurru and Imangara formed only one stop on their three-week timetable, covering about 10,000 kilometers and traversing western Queensland, northern South Australia, and central and southern Northern Territory. We decided that point-to-multipoint wireless was a more cost-effective choice for connecting the computers to the satellite internet services, because installing cable would also have involved digging trenches between all the houses. Additionally, if a house was rebuilt or added (and housing works did occur at Imangara in the last year of the project), more cabling and trenches would be needed.

In choosing an ISP, we took into account the suitability of the available plans, especially the need for one with a high-speed quota, because there would be several computers sharing the service. The service we chose was also 'shaped' to ensure that once the monthly quota was used up, there would be slow-speed residual access to the internet, but no additional charges would accrue.[75] By shaping the services, we avoided a situation where one or more computers might monopolize the internet quota, by spreading the overall usage over the full billing month period, preventing the quota being used up prematurely. However, the low download capacity and speeds undoubtedly influenced the use of the computers.

We began the installation process at Kwale Kwale, because it was closest to Alice Springs (where CAT, the partner most involved in this stage, was located), which made it easier to roadtest the process and any issues that might arise. We chose the large shed near the community's central core of three houses for the satellite dish and service, because

---

75   Essentially, all the computers on each service in the communities shared 17GB per month at full speed (up to 4Mbps), split between morning (12GB) and afternoon/evening (5GB), after which the speed dropped to a much slower speed, comparable to dial-up (64Kbps).

it had mains power, allowed direct connection to two of the four new computers, and had a better (though not ideal) line of sight profile to the other two houses for local WiFi radio connection. Locating the dish in the shed later proved to be a problem, as it required that the community maintain a power supply to the equipment by replenishing pre-paid power cards as needed. Although households were prepared to do this when the dish was co-located with other household appliances, the same commitment did not stretch to a shared space, and the connection would fail due to lack of power.

At Imangara, we had two satellite services installed, so that the level of internet capacity at this larger community would be similar to that available at the two smaller outstations. Originally, two senior residents agreed to be the custodians for these services, so the dishes were to be placed on their respective houses. However, one decided to move to Tennant Creek to support his grandchildren, who were attending school there, and the service intended for his house was moved instead to the Women's Centre, the other most viable option. This change of arrangements took some time to confirm with the ABG staff, and was only approved a short time before the installers visited the community. The degree of mobility amongst remote-community people and the amount of time this change took to process with the ABG group was early evidence of the difficulties associated with subsidized satellite internet programs in remote communities. Movement between houses, and to and from community, was to become a significant factor that influenced people's access to the internet. As recounted in Part III, issues with providers persisted when the households moved to the NBN Interim Satellite Service scheme in 2013.

COMPUTER CHOICES

The second level of infrastructure concerns involved whether the households might want laptops or desktops, a decision that we believed might be important in terms of residents' mobility. On an early visit to Imangara, we found a discarded laptop on the back of a trailer, which was missing a keyboard. After observing this, we pointed out to the residents that desktop computers were tougher, the screens and keyboards were larger and easier to use, desktop computers were also more likely to stay in one place, and the individual parts (keyboard, monitor, mouse) could be replaced. Laptops, we said, were a good idea if they expected to be moving to and from their community on a regular basis. After weighing up the information we gave them, most community members chose desktop computers rather than laptops. Along with computers, we supplied printers, inks and paper, and accessories such as mice, cables, headsets, speakers, keyboards, power boards and spare monitors. People wanted to be able to print pictures and photos in color from the computers, so we provided gel-based, inkjet color printers, because they were cheaper at an entry level and at cost of printing per sheet, and the ink was less likely than conventional inkjet printer ink to dry out in extreme desert temperatures.

As we were interested in whether communal facilities were preferable to home computers, we gave the communities the option to have some or all of the computers in public spaces. Initially, people at the communities weren't sure whether they wanted individual computers in their houses, or whether to share terminals. At Imangara, some senior women felt the equipment would be safer in the only community building available, the Women's Centre. But by our next trip, most households preferred to have their own computer. We put two more computers in the Women's Centre, in any case, for any residents who didn't have computers in their homes, and for use by the couple running the Women's Centre. The use of these computers is discussed further in the next chapter in relation to ownership and sharing.

At Mungalawurru, residents came up with a mix of computers in four houses, and two in what was known as the 'CDEP shed' – a building used for the government's Aboriginal work-for-the-dole scheme. People at Mungalawurru were highly mobile, often shifting between their community, Tennant Creek and other locations, and placing a couple of terminals in a shed seemed like a good option, because more transitory community members could use them. Two residents at Kwale Kwale chose to have a home computer, but a senior couple were unsure about whether they wanted one at home. Ultimately, the senior woman decided that the shed was the best place, and we placed two of the four computers there for them and their family members to use.

In total, we initially installed twenty computers: four at Kwale Kwale, five at Mungalawurru and eleven at Imangara. Although only a few computers ended up in public spaces such as sheds, as discussed in the next chapter, tensions emerged around who got to use the communal computers, who owned them and whether they were up for grabs. The movement of the computers, and people's claims over them, revealed to us dynamics of Western and traditional notions of ownership that were sometimes at odds (see Chapter 3 and Appendix 2).

The residents were concerned about protecting the equipment when they were away from the house, or when they didn't want kids using it. Residents at Kwale Kwale first raised the idea of having lockable computer and printer covers. CAT designed a computer cover with vents around the top to allow heat generated by the equipment to disperse, as well as a hasp that could be secured with a padlock. The Kwale Kwale residents approved the cover, and it became the model for use in the three communities. Tables with a robust metal frame were also provided with each computer, and some of the residents and kids at a couple of the communities helped paint the tables and covers.

When we first discussed with the residents the option of having a computer, some told us they had no room for one. Some residents asked us to build an extra room on their house for the computer, a suggestion we politely refused. However, the issue of space did not turn out to be a major problem for most households. We found the rooms in the larger houses were sparse, possibly reflecting the fact that occupancy varied often, and that individuals did not necessarily lay claim to particular bedrooms.[76] In most cases, the residents opted to place the computer table in the most spacious room – the main living room at the front of the house. A handful of residents decided to put the computer table in a bedroom.

We documented movements of computers between houses in order to understand the implications for home internet. If satellite internet was organized at the household level, with a dish attached to the roof of the dwelling, moving houses would have implications for individuals accessing that internet connection. We developed the hypothesis that community-wide broadband infrastructure – such as a shared WiFi network that could be received at any dwelling – would be necessary, due to such intra-community relocation. As mentioned, by the end of the project, a number of households had chosen individual subscriptions over such an arrangement, with those households having at least some family members who could be considered permanent occupants.

DETRACTORS AND THE FATE OF THE INFRASTRUCTURE

When the project commenced, detractors said that the computers would never last given the harsh environment, distance from repair outlets, overcrowded spaces, and even dogs. Cultural factors to do with communal sharing, mobility and ownership were also raised as likely obstacles to home computing, meaning the computers would be given away or taken out of the homes permanently. A station owner told us it was a 'hare-brained idea' that would give community members another reason 'to sit at home and do nothing'. Essentially, the fact that very few households had purchased computers and entered into internet subscriptions of their own accord was seen as proof that home internet was, at best, not the preferred means of access, and at worst, either inappropriate or unviable.

The detractors were wrong, in that despite equipment failure, loss or damage, an average of seventeen of the twenty computers installed by early August 2011 were still operational by the end of the first year. By the end of the project (twenty-five months since installation), two computers had been lost or taken out of the community. For comparison, a study of computers in offices conducted by an American commercial research company revealed that three and a half computers would typically fail in a twenty-five-month period (see Table 3 in Appendix 2 and Crouch 2014 for a full account).[77]

---

76   Y. Musharbash, *Yuendumu Everyday: Contemporary Life in Remote Aboriginal Australia*, Canberra: Aboriginal Studies Press, 2009.

77   Lenovo, 'TBR Quality Project', http://www.partnerinfo.lenovo.com/partners/us/products/downloads/thinkcentre-mseries/TBR-Quality-Study-ExecSummary.pdf; Crouch, *Home Internet for Remote Indigenous Communities: Technical Report.*

Computer accessories, such as headsets, mice, keyboards, cover padlocks and power boards did not fare as well, being comparatively vulnerable to damage and removal. After the first few months of the project, computer tables were rarely locked and items often disappeared, especially power boards and external speakers, which could be used with other household equipment. Not surprisingly, printers were the equipment to break down most frequently, in some cases irreparably so, with an estimated service lifetime of about two years in these communities. The build-up of dust and grit inside printers, often caused by residents leaving the cover off the paper feed, was a particular source of malfunction. We took one broken printer back to Alice Springs to determine whether it could be rescued, only to find a perfectly formed mouse nest made of shredded paper nestled inside. By contrast, the network equipment (satellite dish, modem, network switch, local area wireless transceiver equipment, roof-mounted antenna and cabling) did not experience any hardware failures; any network failures related to issues with the injector or cabling within households.

Community members asked for technical support for a variety of matters, such as equipment failures, corrupted applications, and password issues. In one email, Andrew was told that one of the printers 'needs pink, red, blue, green, yellow, orange cartridges'. Only a few instances involved problems that prevented the resident from using the computer entirely. Sometimes another computer was available that they could use until repairs took place. Printer problems were relatively frequent, particularly later in the project, although some of these, such as paper feed pick-up issues, usually required working surfaces to be cleaned rather than needing tools, spare parts or software skills to be resolved. Residents often did not attempt to fix these minor mechanical issues themselves, possibly because they knew they could wait for the next support visit to resolve the problem.

We concluded that the difficulties with organizing installation were a far greater barrier to home internet than the maintenance and replacement of equipment. Although replacements and repairs were needed, the frequency of these events did not necessarily warrant a supervised or publicly maintained model of ICT access (such as a shared computer room). We now turn to what happened once the computers arrived, and how particular events impacted on computer use and ownership, including travel, moving house and death. We also discuss who used the computers the most, and what they were used for.

PART II

Chapter 3: Ownership and Values

In 2002, a report commissioned to inform a plan for telecommunications in remote com-munities stated that 'the best solution to provide Internet and higher bandwidth services, such as videoconferencing, will be via **public online access centres**. Public access is more affordable and is well suited to the generally-communal lifestyle of these remote com-munities. It also provides a central point for community support and training' (emphasis in original).[1] The notion that Aboriginal culture requires shared facilities was carried through in a number of subsequent studies. Anne Daly, at the Centre for Aboriginal Economic Policy Research, examined 2001 census data, in which she found that while in 2001 30 per cent of the non-Indigenous population had home internet access, only 10 per cent of the Indigenous population did. This supported the Telecommunications Action Plan for Remote and Indigenous Communities (TAPRIC) findings that computer centers could help overcome the digital divide.[2]

A study of information and communications technology (ICT) centers by McCallum and Papandrea found that 'home use is neither an attainable, nor necessarily desirable, out-come for most remote Indigenous communities. In the remote Indigenous communities that this study visited, the internet was considered to be a community rather than an individual facility, to be managed and used by the whole community'.[3] In its marketing plan setting out the equipment, goods and services that Telstra will supply in fulfillment of the Universal Service Obligation (USO) throughout Australia, Telstra stated that 'the notion of "shared resources" plays a stronger role in many remote Indigenous com-munities than in other areas. This means that the provision of "shared phones" such as payphones can be a more appropriate solution'.[4]

We found no evidence that the 'generally communal lifestyle' of remote-living Aboriginal people negates home internet. In this chapter, we discuss how traditional and Western systems of ownership played out during the home internet trial, and draw on anthro-pological literature to contend that different values are placed on different kinds of objects. Computer ownership was more likely to occur at the household level, while difficulties arose in relation to shared computers (see Chapter 9 for a case study of a

---

1   Regional Telecommunications Inquiry, *Connecting Regional Australia*, Canberra: Department of Communications, Information Technology and the Arts, 2002, p. 7.

2   Daly, *Bridging the Digital Divide*; Telecommunications Action Plan for Remote Indigenous Communities (TAPRIC), *Report on the Strategic Study for Improving Telecommunications in Remote Indigenous Communities*.

3   K. McCallum and F. Papandrea, 'Community Business: The Internet in Remote Australian Indigenous Communities', *New Media & Society* (2009): 1245.

4   Telstra, 'Universal Service Obligation Standard Marketing Plan', https://www.telstra.com.au/ content/dam/tcom/personal/consumer-advice/doc/consumer/uso-standard-marketing-plan.doc.

shared computer facility in Papunya). The related issue of how training is best provided is examined in detail in Chapter 6.

The system of demand sharing, a mechanism for the distribution of goods and services, plays an important role in maintaining socio-economic relationships amongst remote Aboriginal people. This form of exchange is said to have foundations in traditional life-style, when sharing was a matter of survival in a situation of scarcity and unpredictable food supply. Today, demand sharing fulfills social obligations, and acts as a levelling mechanism, whereby those with more resources give, when asked, to those with less. The considered way in which this occurs can be described as a 'calculus of reciprocity'.[5] Anthropologist L.R. Hiatt writes: 'Probably everywhere in Aboriginal Australia the highest secular value is generosity. Readiness to share with others is the main measure of a man's goodness, and hospitality an essential source of his self-esteem'.[6]

Such a worldview may result in ICTs being valued differently from in the mainstream, which in turn may influence adoption and usage. Nicholls' research, for example, found that the Yolngu town of Ramingining 'definitely' did not 'revolve around a computer on a desk', but more recent observations in Ngaanyatjarra communities suggest that personal computers are becoming increasingly important in remote communities, second only to cars, as the most valued commodity.[7]

Understanding the relative importance placed on the maintenance of social relation-ships and concern for others, in contrast to that placed on objects as objects *per se*, is the key to understanding how demand sharing functions. In attempting to establish a critical mass of household computer users in the three communities, we sought to understand what implications the demand sharing system might have for ICT provision in remote Aboriginal Australia. We were aware, for example, that the computers would be subject to types of ownership within the demand sharing system that would be more influential than the Western form of legal ownership we invited participants to take up. We hoped to gain some insights into the interplay between both systems of ownership, and what lessons these might have for ICT policy development and provision in remote Aboriginal contexts.

---

5   R.G. Schwab, *The Calculus of Reciprocity: Principles and Implications of Aboriginal Sharing*, Canberra: Centre for Aboriginal Economic Policy Research, 1995, p. 7.

6   L. Hiatt, 'Traditional Attitudes to Land Resources' in R. M. Berndt (ed.) *Aboriginal Sites: Rites and Resource Development*, Perth: University of Western Australia Press, 1982, pp. 14–15.

7   A.V. Nicholls, *The Social Life of the Computer in Ramingining*, Darwin: Charles Darwin University, 2009, p. 45; D. Featherstone, 'The Aboriginal Invention of Broadband: How Yarnangu Are Using ICTs in the Ngaanyatjarra Lands of Western Australia' in L. Ormond-Parker, A. Corn, C. Fforde, K. Obata and S. O'Sullivan (eds) *Information Technologies and Indigenous Communities*, Canberra: AIATSIS Research Publications, 2013, p. 43.

Previous ethnographic research has documented different types of ownership and associated rights and obligations in relation to different objects, including public and private forms, which operate within demand sharing processes in Aboriginal society. The literature makes a significant distinction between ownership and usage: while an item might be 'owned' by an individual, this does not necessarily equate to exclusive or any usage by that same individual. However, the onus is on a person to ask for use of an object, and giving in response to a legitimate demand fulfills a social obligation. Not only does the practice of demand sharing redistribute resources, but various social alliances and networks are created and maintained in the process, while the autonomy of the giver is acknowledged. In this way, demand sharing is integral to the tension between relatedness and individual autonomy that underpins all Aboriginal social practices.[8]

ABORIGINAL OWNERSHIP AND DEMAND SHARING: RELATEDNESS AND AUTONOMY

In recent times, a popular mainstream view has emerged that all demand sharing equates to 'humbugging': begging relatives to give or share resources.[9] This view provides a limited and erroneous understanding of the true nature and role that demand sharing plays in maintaining Aboriginal socio-economic systems. Drawing on his work amongst the Pintupi people in the Western desert region, anthropologist Fred Myers describes demand sharing as a form of equivalent exchange:

Those who live together must, according to Pintupi notions, 'help each other'. This means that, upon demand at least, co-residents should be willing to give food, clothing, and other material items or, as the case may be now, provide transportation or labor. In Pintupi understanding, the distribution of valued objects and services reflects and creates relatedness. Thus, they insist, those who live – or have regularly lived – together are *walytja*,[10] what we can translate as 'relatives' or 'kin'. They must help each other, and such help, once given, should be reciprocated.[11]

8   N. Peterson, 'Demand Sharing: Reciprocity and the Pressure for Generosity among Foragers', *American Anthropologist* 95.4 (1993): 190.

9   See J. Altman, 'A Genealogy of "Demand Sharing": From Pure Anthropology to Public Policy' in Y. Musharbash and M. Barber (eds) *Ethnography and the Production of Anthropological Knowledge: Essays in Honour of Nicolas Peterson*, Canberra: ANU E Press, 2011.

10   Elsewhere Myers (1986: 109) states that the word *walytja* is used to refer to a sense of belonging or shared identity, possessions, kin, one's own (my own), and oneself.

11   F. Myers, 'Place, Identity and Exchange in a Totemic System: Nurturance and the Process of Social Reproduction in Pintupi Society' in J. Fajans (ed.) *Exchanging Products: Producing Exchange*, Sydney: University of Sydney, 1993, p. 37.

Myers also notes that a wide range of relationships were conceptualized by Pintupi in terms of their own concept or metaphor of *kanyininpa*, a word used to designate the 'having' (as in possession) or 'holding' of an object.[12] Similarly, the term *walytja* refers to a sense of belonging or shared identity, and could be used in relation to possessions, kin, 'one's own (my own) and oneself, as well as to refer to a wider sense of belonging.[13] Here the notion of ownership translates into 'identification', and provides a sense that rights to objects are (and should be) more widely distributed to include others as co-owners.[14]

At the broader level, Myers' work highlights a general attitude towards personal posses-sions amongst the Pintupi: 'property', regardless of what it cost, was considered replace-able, and if faced with a choice of caring for property or caring for people, they preferred to invest in the latter.[15] Indeed, the Pintupi saw non-Aboriginal people as more concerned with the accumulation of individual wealth, money and objects than with their relation-ships to kin, family and friends.[16] Amongst the Pintupi, relationships with relatives were more highly valued than ordinary possessions.[17] For them, ownership of objects provided a mechanism by which social relationships were maintained; the object itself was of less importance than the opportunity to 'give' or participate in the relationship.

Gaynor Macdonald's research amongst the Wiradjuri in New South Wales found that demand sharing did not indicate a system of communal property or an absence of personal ownership. Rather, obligations existed because highly differentiated notions of personal ownership were recognized, and because it was how an individual shared what she or he had rights over that defined that person.[18] The autonomy of the individual was

---

12   F. Myers, *Pintupi Country, Pintupi Self: Sentiment, Place and Politics Among Western Desert Aborigines*, Berkeley, Los Angeles: University of California Press, 1986, p. 145; Myers, 'Place, Identity and Exchange in a Totemic System', p. 38.

13   Myers, *Pintupi Country, Pintupi Self*, p. 109; F. Myers, 'Some Properties of Culture and Persons' in R.A. Ghosh (ed.) *Code: Collaborative Ownership and the Digital Economy*, Cambridge: MIT Press, 2005, pp. 47-48.

14   Myers, *Pintupi Country, Pintupi Self*, p. 109.

15   Myers, *Pintupi Country, Pintupi Self*; F. Myers, 'Burning the Truck and Holding the Country: Pintupi Forms of Property and Identity' in E.N. Wilmsen (ed.) *We Are Here: Politics of Aboriginal Land Tenure*, Los Angeles: University of California Press, 1989.

16   Myers, 'Burning the Truck and Holding the Country'.

17   Myers, *Pintupi Country, Pintupi Self*, p. 111.

18   G. Macdonald, 'Economies and Personhood: Demand Sharing Among the Wiradjuri of New South Wales' in G. Wenzel, G. Hovelsrud-Broda and N. Kishigami (eds) *The Social Economy of Sharing: Resource Allocation and Modern Hunter-Gatherers*, Osaka: National Museum of Ethnology, 2000, p. 94.

maintained in this way within social networks. Many researchers have noted the tension that exists between relatedness and autonomy, and that strategies exist that one may employ to look after one's own interests so items are not parted with indiscriminately. Tonkinson, for example, observed that some individuals carried two tobacco tins, one of which was always kept empty as proof that they had no tobacco to give when asked.[19] Myers also made similar observations during his research with the Pintupi. He noted that people sometimes hid possessions in order to avoid having to relinquish anything when asked; thus one could express compassion without physically giving.[20] However, it was important to maintain a fairly balanced account in one's transactions with others.[21] Sansom recorded that people would sometimes declare items to be 'private': that is, off-limits to normal demands from kin.[22]

OWNERSHIP AND THE ROLE OF PASSWORDS AND PADLOCKS

At the start of the project, the few individuals who had laptops told us that they would hide them from others to keep them safe. When the desktop computers arrived, some community members managed the dynamic between autonomy and relatedness through their use of padlocks and passwords to regulate others' access to the household computers. Virtually all residents with desktop computers said that visitors to their community had used their computers at one time or another, often without permission while they were away. Often this involved people cutting off the padlocks on the computer covers or prizing off the hasp. Some found this highly annoying, and took steps to limit access to their computer when they were out of the community, through passwording, and/or by locking the desk cover, and/or by having an individual room or house where the computer was kept. One woman took the computer cords with her when she traveled. Mostly, houses were not locked, even when people went away.

Once some participants had obtained individual internet accounts and were paying for the internet themselves, we gained the impression that asking permission to use the computers became more common, and that usage became more restricted to the individual household/family (almost two-thirds at this point told us that people had asked to use their computers). One woman at Imangara said she only allowed non-household/family

19   R. Tonkinson, *The Jigalong Mob: Aboriginal Victors of the Desert Crusade*, Menlo Park, California: Cummings Publishing Company, 1974, p. 106.

20   Compare also: A.B. Weiner, 'Cultural Difference and the Density of Objects', *American Ethnologist* 212 (1994).

21   Myers, *Pintupi Country, Pintupi Self*, p. 171.

22   B. Sansom, *The Camp at Wallaby Cross: Aboriginal Fringe Dwellers in Darwin*, Canberra: Australian Institute of Aboriginal Studies, 1980, p. 240.

members to use her computer in exceptional circumstances: for example, when people needed to contact relatives about arranging funerals and had run out of money for a phone card, she would allow them to contact relatives via Facebook on her computer. A woman from Mungalawurru told us that some residents from other households had asked her if she could leave the computer cabinet open while she was in Tennant Creek so they could use it, but that she'd started closing the cabinet because 'they were using it too much', and we observed that it was closed and padlocked. There seemed to be greater awareness that the owner was paying for internet access, and this impacted on the social dynamics and decision-making surrounding requests and permission to use the computers.

Likewise, the use of passwords became a way of managing others' – especially visitors' and to a lesser extent, kids' – access to the computers. Initially, few residents set passwords on their computers, probably because of the inconvenience of having to remember and enter a password, coupled with a limited understanding of computer and internet safety and security generally. But, as the project progressed, more people began asking us for assistance to set a password, usually in the context of managing others' usage, as well as preventing unauthorized access when they were away from the community. One woman, for example, requested we set a password on her computer to 'stop visitors using it and using up all the power', while another asked for a password for her computer so she could 'stop people using it' while she had visitors staying in her house; she started changing the password when too many people had access. A resident reported that someone had cut the padlock off her computer. and consequently she wanted a new and better password. By the end of April 2014, passwords had been established on 65 per cent of computers.

However, others felt that setting passwords for managing kids' usage in particular was not a straightforward solution. One man, who did not have an internet connection at the time, said he'd been thinking of putting a password on the computer, but had decided against it to avoid being humbugged by his grandkids to use the PC, although he also thought that having a password might 'steady them down from using [it too much]'. He added that he would put a password on the computer if he got an internet service.

Rather than being an expression of ownership and attachment, it seems that the setting of passwords on computers by participants during the project was primarily a means of managing others' usage. In this way, individual participants could negotiate their autonomy and relatedness: autonomy through establishing (or changing) a password, and relatedness through sharing that password with select individuals but not others.

ABORIGINAL OWNERSHIP OF 'THINGS'

Existing ethnographic literature explores the different types of ownership that operate within Aboriginal society, demonstrating that these concepts extend beyond simple Western legal notions. Aboriginal ownership of land is conceptualized according to connections to totemic ancestors who created the landscape, kin relations to these ancestors, and among owners, and such relationships are framed in terms of inalienable connections to places, rights and obligations.[23] By contrast, the ownership of consumable and moveable items – such as computers and television sets – is subject to demand sharing, and is not thought of as an inalienable right, although personal ownership of equipment is recognized. As well as the purpose for which they were designed or manufactured, objects may play a role within the processes through which social relationships are structured, mediated, tested and re shaped. Often it is how an object can be used, rather than what it is, that influences and determines the nature of various social interactions and outcomes. Accordingly, some objects may be subject to different kinds of ownership in the course of their use-lives.

Nuances of different kinds of Aboriginal ownership became evident in the ways that certain individuals tested others' ownership of some computers in the project communities. The computers became objects through which relationships were negotiated within the system of demand sharing in each community. These relationships were not necessarily limited to those within the individual household. They also affected the dynamics surrounding computers within shared spaces, such as the Women's Centre at Imangara and the Community Development Employment Projects (CDEP) shed at Mungalawurru. Although most of the computers were installed within individual households, the dynamics surrounding the computers in shared spaces were illuminating, suggesting different forms of Aboriginal ownership at work in these communities, with implications for how to provide equitable access to ICT.

When we installed computers at Imangara, we placed two in the Women's Centre, mainly for use by residents who did not have a desktop computer in their own households, but also for the couple supervising the Centre. In time it became apparent that the couple considered the computers to be 'theirs', restricting access mainly to themselves and some of their family members. They even put a password on their user account on one of the PCs.

In this instance, the couple appeared to be enacting a form of Aboriginal ownership perhaps closest to Western notions: that is, ownership confers exclusive rights to pos-

---

23   I. Keen, 'The Interpretation of Aboriginal "Property" on the Australian Colonial Frontier' in I. Keen
      (ed.) *Aboriginal Participation in Australian Economies: Historical and Anthropological Perspectives*,
      Canberra: ANU Press, 2010.

sess and/or use a particular item. The owner also has the prerogative to determine who else may use that item, and under what circumstances. A distinction is invoked between private and public ownership: that is, the object is 'private' (off-limits to others, including the right to ask) or 'public' (others have a right to ask to use that particular object). Although this example relates to contemporary Western material culture, anthropologists have also documented personal ownership of non-Western or traditional objects such as the *wanari* (short stout digging sticks) used by Pintupi women, which suggests that personal ownership is not necessarily a post-contact phenomenon.[24]

Other residents expressed their irritation about this situation to us, initially in veiled, oblique terms, then more openly. In one instance, a senior woman, whose household did not receive a computer, approached us eight months later, asking if she could get a computer at her house: not for herself, but for her grandchildren. At the time, we didn't have enough funding to buy more desktop computers, so we suggested that her grandchildren use the computers at the Women's Centre. She responded that it 'was too far [away] to walk [to]', which seemed rather unlikely, given that her house was only 200 meters from the Centre. Instead, it seemed that limited access to the computers in the Women's Centre was the real reason.

This couple also dominated usage of other facilities at the Women's Centre, such as the telephone, a practice observed by the Regional Council workers, as well as the local school principal. The disquiet their monopolization of these items caused amongst other community members reflects findings within the anthropological literature that although items non-Aboriginal people own or control within a community are not usually subject to the same level of demand sharing, they may nevertheless still be used to test social relationships.[25] This observation is particularly relevant here, given that Western legal ownership of the computers initially remained with an organization - the Centre for Appropriate Technology (CAT) - prior to being transferred to individual participants. Similarly, Fogarty found, while based at Maningrida, that the school vehicle (a 4WD troop carrier) was not usually the focus of the sort of conflict embedded in ownership of private or community vehicle use, because it was seen as being owned by 'government', an entity not part of the local social organization. This did not mean there weren't any conflicts about the school 4WD, or that local Aboriginal people did not exert some form of claim over the vehicle, but the conflict related to usage constraints, such as the number of passengers, rather than ownership.[26]

---

24 D.F. Thomson, *Bindibu Country*, Melbourne: Thomas Nelson, 1975.

25 W. Fogarty, *'You Got Any Truck?' Vehicles and Decentralised Mobile Service-Provision in Remote Indigenous Australia*, Canberra: ANU Centre for Aboriginal Economic Policy Research, 2005.

26 Fogarty, *'You Got Any Truck?'*, p. 3.

Interestingly, the mother of the woman who worked at the Women's Centre, who was also one of the senior woman's daughters, sometimes used the computer in the Centre, although she had her own computer and internet connection at home. It seems that her close kin association with her daughter facilitated her use of the Centre's computers. Although most of the computers were installed within individual households, the circumstances surrounding the usage of the computers at the Women's Centre – ostensibly a communal space – was indicative of a trend we noticed across the project communities: that residents did not share the computers as much as we had expected, especially beyond family groups.

When we commenced the trial, we developed a system whereby the residents would sign an agreement that transferred ownership of the computers from us to them. The agreement was developed partly for legal reasons, and partly as a means to reinforce to the residents that they could manage the computers however they wished if they chose to take possession of them. Interestingly, despite their possessiveness, neither the couple nor anyone else signed ownership agreements for the two computers while they were at the Centre (which also appeared to be linked to the couple's moderate degree of mobility, as we'll discuss further in Chapter 4). Later, when the couple had left the community, another couple signed a formal ownership agreement for a Women's Centre computer at Imangara within three months of its being relocated from the Centre into their house. This appears to support the understanding that an individual who has non-exclusive usage rights to an item does not gain any additional powers, rights or personal standing, even if he or she is the person primarily associated with it. Musharbash, for example, observed that specific bedrooms in a house were not 'owned' in the exclusive Western sense; rather, each room would be primarily associated with a particular person, who would nevertheless share access and use of it with others, usually those of the *jilimi* (women's camp) or close relatives.[27] When that individual moved to another camp, the room then became associated with someone else. An association with a particular room did not confer any additional rights or power over other spaces in the house or *jilimi*; nor did it add any personal standing to that individual.[28] In the same way, although the couple was primarily associated with the computer and other facilities in the Women's Centre, they did not have any exclusive rights to them once they had left the community.

Initially, we installed two PCs in the CDEP shed at Mungalawurru for residents' general use, but soon afterwards, one of these was relocated within the community. A woman signed a formal ownership agreement for the one that remained in the shed, and although it was still available for use by other residents, they consistently referred to it as the woman's computer. While her ownership of this computer appeared to approximate

---

27   Musharbash, *Yuendumu Everyday*, p. 55.

28   Musharbash, *Yuendumu Everyday*, p. 55.

Western notions, the events that ensued when the woman left the community suggest that although her individual ownership was recognized, it did not confer exclusive use.

Several weeks after the woman relocated more or less permanently to Tennant Creek, a couple moved the computer into their house, placing their own computer on a table to one side because it had technical problems. A month later, prior to visiting Mungalawurru, we ran into the woman in Tennant Creek, and she made a point of telling us that she wanted 'her' computer back.

Several interpretations of these events are possible. Other residents may have consid- ered this computer to be communal or shared property, available for use when required, given its public location in the CDEP shed, despite the fact that the woman owned it in a Western legal sense, and was primarily associated with it. While the woman's individual ownership of the computer was recognized (i.e. in how it was named), this did not confer exclusive rights of usage on her: only the right to determine who could use the computer, for as long as she was perceived to be a permanent resident at Mungalawurru. Once she had moved to Tennant Creek, others may have felt that she had relinquished her ownership of the computer and abandoned it, and that it was now available for others to take up.

In his work amongst Darwin's town campers, anthropologist Basil Sansom (1980) observed a distinction between private and public ownership of items, including cash. Specifically, he used the term 'routine' ownership to refer to things, persons and words that were potentially available to other individuals through the mechanism of demand sharing. In contrast, when something was declared 'private', it was removed from the realm of social relationships and associated obligations, and was essentially 'off-limits' to others. However, ownership of such items may move back and forth between the private and public domains over a period of time, according to the location (whether it is a private or public space) and other circumstances.[29]

The fact that the computer was in a public space may have signalled the potential for a change in ownership once the woman had left the community. The anthropological literature also distinguishes between the dynamics surrounding ownership of 'high end' items, such as vehicles, and scarce or 'luxury' goods, compared with those considered for 'everyday' use. Myers observed that Pintupi people distinguished between private and community property in relation to vehicle ownership.[30] 'Private' vehicles were those purchased with an individual's own money, with the result that he or she was recognized as the proprietor of that vehicle with the right to make decisions regarding its use. In

29   For example of flour, see also Musharbash, *Yuendumu Everyday*.

30   Myers, 'Burning the Truck and Holding the Country', pp. 23-25.

contrast, 'community' or company vehicles, usually purchased through government or foundation grants, were often the subject of conflict arising from the problem of who could be said to 'own' something that was owned by 'the community'.

The couple's decision to move the computer into their house may have been based on a pragmatic rationale that the computers had been 'abandoned' and were available for re use: that since the woman was absent from Mungalawurru, she wouldn't need the computer and that it was more convenient to move the computer into their house rather than wait for theirs to be fixed, or use it in the CDEP shed. O'Connell's observations about Alyawarr ownership of physical objects, such as everyday items found in houses, suggests that in addition to an item's function, its cost and/or relative availability may be a factor in determining whether or not ownership remains with the individual purchaser, or whether the item becomes part of the assemblage owned by the household.[31] Amongst the Alyawarr, ownership and control of structural materials was usually vested in the household unit as long as the materials were being used.[32] Once community members perceived such items to be abandoned, they were available for reclamation by anyone. Items that were costly but relatively portable, such as tents, tended to remain the property of an individual or a household for as long as they were useful, unless they were specifically sold, traded or given away.

These stories about desktop computers in shared spaces at Imangara and Mungalawurru highlight the strength of Aboriginal forms of ownership in remote communities. They also strongly suggest that the location of individual computers influences notions of, and the strength of, this ownership: i.e. that people with a desktop computer in their own house had a stronger claim/right to ownership of that computer (and by extension, demonstrated a particular type of ownership). By contrast, people who were notionally responsible for computers located in public spaces appeared to have weaker claims to some form of 'ownership', and/or demonstrated a different type of ownership, even though they were strongly associated with use and access to these computers. Ownership of computers in individual houses appeared to possess an exclusivity similar to Western legal notions, compared to computers in public spaces, where ownership constituted a primary or shared/collective association.

Contrary to our original expectations that Aboriginal social structures and practices might automatically foster greater sharing of ICT resources and skills amongst participants, with positive implications for diminishing the digital divide, the sharing of resources was concentrated on kinship networks between families and across households, and

---

31   J.F. O'Connell, 'Room to Move: Contemporary Alyawara Settlement Patterns and Their Implications for Aboriginal Housing Policy' in M. Heppell (ed.) *A Black Reality: Aboriginal Camps and Housing in Remote Australia*, Canberra: Australian Institute of Aboriginal Studies, 1979.

32   O'Connell, 'Room to Move'.

amongst individual families within houses. Even when computers were situated in public spaces, and not formally owned by a particular individual, this did not necessarily result in equitable access to ICT devices and the internet. In Chapter 9 we discuss how this has proven difficult in relation to shared internet facilities in a larger community.

Another factor that came into play here was the implications that relationships between families and households had, not only for individuals' access to computers and the internet, but also for installation of ICT equipment and networks. These became more apparent through the affiliations along household and family lines that emerged towards the project's end, when we began discussing with community members whether their household wanted to pay for an internet plan or to share a connection with others. The following story highlights how these family affiliations, as well as the influence of elders on decision-making, shaped the distribution of ICT resources.

FAMILY DISTINCTIONS AND THE INFLUENCE OF ELDERS ON ICT AR-RANGEMENTS

While discussing with us potential options for sharing internet connections after the project, one of the senior women at Imangara said she wanted her own 'dish', and that she only wanted to pay for her household's usage. We asked if she would consider sharing a connection with the house next door, which was occupied by her daughter, her children and grandchildren. Her sister (by kinship), Mary, then interjected, pointing out that the arrangement might work, referring to her sister's house as 'you mob' and her niece's house as 'that mob'.

Mary was the senior person most often involved in liaising with us, and in working out ICT arrangements in the community. She had significant responsibilities representing the community in external organizations, and was thus a key liaison for various visitors (including a linguist working in the community at the time). Mary, as we will see, was one of the few residents who came to rely on email for correspondence with outside agencies, although she did so with assistance from others. On this occasion, Mary pointed at a map of Imangara showing the location of the two existing satellite dishes and all the houses connected to the internet, indicating that she would share a dish with her mob. This included not only her immediate household but also her grandson and grand daughter-in-law in the house next door, another grandson and grand daughter-in-law in a house a bit further away, and another granddaughter and grandson-in-law, whose house was still further away, with other households in between.

But on one of our previous visits, Mary's granddaughter-in-law, Emily, had strongly asserted that everyone should have their own internet connection, and only pay for what each individual household used. Emily, who worked at the school and had a young family, had become one of the more confident users in the community. Emily was also quite financially literate, and likely to understand the difficulties that a shared arrangement would involve in terms of payment. Basically, payment for an internet plan can only be made from one individual's account, which means that he or she would then have to extract a share of that payment from all the others who shared that connection. This would place an extra burden and responsibility on that individual.

Mary seemed willing to take on this responsibility for her 'mob' when we next visited, even though she had been at pains to point out to us during an earlier trip that the extra electricity required to run the satellite dish on her roof, which provides connectivity for her own house plus three others, was too much for her and her partner to pay. Although Emily had previously expressed the view that everyone should have their own dish, she deferred to Mary on this occasion, appearing to accept her decision regarding a new arrangement in which only her household would share with Mary's. Notably, by this time Mary's two grandsons and their partners were not to share with Mary, but to have their own internet connections. It seemed that Mary had not pressed them to review this decision, perhaps because it was her grandsons rather than her granddaughters who were involved, although it was two of her granddaughters-in-law, including Emily, who told us about this decision.

Emily may also have agreed to share with Mary out of a concern for Mary's ability to pay for the internet connection on her own. The other reason for Emily's change of mind might have been that her personal situation had altered between our two visits: her household income had halved after her partner lost his job. However, Emily later chose to have her own internet connection, while Mary and another granddaughter, who was looking after the house next door while its residents were interstate, decided they would share Mary's connection. It seems that Emily had wanted to have her own connection all along.

These developments were in keeping with the trend that emerged during the project on sharing ICT resources amongst kinship networks, between families, across households, and amongst individual families within houses. Both Western legal ownership and Aboriginal ownership of the majority of the computers appear to have been vested in particular individuals, rather than to have taken the form of collective ownership by households or families. Eventually, all participants who decided to retain internet access chose to establish an individual household connection and account, with one exception (see Chapter 9). Another factor in the trend towards individual ownership was probably residents' increasing awareness that a computer's formal owner would have to bear the brunt of power and internet bill costs.

VALUING HARDWARE AND THE INTERNET

During the project, we were interested in seeing whether participants would value computers differently from mainstream users, and how this might influence adoption and usage. Attitudes towards property in Aboriginal society operate on two levels: as a broad 'world view' perspective, and on a more personal level that allows for changes in individual attitudes according to various circumstances. As an example of the latter, Taylor observed a change in attitudes towards material possessions, from relatively frugal and generally confined to simple items (i.e. clothing, bedding, tools, weapons, utensils) to a desire for new furniture, furnishings and household appliances once people occupied permanent dwellings.[33]

According to the anthropological literature, objects may be valued for various reasons, not all necessarily related solely to usage. Tanner suggests that 'defining modes of value for digital culture that are not solely economically driven but which do contain indicators of value that can be measured and can demonstrate change' is important when considering the impact of digital resources.[34] He identifies four values in addition to utility: existence and/or prestige, education, community (being part of a community that is afforded by the digital resource) and inheritance/bequest value. Additionally, values are not fixed, nor static. For example, Renfrew's work highlights how the value of certain objects may alter over time, reflecting new uses and forms of political control. Davenport has observed that particular objects can possess multiple values depending on circumstances, and that these values are not limited to those held by the owner or end user, but may be held collectively by a community.[35] Myers notes that the value possessed by objects is characterized by what he called 'slippage', in which the relative value of the object (whether quantitative or qualitative) declines.[36] Regarding computers, Brown et al. suggest that they change from being considered luxury items to being thought of as necessities, which in turn may also influence adoption and usage.[37]

---

33   J. Taylor, 'Housing Programs at Edward River and Mitchell River Aboriginal Reserves' in M. Heppell (ed.) *A Black Reality: Aboriginal Camps and Housing in Remote Australia*, Canberra: Australian Institute of Aboriginal Studies, 1979, p. 213.

34   S. Tanner, *Measuring the Impact of Digital Resources: The Balanced Value Impact Model*, London: King's College, 2012, p. 26.

35   C. Renfrew, 'Varna and the Emergence of Wealth in Prehistoric Europe' in A. Appadurai (ed.) *The Social Life of Things: Commodities in Cultural Perspective*, Cambridge: Cambridge University Press, 1988; W.H. Davenport, 'Two Kinds of Value in the Eastern Solomon Islands' in A. Appadurai (ed.) *The Social Life of Things: Commodities in Cultural Perspective*, Cambridge: Cambridge University Press, 1988, p. 108.

36   F. Myers, 'Introduction: The Empire of Things' in F. Myers (ed.) *The Empire of Things: Regimes of Value and Material Culture*, Santa Fe: School of American Research Press, 2001, p. 6.

37   S.A. Brown, V. Venkatesh and H. Bala, 'Household Technology Use: Integrating Household Life Cycle and the Model of Adoption of Technology in Households', *The Information Society* 22.4 (2006): 216.

In the case of the three communities, we considered the nature and extent to which participants valued the computers and internet access, and whether any changes in how they valued the ICTs emerged across the project. We took into account factors such as participants' readiness to maintain internet access, what they were prepared to pay, and how community members personalized their computers as indicators of what value they placed on home computers and internet access. We also attempted to assess the comparative value of the computers in relation to other material objects used by participants, such as cars, mobile phones, Xboxes, fridges and TVs, as well as the community payphone, as a means of gauging their significance in remote community life.

By the end of September 2013, there were relatively high rates of formal ownership (signed agreements) of the computers and payment for internet plans at Imangara and Mungalawurru, suggesting that most participants valued the PCs and internet access. In the initial phases of the project, community members' interest in having internet access grew considerably. Between February and November 2012, when we asked individuals regularly present in both these communities whether they'd be prepared to pay for their own internet service, the proportion of participants willing to pay increased from 40 to 77 per cent. Eventually, two-thirds of participants actually retained internet access; the remaining third did not because of mobility issues (i.e. they had moved or were anticipating moving from the community), or because they found the payment methods too difficult to manage. Given that project funding supported payment for internet use until September 2013, these results suggest that participants attached real value to maintaining connectivity at a tangible cost to themselves.

We also periodically asked participants how much they'd be prepared to pay for internet access at the end of the project, as a gross measure of how much they valued the ICTs in monetary terms. When we first asked them in February 2012, only two individuals (a couple) out of fifteen nominated an actual amount. By contrast, in November 2012, twelve out of thirteen individuals nominated a sum of money, varying from $20/month up to $200-$300/month, with three people saying they'd be prepared to pay at least $100/month. However, by March 2013, the amounts they named had moderated, coalescing around $40-$60/month, most likely as residents became better informed of the various plans available. Overall, it seems that a more pragmatic attitude emerged as the project progressed and once funding support ended.

Psychologists Pierce and colleagues suggest that feelings of ownership are created first by controlling an object through possession, then by becoming familiar with it through actual or imagined use, and/or investing the self into it (e.g. through identification).[38] As an indication of the potential value people placed on their desktop computers, we examined how the residents personalized them, for example by posting photographs, usually

---

38   J.L. Pierce, T. Kostova, and K.T. Dirks. 'The State of Psychological Ownership: Integrating and Extending a Century of Research', *Review of General Psychology* 7.1 (2003): 84.

of family members, as wallpaper and/or screensavers. When we visited the communities in 2014, almost half those we interviewed said they had personalized their computer. Of two people who stated that they hadn't personalized their computers, we'd observed that one of these had changed her computer's wallpaper before. Three said they couldn't remember, although we'd previously noticed they had personally configured or chosen their computers' wallpaper, and one individual had replaced the particular photograph she'd used earlier as wallpaper on her computer.

Those who personalized the computers in this way were not necessarily their formal owners, and we do not know whether they had asked the owner's permission in each instance. However, one example suggests that such personalization by users was not always with the owner's approval. In September 2013, Mary asked one of the researchers to change the wallpaper on her computer, from the rather violent gaming image, which one of the younger male residents in her house had probably installed, to feature a gospel image. Personalization also occurred on computers in shared spaces: those managing the Women's Centre put wallpaper featuring sports cars on the computers, although this may have been part of their attempt at possession of these computers.

At the end of the project, we asked people how important the computer was to them, compared to other household items such as TVs, mobile phones and refrigerators, commonly using the television as an item for comparison. Most of those who responded to this question said that the computer was more important than the TV, regardless of whether they were adept users.

These perceptions of the computers' comparative value did not appear to reflect the phenomenon known as 'source dependence', either, whereby people become attached to objects because of how they were obtained, such as whether they'd paid for them or received them by chance.[39] Specifically, source dependence is where objects are more highly valued when people believe that they have obtained them as a result of their own efforts.[40] According to this logic, we would expect most community members to value TVs more highly than the computers, because they'd bought the televisions themselves, but this was not always the case. This preference for the computers may reflect individual personal interests and awareness of the computers' potential uses, the presence of some sort of existence/status and community value, that the TVs were considered to be more of an 'everyday' item, or a combination of all these factors.

39   G. Loewenstein and S. Issacharoff, 'Source Dependence in the Valuation of Objects', *Journal of Behavioral Decision Making* 7.3 (1994).

40   Loewenstein and Issacharoff, 'Source Dependence in the Valuation of Objects': 160.

CONCLUSION

In opening this chapter, we suggested that Aboriginal people living in remote communities might value computers and the internet differently from the mainstream, with
implications for their adoption and usage. The outstation residents clearly valued the
computers and internet access, although, as we will see in later chapters, their relative
value – as expressed in how they personalized the computers and valued them in relation to other household items – changed over the project. As we will see in later chapters,
the amounts of money people were prepared to pay for internet access also changed
as participants became increasingly aware of the real costs of retaining internet access,
ownership and maintenance of the computer, especially electricity bills. The relative
value of ICTs is also likely to fluctuate depending on an individual's life circumstances;
for example, when money is short, basics such as food, power and transport may take
priority rather than fixing a computer or paying for an internet plan.

Contrary to the idea that the 'caring and sharing' ethic (that non-Indigenous people often
associate with Aboriginal culture) might result in more collective possession and use
of the computers, ownership of most of the computers in the project became invested
in particular individuals. Access, and by extension usage, was largely restricted to the
household/immediate family members, with the owner determining who could use the
computer. The use of passwords emerged as a key mechanism in managing demands,
particularly from visitors and kids, and as a way of preventing unauthorized or excessive
use of the computers when the owners were absent.

Ownership is embedded within the system of demand sharing, in which objects may
function as a mechanism through which social relationships are continually tested, mediated and re negotiated. This understanding has implications for the design of future ICT
arrangements, including payment methods for internet access (discussed in Chapters 8
and 9). In particular, flexibility to allow for changes in ownership and residential mobility
needs to be incorporated into ICT provision to these communities, a subject that will be
taken up in the next chapter.

Chapter 4: Mobility

Six months after computers and internet access were installed at Kwale Kwale, Rhonda, a middle-aged woman who had been using computers at work, expressed concern to us that some of her older relatives drove 40 kilometers to Alice Springs almost every day to shop, estimating that they spent about $30 per trip on fuel. She was hoping to teach them and other community members how to shop online for groceries and other supplies to reduce their transport costs. Her older relatives had already told us that they wished to avoid having to live in town to access medical services, and seemed stressed at the prospect of being away from country and family for any length of time. The older relatives had moved into a caravan when another daughter and her family moved in, due to maintenance issues in their house. The family's concerns are indicative of three types of mobility typical of outstations: the costs and inconveniences associated with living on an outstation, relocation to towns to access services, and individuals moving from house to house within a community, all of which we discuss in this chapter in relation to ICT.

These seemingly ordinary concerns – relocation and travel – have a social dimension, in that living at a distance from essential services can contribute to hardship. The resulting fluctuating occupancy of remote settlements and the expense that their remoteness confers on individuals and services have been ever-present themes in the debate on government resourcing of outstations. The Commonwealth's decision to direct resources to larger towns only (see Chapter 1) and its divestment of funding to the states have resulted in a significant and (at the time of writing) ongoing social movement against the so-called 'closure' of remote communities. Underlying these developments has been what some consider a new policy trend of 'mainstreaming', whereby those living in outstations are expected to move to larger towns to reduce public expense. As discussed in previous chapters, researchers have been divided over the benefits of staying on country versus relocation, and the cultural and wellbeing advantages associated with each scenario.[41]

Our particular interest was whether broadband delivery of services and the conveniences of online transactions might alleviate some of the day-to-day difficulties associated with remote living. For instance, could it minimize the expense of travelling into town, or overcome difficulties in carrying out personal or household administration? Rather than treat the issue of remote living as one of citizenry rights and entitlements, we focused instead on the more mundane dimensions of remote community life.[42] Understanding the tangible benefits of internet use required knowing the extent to which residents moved between town and community, why they did so, and whether internet access and use altered patterns of movement in and out of each locality.

---

41   See P. Sutton, *The Politics of Suffering: Indigenous Australia and the End of the Liberal Consensus*, Carlton: Melbourne University Publishing, 2009; N. Pearson, *Radical Hope: Education and Equality in Australia*, Melbourne: Schwartz Publishing Pty Ltd, 2011.

42   Such as: Kerins, *The First-Ever Northern Territory Homelands/Outstations Policy*.

The frequency with which people travel and move also influences infrastructure and hardware choices. If travel was a common feature of everyone's life, then this might explain why fixed satellite connections and desktop computers were scarce in remote communities when we commenced (as these cannot easily be moved). As we were to discover, mobility did affect internet access and use, not only for those who moved in and out of their community, but also for individuals and whole families moving to different houses within the community. The latter turned out to be a more significant issue for understanding the digital divide, adding further to our doubts about the appropriateness of the extant satellite internet offerings as a solution for remote consumers.

COST-SAVING AND GEOGRAPHIC DISADVANTAGE

It was often the case that, however many messages we sent by email or through calling public phones, and however much we checked potential competing activities, some, or even all, of the community members wouldn't be there on our visits. They had other priorities and many reasons to travel. Native title and royalty meetings invariably had more clout than our visits; sorry business (funeral rites) would lay heavy and unexpected claims on people's time. On one trip, the Imangara people had gone to Lake Nash for a funeral and a sing-along, and then travelled on to a rodeo at Mount Isa.

At the project's outset, we anticipated, like Rhonda, that participants would save on transport costs as they would have less need to travel to regional centers and hub communities because they could access banking and services and shop online. We asked the residents whether having a computer reduced the frequency with which they travelled into town.

At Imangara some commented that there wasn't 'much need' for community members to go to Tennant Creek or Alice Springs because of the proximity of the station store (1 kilometer away) and Ali Curung (35 kilometers away), where they could shop. However, they observed that now that they could check their balances online, they didn't have to go into town to bank. One man said he transferred money into his wife's bank account over the internet, whereas previously he would have travelled to Alice Springs to withdraw money. Two of the community's more adept computer users (Emily and another young mother), said that they did not visit town as often now that they had computers.

For Imangara residents, goods purchased at the station store and at nearby Ali Curung were expensive. A 2009 Commonwealth inquiry into remote community stores reported that a basket of food cost around 30 per cent more in very remote communities than in the cities.[43] Although freight refrigeration might explain the margin on food, even non-perishable goods tend to be more expensive. On one trip, Mary, a grandmother, complained to us about the cost of a child's mattress, pointing out that she paid over $100 for a piece of foam. As a result of this purchase, she said she had no money left for necessities that week.

The younger women in the community had meanwhile been buying children's toys and clothes online. Emily and the other young mother had taught themselves online shopping, having only had some introductory computer skills sessions with us. Emily said that she had 'worked out how to shop for clothes, runners, toys and other small purchases for the kids online, at eBay, etc.', which were delivered to the neighboring cattle station 1 kilometer away. They both commented that they'd started shopping online to make 'less trips to shops in Tennant Creek', and because it was 'easier than going into town; [there was] more choice.' A man at Imangara even bought a car from Adelaide on the website Gumtree fairly early in the project. Other community members followed suit; they were able to shop around for vehicles online, avoiding high mark-ups on cars at 'shark' dealers in town known to exploit Aboriginal people.[44]

Some participants wanted to learn how to shop online, but ran into difficulties because they didn't have a debit or credit card, or they found having several passwords for different accounts confusing (a situation not uncommon amongst mainstream ICT users). In Mungalwurru a woman remarked: 'I've got Facebook; I've got eBay. I get mixed up with all these passwords. So I just gave up'. Two-stage verification, which is becoming the norm for accessing accounts when the user has forgotten his or her password, is not possible in communities where there is no mobile reception.

Overall, community members at Mungalawurru were less successful in learning to shop online, although there was probably less incentive for them to learn because Tennant Creek was only 80 kilometers away, and people frequented town for social reasons. People at Imangara, however, had much greater distances to travel to shop in either Alice Springs or Tennant Creek. For them, if they could not access a car or get a lift, then the next best option would be to get the bus from Ali Curung to Alice Springs, which costs around $80 for a one-way trip.

While being able to purchase some items – even vehicles – over the internet contributed to the ease and convenience of community members' lives, and most participants began

43   Aboriginal and Torres Strait Islander Committee, *Everybody's Business: Remote Aboriginal and Torres Strait Community Stores*, Canberra: Commonwealth of Australia, 2009, p. 10.

44   See J. Altman, M.C. Dillon and K. Jordan, 'Submission to the House of Representatives Standing Committee on Aboriginal and Torres Strait Islander Affairs Inquiry into Community Stores in Remote Aboriginal and Torres Strait Islander Communities', *CAEPR Topical Issue No 04/2009*, Canberra: Australian National University, 2009.

regularly checking bank and Centrelink accounts online, these facilities did not, as we had speculated, lead to substantial changes in the frequency of their trips to regional centers for all residents. In 2012, when we asked the residents how often they visited town now that they had a home computer, almost half said that they made the trip about as often as before, and the other half said that they traveled less or never to town. The frequency of visits varied from daily (only residents of Mungalawurru and Kwale Kwale, both of which are relatively close to town) to every six weeks (an Imangara resident). The reasons most often given for visiting town were catching up with family and friends, followed by shopping; they particularly mentioned accessing health services, but went also to visit the Central Land Council (CLC), banks and Centrelink, and to attend parties and sporting events.

DEATH AND RELOCATION

In late November 2011, the CLC informed us that there had been a road accident near the Ali Curung turnoff, which resulted in a triple fatality and multiple critical injuries, and that the accident involved Imangara residents. One young woman who had been closely involved with the computer trial, including working as a research assistant for us, was killed. We postponed our visits to Imangara, but the tragedy had a profound and extended impact on the community. The family, which occupied five houses in the community, initially moved out of Imangara - some to stay with relatives at 6 Mile at Ti Tree, and others to Utopia locations. The family's relocation was part of the Alyawarr practice of memory and name suppression, a deliberate process of 'forgetting' in order to cope with grief.[45] Less than two months later, the mother of the daughter also passed away. Around this time, the family returned to Imangara because the children were not happy at the Ti Tree school, where the other kids spoke a different language. However, they did not return to the house where the deceased had lived. Instead it was boarded up and scheduled for redevelopment, after which a different family from the community would move in. The father approached us and asked that we take the computer from the family's original house and remove the images, as they needed to avoid viewing images or reading the names of the deceased.

The deaths in Imangara were a particularly tragic event that caused major changes to house occupancy.[46] Other instances were practical and social rather than cultural. For

45 C. Elliot, 'Social Death and Disenfranchised Grief: An Alyawarr Case Study' in K. Glaskin (ed.) *Mortality, Mourning and Mortuary Practices in Indigenous Australia*, London: Ashgate Publishing, 2008.

46 Subsequently, Imangara residents made the decision that people would be allowed to return to the same house if they moved out for a period due to death, and that houses would not be reallocated to other families in the interim. The residents specified that this was a decision specific to Imangara and did not necessarily apply in other communities.

instance, Mungalawurru residents were forced to stay in Tennant Creek for a stretch of time as the roads had flooded, and told us of being forced to walk the long distance into town on past occasions. Some left for medical reasons (their own or others'), or to spend time with family in other communities. A couple of community members with young families became temporary migrants, moving to town so their children or grandchildren could attend school. An older man, who'd initially been fairly active in discussions about having computers and internet access at Imangara, moved to Tennant Creek for this purpose not long after the ICTs had been installed, as did a young family from Mungalawurru towards the end of the project. Such temporary relocation, of varying duration, was a recurring feature in our interaction with the residents. As John Taylor writes, 'Much temporary movement is generated by a spatial dichotomy between the concentration of services and dispersion of population, with the result that regional centers, especially in remote Australia, are net recipients of temporary migrants'.[47] We observed that the house in a Tennant Creek town camp, where a close relative of the Mungalawurru residents lived, was sometimes bursting at the seams with visitors from more remote areas, including the Mungalawurru family members.

Some individuals were not particularly mobile, such as younger women with families, and also older women, for whom the young women often played a support role. Generally we found that these residents were more likely to identify themselves as the owner of a computer, and sooner than their more mobile counterparts. Taylor has observed that young Aboriginal people in very remote areas appear to be less mobile than their counterparts in the non-Aboriginal and urban Aboriginal populations (in terms of moving for work, etc.). He attributes the relatively low rates of out-migration by young people from remote and very remote Aboriginal settlements to 'a cultural setting that places emphasis on maintaining extended kinship ties' in which the establishment of independent living arrangements is 'likely to be less of a stimulus for migration among young Aboriginal adults'.[48] Housing shortages, as well as high dependence on rental housing, are further constraints.[49]

We discovered a clear association between residents' degree of mobility and the likelihood that they would take up ownership of, and make use of, the computers. As a measure, we used the number of post-installation field visits where each individual was present in the community up to and including the time when the formal agreement was signed. Participants designated as exhibiting a relatively high degree of mobility were those present for less than a third of the field visits; those present for between one-third

47   J. Taylor, *Population and Diversity: Policy Implications of Emerging Indigenous Demographic Trends*, Canberra: Centre for Aboriginal Economic Policy Research, 2006, p. 64.

48   Taylor, *Population and Diversity*, p. 32.

49   Taylor, *Population and Diversity*.

and two-thirds of visits, a moderate degree of mobility; and those present for more than two-thirds of visits, a low degree of mobility.

Overall, highly mobile individuals tended not to take up formal ownership of the computers (by signing an agreement stating it was their possession) as quickly or to the same extent as those who were less mobile. Of those who signed ownership agreements, the two-thirds who signed agreements in the first year (nine) were all less mobile, while the highly mobile individuals signed the remaining third (six) towards the end of the project. Fourteen people whom we approached to sign did not, and these were all highly mobile. For example, one man moved to another community by mid-November 2012 and did not return, while another spent some months living in a different community. One individual spent some time in jail, and by the time he was released, someone else had taken possession of his desktop computer. It is likely that highly mobile people perceived ownership of a desktop computer as something of a tie or a constraint, indicating that internet services that are fixed to a particular residence are not viable for a significant proportion of people.

Almost all participants chose desktops, which do not readily lend themselves to relocation. Mary, the senior woman at Imangara, hinted at this when we asked her how often the young men in her community used the computers. Gesturing at herself, her daughter, Emily, and another senior woman, she replied that 'we don't move around 'cos we got the [satellite] dish on the house', but the young men 'move around a lot'. Mary's house had one of two satellite dishes at Imangara, and her dish facilitated internet access for five other houses. Although Emily and the other senior woman did not have satellite dishes on their houses, they also became identified during the project as 'the providers' of the computers in their respective households. All three women were also amongst the least mobile of community members at Imangara. As Mary implied, this was in contrast to the young men, who were highly mobile (see discussion of gender in Chapter 7).

INTRA-COMMUNITY MOBILITY

While participants often moved out of the community, even for short periods, they were also comparatively mobile between houses within the communities, which sometimes resulted in them moving computers. As mentioned above, aside from death, the habitability of houses and buildings often played a role in families' relocations within a community. At Mungalawurru, for example, a family moved back into a dwelling that had been vacant for a while after repairs to damage (caused by wasps) were made. Participants also moved out of houses, sometimes on a temporary basis, sometimes more permanently to another dwelling, when housing renovations and rebuilding occurred at Imangara.

Several computers were moved within and from the communities during the project. In some instances, we removed computers because of technical problems, returning them to Alice Springs for repair or replacement. In other cases, participants moved computers themselves. For instance, after the tragedy in Imangara, we did as requested and removed the images off the computer, taking it back to Alice Springs to do so. We later returned the computer to the original house, as the family seemed unsure about what to do with it. However, another family, who were not closely related to the deceased, had since occupied the house. That family later moved to another community, taking the computer with them. Later, when we visited Imangara in April 2014, we found that they had returned with the computer, and were living in another house.

In another incident at Imangara, a young woman left to live in a community 100 kilometers away, taking her household's computer with her. Other community members contacted the Centre for Appropriate Technology (CAT) expressing their concern. When we next visited Imangara, the senior male elder made a point of saying that she should not have taken the computer with her without consulting us. Clearly the young woman felt she had the right to take the computer with her, and considered that it was 'hers', whereas others saw it as a resource provided for all, but also that we had some power over the situation, having given it to the family in the first instance. Of the computers remaining at Mungalawurru, the only computer to 'stay put' in one house throughout the project was owned by the resident we most often found at home in the community (see Appendix 2).

LOCATION AND THE NEED FOR GREATER FLEXIBILITY

Participants' degree of mobility, both within and outside the communities, has clear implications for ICT provision, including ownership of and access to computers and the internet. As to be expected, we found that less mobile participants – those more likely to stay put – took up computer ownership and internet plans sooner and more often than highly mobile community members. Observing the degree and types of mobility, and the diverse reasons for moving within and out of the community, was revealing in other ways, providing a framework for understanding aspects of remote community living. For instance, cultural practices, including those associated with death, can impact significantly on housing and infrastructure needs. In terms of shopping, we observed how geographic isolation could lead to economic hardship (at worst caused by exploitative practices of businesses), and that internet access could provide people with a degree of agency over such transactions, a topic we explore further in the next chapter.

Although we were initially interested in discovering the extent to which internet access might reduce community members' amount of travel and the accompanying costs, the most significant findings related to infrastructure and hardware. As discussed in Chapter 2, most of the community members had opted for desktops, which they perceived as easier to manage, both for the replacement of parts and for ensuring that the computers were not taken out of the community. A family that is moving house and wants to retain the use of the computer for internet access must thus relocate the computer and associated accessories to a house with an existing broadband connection.

The consequences for infrastructure arrangements are significant. For instance, the National Broadband Network (NBN) satellite scheme entails a fixed satellite dish and an account that is tied to a particular dwelling. Such arrangements mean that the somewhat informal movements within the community (such as moving in with relatives when there is no power in one house) will require going without internet access. Those who move a lot are not likely to enter into a contract with a retail service provider, and will therefore go without internet, at least when outside mobile broadband coverage. Indeed, devices such as smartphones, tablets and laptops may have encouraged greater use of the internet for those who travelled frequently, or had responsibilities that took them away from home for extended durations. As the project progressed, we noticed a significant rise in smartphones and tablets, both in the communities and elsewhere. The evolving ecology of internet-enabled hardware in remote communities may ultimately involve a high proportion of mobile devices. However, the desirability of home computers should not be underestimated, especially for those permanently living in outstations, particularly if they wish to manage and restrict access, or to maintain and replace parts easily.

In terms of internet infrastructure arrangements, we concluded that the most viable means of overcoming mobility-related barriers to internet access is to establish community WiFi systems that would reach all dwellings and public spaces. We discuss this issue further in Chapter 9.

Chapter 5: Uses

On one visit, two years after the computers had arrived, a few women were at home in Mungalawurru while the men were off mustering cattle. Karen, a woman in her mid-20s, and one of the community's keenest participants, greeted us, saying that she and her three kids were about to have health check-ups with Anyinginyi, the visiting regional Aboriginal health service. After that, she'd have time to talk to us.

While we were waiting for Karen, we decamped to a shed, where one of the computers had been placed for shared usage, to talk to another young woman, who was next in line with her son and her brother-law to see the health workers. The young woman's skills and use of the home computer had plateaued, like many of the participants', since the project started. She'd worked out how to download movies from the internet, and she'd learnt some new things, like how to import photos from a mobile phone to the computer, and pictures and movies from the computer to a USB stick. But otherwise, she was only using the computer for about half an hour a week, 'sometimes to check Centrelink BasicsCards, sometimes Facebook [...] I used to play games – now I [use the computer] for Centrelink'. Other relatives – her partner, and her mother-in-law, who lives in the house next door – used the computer 'the same' amount in her household.

The young woman was proudest of having used the computer to download and print out an article about her father-in-law and his participation as a young man in a fruit-picking program in Victoria during the 1960s. Now white-whiskered but still wearing a cowboy hat, he sat in his wheelchair on the back veranda of a nearby house, looking out towards the road along which the young men would later return from their day's cattle work.

'But I'm not really like her', the young woman said, stabbing a finger towards the health clinic, where Karen waited outside in the shade. 'She knows everything about computers.'

Karen was one of a core of residents who'd quickly become adept with the computers, and often provided ad hoc ICT assistance for other community members. She was also a research assistant during early interviews when we needed someone to explain to others what we were doing (sometimes in language). She'd maintained an enthusiasm for digital technology, making comments less than a year after receiving a home computer such as: 'The only thing that stops [me] using it is when the power is turned off.' By the end of 2012, she said that she would be willing to pay $100 per month for an internet plan for her household once the project had finished.

When Karen joined us after her family's check-up, she estimated that she used the computer for two to three hours each day for games, music and pictures, including to put these on USB sticks for others, as well as videos for her and her children to watch. She ranked educational and child-rearing activities as the most important uses of the computer: 'Print ABCs for kids or 123 is number one'; download 'kid's music video', 'kid learning to sing with action music' featured in the top six, along with administrative uses such as accessing bank and Centrelink accounts.

Karen's story, but also the other young woman's, relates to the uses of computers, and the ways in which the computers became ordinary features of daily life - tools that assisted them to undertake everyday activities. In this chapter, we discuss what residents used the internet and computer *for*, and how this can be understood in relation to tangible change within the residents' daily lives, including individual agency and enterprise. We also discuss the perceived, if not real, threats of internet use, including concerns around cyber-bullying that emerged within the region during this time.

TANGIBLE OUTCOMES

As discussed in Chapter 2, statistical analysis of internet uses, such as that conducted in the Netherlands by Van Deursen and Van Dijk, have set out to determine whether there are correlations in what people use the internet for and factors such as age, gender and income.[50] They found that those higher up the ladder are likely to undertake self-development online activities, and thus may profit more from internet use.

However, evidence of unequal participation across large data sets cannot tell us about the relationship of online use to resulting changes in an individual's life. As Helsper writes, highlighting the complexity of the area: 'Only when digital experiences are relevant to everyday situations, if they are positive in nature and only if the person feels that online actions lead to the reactions/actions of others, will digital inclusion influence social inclusion.'[51]

When we asked community members in our initial discussions how they would find out simple information such as weather forecasts, road conditions or football scores, they commonly said they would access such information on the television (where available and not necessarily their own) and by word of mouth. Some people said they would use the telephone, but this was far from straightforward (see telephone situation in Chapter 2). The only person amongst the three communities who was using computers at work told us that she printed out information 'like a leaflet' to give to others. A man commented that you had to be careful not to 'shoot the messenger' if you wanted to know what was going on.

---

50   Van Deursen, Van Dijk and Ten Klooster, 'Increasing Inequalities in What We Do Online'.

51   Helsper, *Digital Inclusion*, p. 31.

To gain some insights into what they most valued using the computers and internet access for by the project's end, on our final trips to the communities in April 2014, we asked participants what was the *first thing* they did when they logged onto their computers. Most responses fell evenly within the categories of either functional (Centrelink, Gumtree) or entertainment activities (movies, games, listening to songs, YouTube). These categories were similar to those that emerged when the residents were asked almost eighteen months earlier in November 2012 what activities they used the computers and internet for (see Appendix 3). This suggests that their main areas of use hadn't changed significantly in that time. The community members' reported in November 2012 that usage for banking, downloading music, and viewing videos and photos were also amongst the types of activities they thought the computers and internet would be useful for at the project's start. As discussed further below, use of the internet for email communication and educational purposes was fairly modest.

In order to confirm uses, we took data off the filter for a sub-set of the computers (with the permission of the owner of that computer) and analyzed what websites people were visiting the most. Around half of the websites visited we categorized as 'miscellaneous' sites, and search was regularly used to find information. The second-largest group of websites visited were videos, followed by religious sites and shopping. These uses indicate that the internet was a continuation of everyday activities for the residents, occurring within the same spread of priorities and concerns they had before the computers arrived, rather than seeking out new opportunities. For instance, although online education was theoretically accessible to residents, none took it up (although computers were used for existing educational activities, including supplementing kids' school work in the form of educational games).

When seen in the context of life in remote communities, these uses are providing a level of autonomy over personal affairs that was difficult for them to achieve before. The young woman from Mungalawurru, while waiting in the queue for her health check, said that having internet in the community had been 'all right', but that it hasn't made 'much difference'. She also told us, however, that she was relying on Facebook to keep up with family and friends outside Mungalawurru, 'now the phone isn't working' (the community's public telephone was on the blink). She looked up the *Tennant Times* online on Fridays to see what was happening in town on the weekend. She could also transfer 'kid's money' (parenting payments) over the internet on the weekend, whereas she could only do it by phone before Friday at 5 pm. Although she said the internet hadn't made much difference to life in the community, her comments suggested that the convenience, agency and autonomy it provided in accessing services and information, and in keeping up with friends and family, had become a matter-of-course by then for active participants like her, impacting in subtle, yet important, ways on her lifestyle.

The high interest in religious websites also reflected community activities and priorities at the time. Residents used the computers for personal and community-based religious activities such as downloading and playing gospel songs, printing out posters, and producing songbooks to use in the local church. It was not uncommon to find a picture of Jesus, printed on a home computer and captioned with, 'He is coming', taped to a community member's front door, or to see Christian iconography used as a screensaver. One woman reported doing a Bible study online with someone in Mexico. On some of our visits, we were told that various people were absent because they were attending a sing-along or a gospel meeting at another community. On our last trip to Mungalawurru, a man who'd experienced a conversion during a stint in prison was reading the Bible on his house's verandah while listening to Warlpiri, Pitjantjatjara and Waramunga gospel music he'd downloaded onto a USB stick. He told us that it had changed his life for the better, including leading him to sobriety.

Although we were not clear on the extent of it, we knew that missionaries had been using ICTs to reach out to these communities, particularly through music sharing. In previous chapters, we have discussed how various programs have resulted in a patchwork of infrastructures in remote communities, resulting in different types of access and levels of adoption. The same can be observed of the level of uses, with short-term or ongoing programs encouraging or enabling certain uses in particular localities. For instance, the cultural archive Ara Irititja appears popular amongst the Ngaanyatjarra, Pitjantjatjara and Yankunytjatjara people for whom it was created, but no such online archive exists for the language groups we were working with.[52] As discussed further in the next chapter, Inge Kral observed the popularity of GarageBand (sound mixing) software in Wingelina, where a media center was active in music development at the time.[53] Other programs have focused on the use of computers as part of diversionary youth programs. In Chapter 9, we discuss how internet use at the Papunya Computer Room differed from what we observed in the outstations, possibly due to a history of creative enterprise in that community, as well as greater access to face-to-face services and the circumstances surrounding its establishment. Keeping these differences in mind, the idea that use can be linked to cultural characteristics separate from the contemporary cultural landscape of remote communities is flawed. Internet use reflects daily life, but also the various activities and programs of outsiders that work in communities – including religious organizations.

ONLINE BANKING AND MONEY MANAGEMENT

A year after the computers were installed, Mary asked us how to check her BasicsCard balance online: 'I don't want to have to ask the woman at the store to check it for me anymore', she told us. After a lengthy wait on the Centrelink helpline – in the freezing wind

---

52   Although Kimberly Christen has produced innovative digital content and databases for Warumungu.

53   I. Kral, *Plugged In: Remote Australian Indigenous Youth and Digital Culture.*

on the community's only telephone – we managed to set her up with an online account and showed her how to log on using her home computer. The satellite internet speed was so slow that the site's security system kept locking us out (the communities had not yet moved to the National Broadband Network (NBN) Interim Satellite Service, which provides faster internet); and once we did get in, the website was unnecessarily complex. Regardless, Mary was willing to try to navigate the site in order to have some level of financial control, even if it was simply to know how much money was available that day.

In the previous chapter, we discussed how online banking reduced travel for some. Banking also provided a level of control over finances that is significant, given that Aboriginal people living in remote areas are the most 'underbanked' in the country. A study by Vinita Godinho has looked at the reasons for underbanking, and found that money is regularly shared amongst a wide network of kin, and that many people see money as a problem, lacking the financial knowledge to control it.[54] In addition, 'Lower levels of access and usage of information and communications technology (ICT) combined with lower digital literacy further restrict Indigenous financial inclusion, by limiting their ability to access electronic banking delivery channels'.[55]

In our first meetings with the communities, residents identified banking as one of the main services they'd like to access online. At the time, less than 20 per cent of participants had used internet banking, and around half expressed an interest in doing so.[56] A woman who was involved in a financial literacy organization did not know how to use internet banking, but wanted to learn. By the end of the project, all regular adult internet users were using online banking. Even an old man, who had shown no interest in computers and declined the offer of having one in his house, was asking for assistance from others for money-related purposes.[57]

When we commenced the project, those living in remote communities were known to be paying more for banking than other Australians.[58] A 2011 Department of Treasury

---

54   V. Godinho, *Money, Financial Capability and Well-Being in Indigenous Australia*, Melbourne: RMIT University, 2014, p. 8.

55   Godinho, *Money, Financial Capability and Well-Being in Indigenous Australia*, p. 2; See also L. Hems, C. Connolly and M. Georgouras, 'Measuring Financial Exclusion in Australia' for National Australia Bank, Sydney: Centre for Social Impact (CSI), University of New South Wales, 2012.

56   Rennie et al., *Home Internet for Remote Indigenous Communities*, pp. 46-47.

57   Asking for assistance with online banking is also problematic for some people, leading to privacy breaches and theft. Financial abuse by family members through online banking is an area that requires further research.

58   See Australian Financial Counselling and Credit Reform Association, 'ATM Fees in Indigenous Communities', http://www.afccra.org/media%20releases%20documents/ATM%20Fees%20in%20 Remote%20Indigenous%20Communities.pdf.

Taskforce on ATMs in remote communities found that there was a tendency amongst this population to check balances and make withdrawals frequently, and that this resulted in significant costs, as consumers in remote communities did not have a choice of ATMs as do those in larger towns. Independent ATM providers owned nearly 80 per cent of to the 600 ATMs in remote communities across the country at the time we commenced our study, and were depending on revenue from these ATMs (usually $2 per transaction). The taskforce report found that people were often checking balances and making withdrawals for various reasons, including the inability to store food and therefore a need to shop on a daily basis, the obligation to give money to relatives acting as a disincentive to hold large amounts of money at a time, and low withdrawal limits on ATMs if cash was in short supply.[59] The taskforce also found 'many more balance enquiries relative to withdrawals than the Australian average', which was likely caused by not knowing when Centrelink payments or direct debits would be made.[60] The report noted that those living in remote communities were either unable or unwilling to use internet banking. As a result of the taskforce, the Australian Bankers' Association put forward a proposal to eliminate fees on withdrawals and balance enquiries at selected ATMs in remote communities, and this was accepted by the competition regulator in late 2012.

A significant and controversial change in how welfare was administered in remote Northern Territory communities also had consequences for personal finance control. As part of the Northern Territory Emergency Response (the Intervention, 2007-2012), welfare recipients in prescribed communities were subject to new measures from 2007 that meant that part of their payments (50-70 per cent) were quarantined and could only be spent on 'basics'. To spend that money, individuals would use a BasicsCard to buy groceries and approved items (not alcohol or cigarettes, for instance) through an EFTPOS-style system. People were automatically enrolled in the scheme, although they could apply to be made exempt from it, assessed on whether their children were attending school regularly, and whether they were shown by Centrelink to have reasonable financial stability.

We did not ask the residents about their spending and withdrawal practices. However, it was clear that the ability to check online banking and BasicsCard balances offered significant convenience to community members, as they could avoid the time-consuming processes involved in contacting services by phone. It was not uncommon to see people sitting around the sole community phone on old chairs, sometimes in harsh sunlight or in strong winds, or in the mud if the weather had been wet, for lengthy periods. Accessing social security services via satellite broadband at home was also cheaper than doing so by mobile phone, as 1800 numbers were metered at that time (Telstra, the sole provider in most remote areas, has since made 1800 numbers free for mobiles).

---

59   See Australian Financial Counselling and Credit Reform Association, 'ATM Fees in Indigenous Communities', p. 8.

60   See Australian Financial Counselling and Credit Reform Association, 'ATM Fees in Indigenous Communities', p. 7.

As early as February 2012, residents began mentioning using the internet to access these services, with comments like those from two young women at Imangara that they went online 'definitely once a week on "payday" to check their keycard', or 'I access Centrelink every day' becoming increasingly common. Women tended to make greater use of the computers and internet access for household administrative activities than men (discussed further in Chapter 7). Karen observed the relative accessibility of the home computers to us, saying that while a couple of people kept wanting to come into town to check their Centrelink account, 'I tell them to get registered, just phone them [Centrelink] then get back on the computer.'

This use of the home computers and the internet to access services online might suggest increasing the ease of access by government for the control and surveillance of remote Aboriginal people's daily lives. Lattas and Morris have described how the state's implementation of measures such as the BasicsCard through the Northern Territory Intervention increased the 'forms of sociocultural surveillance and policing that seek to instil new cultural habits' within Indigenous lives in an 'urgent need to normalise Indigenous familial relations of reciprocity'.[61] At a more general level, governments have historically led the digital divide agenda. It aligns with efficiency measures, as well as an internal bureaucratic push for data-driven policy.[62] These motivations spur a wide-reaching range of technological changes that do not always serve the citizens whom they are purportedly supposed to be helping.

Nonetheless, the greater reach and accessibility of online government services available through home ICTs can also be seen within the broader canvas of increasing online participation for Aboriginal people, and potentially removing barriers to social inclusion. Discussing the impact of the introduction of cheap mobile phones to India, Robin Jeffrey and Assa Doron observe how 'the mobile phone offered greater potential to connect people regularly to state institutions', and that it 'drew India's people into relations with the record-keeping capitalist state more comprehensively than any previous mechanism or technology'.[63] This is offset, however, by the democratic nature of mobile phones in enabling vast numbers of people, from across different classes and hierarchies, and different genders, to become part of a network society. Jeffrey and Doron stress the democratization of information-sharing that has become possible through this cheap and simple form of ICT access, as well as other capabilities such as increased

61   A. Lattas and B. Morris, 'The Politics of Suffering and the Politics of Anthropology' in J. Altman and M. Hinkson (eds) *Culture Crisis: Anthropology and Politics in Aboriginal Australia*, Chicago: University of New South Wales Press, 2010, pp. 123-124.

62   Coalition, 'The Coalition's Policy for E-Government and the Digital Economy'.

63   A. Doron and R. Jeffrey, *The Great Indian Phone Book: How the Cheap Cell Phone Changes Business, Politics, and Daily Life*, Cambridge: Harvard University Press, 2013, pp. 222, 224.

capacity to connect, mobilize and broadcast, improving citizens' ability to advocate for improved governance.[64] While 'none of this [has] overturned power structures or ironed out inequality yet', Jeffrey and Doron comment that 'it did make conditions "faster, more efficient and" – a matter of hope and promise – "more democratic"'.[65]

ENTERPRISE DEVELOPMENT

Altman describes the 'hybrid' set of economic and administrative variables underpinning the fabric of outstation settlements as a combination of state sector, private sector and customary economic activities (for instance, land management and visual art).[66]

The hybrid economy was visible within all three communities insofar as residents supported themselves on a mixture of social security payments and local employment. The cattle project at Mungalawurru, aspirations to develop cultural tourism at Kwale Kwale, and bush foods at Imangara were instances of the customary activities that represented the possibility of enterprise. One question we had was whether improved telecommunications could assist these 'off-the-grid' communities in developing a base for economic sustainability, assisting Aboriginal people to live on their traditional lands.

Initially, several residents within the communities expressed interest in using the computers for local cultural, social and/or economic enterprises. At Kwale Kwale, Rhonda said she wished to use the computer and printer to self-publish cultural resources, and to keep the books for a cultural tourism enterprise. Another man who ran a youth respite service suggested he might use a computer to keep a database tracking outcomes across five projects. Mungalawurru residents were interested in keeping a database of stock for their cattle business on their computers, and a local artist wanted to use the internet to liaise with Barkly Arts to display her work.

However, the enterprises that were occurring had administrative assistance from outsiders, and these were the individuals who generally made use of the computers and internet for business-related purposes. A church worker who assisted the man running the youth respite center used his computer, and when the live-in visitor moved on, the man did not use the computer at all. While individuals mentioned using the computer

64   Doron and Jeffrey, *The Great Indian Phone Book*.

65   Doron and Jeffrey, *The Great Indian Phone Book*, p. 224.

66   See J. Altman, 'Development Options on Aboriginal Land: Sustainable Indigenous Hybrid Economies in the Twenty-First Century' in L. Taylor, G. Ward, G. Henderson, R. Davis and L. Wallis (eds) *The Power of Knowledge, the Resonance of Tradition*, Canberra: Aboriginal Studies Press, 2005.

and printer for individual and family-oriented purposes such as printing out 'kids' stories, put[ting] them in folders', and or historical documents they found on the net,[67] very few reported using the computer equipment in a work-related context, such as for printing out spread-sheets.

Given the lack of infrastructure and skills base that small settlements such as outstations possess, it would have been unrealistic to expect economic and/or creative ventures to emerge during the timespan of the project simply through access to ICTs. Kwale Kwale was one community where this seemed possible, but again outsiders had significant influence in determining how and when that occurred.

During the years that we visited Kwale Kwale, we witnessed various efforts towards enterprise development, and even community self-sustainability. At times community members were enthusiastic at the prospect of using the internet for enterprise purposes, while at other times the computers and internet were cast aside.

In October 2011, we were told that the Apostolic (Baptist) church was providing resources to partly refurbish some houses, and to build a small backpacker camping ground, a vegetable garden and a shop. The computers were initially seen as an asset in this overall plan. By early 2012, considerable work had been done, and we were told that the community was aiming for self-sufficiency over ten years. The church members were living onsite, and appeared to have a significant influence in guiding the direction of the community, although it was difficult to ascertain whether the ideas were coming from the church or from the community. A few months later, one of the visiting pastors advised us that the computers had been declared off-limits in order to stop kids from playing games, and to prevent any other inappropriate use. At the pastor's request, we took the computers away to 'clean' them, but found no evidence of inappropriate material, and both machines still had their filters set to 'child' (the highest level of filtering).

By September 2012, there was a sign by the turn-off to Kwale Kwale that read, 'Art for sale', and the vegetable patch was producing crops that were consumed by the residents during an evening meal organized by the pastor. The elder woman in the community, while painting gumnuts, told us that she wanted the children to be able to play games, and that it wasn't up to the pastor to determine what the children did. One of the derelict houses was undergoing repairs for an intended arts center. The work had been carried out by the church members, with some assistance from the residents, and we were informed that Rhonda was the driving force behind the project. The next stage of the project would be to build a walking trail for tours, and to establish a restaurant and small caravan park. While relaying this, the pastor asked that two computers originally

---

67   The young woman in the story opening this chapter made a wall poster from an online article
      about her grandfather's days as a stockman.

placed in the community shed be returned – one of the computers into the building being refurbished for the arts center for use by the business, and the other to a house for one of the residents to use. These moves required some significant reconfiguring of the technical arrangements, which CAT set about organizing. While one computer was eventually moved into the resident's house, months later it seemed that progress on the art gallery had stalled due to lack of money, and the community's artists had begun making their art work and selling it through Tangentyere Art Centre. Over time, our visits to Kwale Kwale slowed compared to the other two communities. Rhonda, who had access to computers at work, requested assistance from us from time to time, but we received mixed messages as to the value and use of the computers in Kwale Kwale. No-one chose to continue a subscription to internet services at the completion of the funded period.

The church's involvement in the community was an instance of the non-government sector stepping in to assist in the absence of other programs. The moral influence of the church may have been a factor in the community's oscillating attitudes towards ICTs and how they should best be provided. Although it was not possible to fully know how these events were impacting on the community, Kwale Kwale does illustrate the ways in which some communities are actively pursuing enterprise and sustainability, in this case with assistance from willing workers and missionaries. As mentioned previously, downloading Aboriginal gospel music was popular in both Imangara and Mungalawurru, and the influence of various Christian churches was apparent throughout the region.[68]

Meanwhile, the man living on the far side of the community – the only resident who had his own computer and internet when we commenced – had developed a substantial tomato garden, and was selling to Alice Springs caterers. The other enterprise, a youth respite center, continued to operate intermittently over this time.

EMAIL AND SOCIAL NETWORKING

In July 2012, Karen at Mungalawurru announced to us: 'I don't run up to answer the phone because I get email'. Like her comments about the convenience of having a home computer to check online banking and Centrelink accounts, she'd realized it was easier to rely on email for communications than on the community payphone. Karen described emailing more people, maybe five a week, and receiving emails from the cattle project, the CLC and friends. But she was also one of a handful of residents on whom organizations like the CLC and CAT relied to communicate with the community about matters such as scheduling visits.

---

68   In January 2014, ABC news reported that the community of Haasts Bluff had started fundraising to erect a 20-meter-high neon crucifix on a hill, with an estimated cost of $1.2 million. G. Liston, 'Remote Community Hopes to Erect Giant Neon Crucifix', http://www.abc.net.au/news/2008-09-25/fiery-debate-over-dpp-decision/521100.

Although people identified contacting friends and family outside the community as one of the main advantages of having ICT access, extensive social use of email did not develop during the project. It soon became apparent that apart from having the basic applications, both parties needed ready access to the internet to have the regular habit of checking their email, and to leave their Skype application turned on. Initially, we tried to speed up the process by passing on to the residents the email addresses of regular contacts (a local accountant, the CLC, Barkly Arts), with their permission. We also tried to increase community members' familiarity with e-communication by activating programs such as Outlook and Skype at start-up, and by regularly sending email messages to all the computers to maximize their chance of being read. Co-author Andrew Crouch at CAT received some emails from Imangara in the next few months, with queries like: 'How can I do such-and-such' or, 'How can I obtain a Hotmail account?', which he was able to resolve online. In total, between when the computers were installed in 2011 and the end of 2012, Andrew had only a total of only 109 emails from residents, either initiated by them or in response to an email he sent. Nonetheless, when asked whom they emailed, those using email mostly responded that Andrew was the main person they liaised with. It seemed the main reason why e-communication did not emerge as one of the major uses of ICT was because people didn't have friends and family outside the communities with functional email accounts.

Given that the use of email is somewhat waning as a form of online communication, it is more likely that social media will be the dominant means of connecting with outside networks and finding information, particularly amongst younger people.[69] Use of social media in the project was fairly modest. While social media users reported spending significant amounts of time on Facebook, only ten community members said they regularly accessed Facebook and other social networking sites such as Divas Chat,[70] and several more said they wished to learn, or had forgotten how to use, social media. Unsurprisingly, social media users were also youthful: most were women aged 18-29 years, plus a man in the same age group, a teenage girl and two women in their 30s.

Facebook appeared to become increasingly popular as a form of communication amongst remote central Australian Aboriginal populations during 2013 and 2014. For example, when we visited the Papunya Computer Room in May 2012, almost no-one was using Facebook. However, two years later, the computer room staff claimed that: 'Everyone has a Facebook account. It's the easiest way to communicate with outside'; and:

---

69   P. Olsen, 'Teenagers Say Goodbye to Facebook and Hello to Messenger Apps', *The Guardian*, 10 November 2013.

70   Divas Chat is a dating and messaging service owned by Canadian company airG and contracted to Telstra. It is popular amongst remote-living Aboriginal people as it can be accessed from a phone that has run out of credit. Debt accrued through subscription to airG (95c a day) is then deducted from the user's Telstra credit when the mobile is recharged.

'They talk to friends in other parts of Australia. Facebook Hermannsburg, South Australia, Santa Teresa'. In the Remote Indigenous Public Internet Access's (RIPIA's) *Cyber Safety Program Report*, which interviewed people in six central Australian remote communities, including Ali Curung and Papunya, 37 per cent of participants 'claimed they/and or their family members enjoy using social media for keeping in touch with friends and family, while 40 per cent claim they do not know why people like it or find it useful'.[71] When we discussed ICT use with Ali Curung community members in October 2013, roughly half of those we interviewed who were using the internet at the time said they used a social media site such as Facebook or Divas Chat.[72] A woman told us that she would often ask neighbours via Facebook whether they had any sugar or tea rather than walk over to their house.

In late 2013, workers in Tennant Creek local agencies and organizations told us that they were now 'Facebooking' clients from in town and remote communities because it was the quickest way of contacting them: 'It's much easier to use social networking to find people.' One interviewee said that 90 per cent of her communication with board and staff in the community organization where she worked 'is text-based [i.e. via mobile phone] or is messaged via Facebook'.

A survey by a commercial research agency, McNair Ingenuity Research in 2014 also observed the prevalence and popularity of Facebook usage amongst Indigenous Australians, particularly in remote areas, noting: 'First Australians are significantly more likely to join and participate in Facebook than the overall population', with 'six-in-ten adult Indigenous Australians us[ing] Facebook, compared to 42 per cent of adult Australians nationally'. At 44 per cent, Facebook usage amongst remote Indigenous people was 'slightly above the overall national average', even though home computer usage was low, and ADSL was often unavailable: people generally accessed the internet on mobile phones.[73] Urban Indigenous scholar Bronwyn Carlson has also documented an increasing trend amongst Indigenous Australians to use Facebook 'to build, display, and perform Aboriginal identities', as a 'key self-representational tool'.[74]

---

71   L. Iten, *Cyber Safety Program Report,* Alice Springs: Northern Territory Library and Central Australian Youth Link Up Service, 2014, p. 10.

72   This finding differs somewhat to Iten's (2014); however, Iten interviewed a smaller sample and did not include 'nil' responses.

73   M. Balogh, 'Indigenous Australia Addicted to Facebook', news release, 26 August 2014.

74   B. Carlson, 'The "New Frontier": Emergent Indigenous Identities and Social Media', in M. Harris, M. Nakata and B. Carlson (eds) *The Politics of Identity: Emerging Indigeneity,* Sydney: University of Technology Sydney E-Press, 2013.

KIDS AND ICT USAGE

When we asked community members in our early discussions whether they thought having computers would be good for children, most were positive about their educational value for young people. They did not express much 'worry about kids' regarding what they might access online; instead, they were concerned about addiction to games and time-wasting behavior. Adults thought kids were pests when it came to media devices, especially as they 'get upset when they don't get to use it'. They also spoke of kids bugging them to play games on mobile phones, and of locking their games console away, saying they would do the same with a computer when they had one and, as discussed in Chapter 3, they began to set passwords to restrict access to computers later in the project.

Once the computers were installed, adults had mixed responses to children's use of them, some expressing surprise at their aptitude on the computers, others complaining about time-wasting. Adults described the children using the computers for both educational and entertainment purposes, including playing games, internet browsing, Indigitube,[75] downloading photos and drawing pictures. Playing games was by far the most popular use (50 per cent) of the computers for children, with frequent mentions of educational games, particularly a maths game. Young women often described activities on the computers involving kids, such as 'play music video for kids', 'kids write stories', 'kids do paintings' and 'kids play educational games'. Emily showed us books with photos and stories that she had created with her children on the home computer. Several people also thought kids' activities on the household computers supplemented schoolwork: 'Yes! – counting, alphabet', and 'Kids use at school, then come home and use. Has been helping for maths and reading'.

When we asked community members whether they thought computers had been a source of time-wasting, some disagreed, saying they 'just sit there for a little while and then run around', 'spend most time outside, only on computer a bit', 'probably about half an hour, then go out and play'. Just under a third, all young adults, who were also most often the parents of young children, gave an unqualified 'yes' in response. Children using up the internet quota or power was, however, a continuing source of irritation, with one man remarking that his household needed to 'manage power use' as a result of kids' frequent computer use. As part of its Codey cybersmart project, arts provider Barkly Arts produced an educational poster captioned 'Plugging in your phone at home to get on the Internet uses power and costs money. Power at home is for everyone to share and must be respected.'[76] As discussed in Chapter 3, towards the end of the project, people commented that they'd put passwords on their computers to regulate kids', as well as

---

75   In early 2016, Indigitube was not available and the site was redirecting to ICTV Play, a video-on-demand service for the remote Indigenous community television service, ICTV.

76   Barkly Arts, 8 August 2014. In fact, mobile phone charging uses a trivial amount of power.

visitors' and other residents' use of them, so that they would not use up all the power when they were away from the community. They also mentioned locking the desktop lid, so that kids did not 'always use it', and providing adult supervision to kids: I 'encourage them to behave properly/set some rules – e.g. switch on and off properly', and they can use the computer 'when I'm around, yes, but not when I'm not around'.

CYBER-SAFETY

In our initial conversations with the communities, their concern about potential cyber-safety issues was low, and difficult to gauge compared to their quite strong opinions about time-wasting activities. By contrast, a 2010 report commissioned by the Australian Media and Communications Authority (ACMA) found that 71 per cent of Australian parents 'were concerned about cyber-safety, with 32% of this group reporting that they were "very concerned".[77] Notably, most Australian parents were regularly using the internet (88 per cent) and accessing the internet from home at least several times a week (81 per cent) in comparison with the outstation residents at that time. It was possible that adult community members' limited exposure to ICTs was the main reason for their lack of concern about cyber-safety.

The term 'cyber-safety' encompasses the protection of internet users from online risks and security breaches such as 'exposure to illegal or inappropriate material, stranger danger, identity theft, invasion of privacy, harassment and cyber-bullying'.[78] Cyber-bullying refers more specifically to incidents of harassment, usually involving sending messages (text and images) via the internet or mobile phones to other parties.[79] While the more dramatic and disturbing aspects of cyber-safety are often quick to capture public attention, these are symptomatic of a range of issues relating to online literacy.

Currently, little research is available on the nature and extent of cyber-safety issues in remote Aboriginal communities, although there is a growing body of national and international academic and policy literature, such as *EU Kids Online* and its Australian counterpart, *AU Kids Online*, and reports by the Australian government's Joint Select

---

77   Australian Communications and Media Authority (ACMA), 'Cybersmart Parents: Connecting Parents to Cyber-Safety Resources', Canberra: Australian Media and Communications Authority, 2010, p. 6.

78   ACMA, 'Cybersmart Parents', p. 6.

79   ACMA, 'Cybersmart Parents', p. 52.

Committee on Cyber-Safety.[80] Some limited reporting on cyber-safety in remote northern Australia appears in the Commonwealth Department of Families, Housing, Community Services and Indigenous Affairs (FaHCSIA)'s *Community Safety and Wellbeing Research Study*, which surveyed seventeen Aboriginal communities across the Northern Territory between December 2010 and June 2011, with 76 per cent of respondents classifying nasty phone texts as a 'very big' or 'big' problem.[81] Similarly, RIPIA's *Cyber Safety Program Report* identified 'swearing and arguments' online as the most common cyber-safety-related problem.[82]

We did hear concern expressed about potential and actual outbreaks of cyber-bullying in central Australia. When we visited Papunya in May 2012, some elders were worried about cyber-bullying occurring if mobile phone towers were installed in the community (which did not happen until 2014). They said being at Papunya gave young people a break from the 'trash talk' on mobile phones that went on when they were in Alice Springs and Tennant Creek, and they didn't want conflict emerging from cyber-bullying and sexting in their community.

They were particularly aware of how cyber-bullying had fed conflict between two camps aligned with different families in Yuendumu, a major Aboriginal community 262 kilometers' drive away, which was exacerbated when people from Hermannsburg (420 kilometers from Yuendumu) began to send inflammatory phone messages. Some of these were sent anonymously through false identities created on the social media platform Divas Chat (airG) using the names of deceased relatives from the other camp, a highly provocative gesture given the restrictions in local Aboriginal culture on naming or viewing images of the dead. Ultimately, the situation was managed with the assistance of the Australian Federal Police and ISP to identify and close the social networking accounts of people sending offensive messages, and to appoint monitors (e.g. 'Diva Cops') in chat rooms to identify and report potential concerns.[83]

---

80   S. Livingstone and L. Haddon, *EU Kids Online: Final Report,* London: EU Kids Online, 2009; L. Green, D. Brady, K. Olafsson, J. Hartley and C. Lumby, 'Risks and Safety for Australian Children on the Internet: Full Findings from the Au Kids Online Survey of 9-16 Year Olds and Their Parents', *Cultural Science Journal* 4.1 (2011); Joint Select Committee on Cyber-Safety, 'High-Wire Act: Cyber-Safety and the Young', *Interim Report,* Canberra, 2011.

81   G. Shaw and P. D'Abbs, *Community Safety and Wellbeing Research Study: Consolidated Report,* Canberra: Department of Families, Housing, Community Services and Indigenous Affairs, 2011, pp. 8-9.

82   L. Iten, *Cyber Safety Program Report,* Alice Springs: Northern Territory Library and Central Australian Youth Link Up Service, 2014.

83   Central Land Council (CLC), 'Divas Chat Causing Social Chaos', *Land Rights News,* Alice Springs: Central Land Council, 2012, pp. 4-6; Human Rights Equal Opportunity Commission, *Social Justice Report 2011,* Sydney: Commonwealth of Australia, 2011.

At Ali Curung, the women who assisted us with our survey also expressed concern about cyber-bullying, commenting that it was a problem amongst young people, but also that social networking sites like Facebook were causing domestic problems for couples, presumably due to jealousy (an observation confirmed by the local policeman). Although the women asked us to include questions related to cyber-safety in our survey of eighty-five Ali Curung residents, we found that any direct line of questioning on the topic closed down discussion almost immediately, and we all agreed to cease raising it in our interviews.

Tennant Creek provides a hub for many residents from Aboriginal settlements in the surrounding Barkly region, which has a population of 7,500, approximately 70 per cent of whom are Indigenous. We began to hear from local organizations that some Aboriginal elders and parents were disturbed by reports that kids had been involved in cyber-bullying, something they knew little about. Children had been texting each other during school hours, with physical fights erupting from arguments online. Sometimes, older relatives weighed into kids' spats on Facebook; on other occasions, the conflict spread beyond families to communities outside Tennant Creek, to people they might have met once or twice, and even to total strangers. As at Yuendumu, people set up false profiles on social media using names and images of the deceased to taunt others.

Most of the activity was associated with mobile phones, and some kids from nearby communities without mobile coverage were going to great lengths to access social media. In some cases, kids stole their parents' cars and drove to get service to be able to text their girlfriends or find out the footy scores, so keen were they to keep up with what was happening. There were also stories of inter-racial cyber-bullying erupting around tension at football matches, and of racist comments being posted on Facebook walls, especially under photos of different racial groups in Tennant Creek.[84]

To follow up on these concerns, we spoke to a number of professionals, including lawyers, police, teachers, youth workers and other community workers at Aboriginal and non-Aboriginal social service, arts and educational agencies at Tennant Creek, and at three other remote communities in the Barkly region. Because of the high degree of sensitivity surrounding research using Indigenous subjects, and because of our experience in Ali Curung, we thought it was better to proceed by canvassing a group of professionals first to gauge how serious an issue cyber-bullying was in the area.[85] We were interested in what forms it took (whether it was confined to bullying or took other forms like security

---

84   See E. Hogan, 'Behind the Mulga Curtain', *Inside Story*, 2014; E. Hogan, E. Rennie, A. Crouch, A. Wright, R. Gregory and J. Thomas, *Submission to the Inquiry into Issues Surrounding Cyber-Safety for Indigenous Australians*, Brisbane: ARC Centre of Excellence for Creative Industries and Innovation, Queensland University of Technology, 2013.

85   G. Cowlishaw, 'A New Protection Policy?', *Inside Story*, 2013.

threats), what responses had been developed, and what implications there might be for Aboriginal people's access to the ICTs. Tennant Creek was an appropriate location for this research, not only because of the local reports of cyber-bullying, but also because of its centrality to Aboriginal people in the region, and because the town had long possessed mobile coverage.

Most interviewees did not think the incidence of cyber-bullying in Tennant Creek 'was different to anywhere else', and emphasized that cyber-safety was a problem worldwide, and not limited to particular race or community groups. Texting and messaging provided the main avenues for cyber-bullying in the Tennant Creek survey, particularly on social networking platforms Divas Chat and Facebook.

On our last visit to Mungalawurru, which does not have mobile access, a middle-aged woman told us she wasn't interested in using social media, because it caused too much fighting, and told us how when she'd stayed with family in a mid-sized town, her nieces had been arguing on Facebook even though they were in the same house. In Tennant Creek, young women, from 10 years old through to high-school age, were described as tending 'to be more bitchy and more often on social media' and 'to be a bit more technically functional' than young men, who were described as 'more reserved' in commenting, but more sexually forthright in their content. Similarly, FaHCSIA's *Community Safety and Wellbeing Research Study* reported that cyber-bullying was 'particularly problematic for young girls', and that it emerged in contexts such as same-sex fights (including 'jealousing' fights between girls over boyfriends and boys teasing each other), between couples and amongst groups of young men and women in communities'.[86] The RIPIA Report also identified '[f]emale dominated social networking service use' as 'the group most commonly experiencing problems', with 'jealousing' as 'an issue voiced overwhelmingly by females (78%)'.[87] Sexting, by contrast, was negligible, being 'recognised and voiced as a problem only by males, at just 2% of the response'.[88]

Although older people were reportedly mystified by local outbursts of cyber-bullying, they could also be implicated in online fights via their children. A school representative explained: 'Often what happens as well is that parents will get on their kids' accounts and write things back. I've had that before actually where on Facebook they said, "But such-and-such's mum was there giving me a serve", and all sorts of things.'

Older, remote communities were said to be particularly vulnerable to online frauds and

---

86   Shaw and D'Abbs, *Community Safety and Wellbeing Research Study: Consolidated Report*, p. 82, 106.

87   Iten, *Cyber Safety Program Report*, p. 9, 12.

88   Iten, *Cyber Safety Program Report*, p. 12.

scams, tending to take offers of financial remuneration over the internet at face value. A project officer for a royalties organization said, 'We have those all the time. The number of scams that are going on at any given time [...] We have old ladies saying, "I'm going to win a million dollars. Look at this [...] I've got this on my phone", and I'm like, "No. Don't reply. Don't engage". They just don't understand that it's not - it's coming on a phone, it's [not] coming on an official [basis].'

Despite the emergence of cyber-safety and related issues in Tennant Creek, no-one suggested that social media and digital technology should be banned: instead they thought internet connectivity had too many benefits for remote populations for its use to be restricted. Elders and older generations decided they needed to become 'digi-smart' to engage with the emerging local cyber-culture: 'We need to understand more about the digital world, or otherwise, get rid of it. And obviously, we can't get rid of it because it's here and it's important. It will just mean people are becoming further and further away from what the rest of the world is sort of doing.'

The key issues identified in our Tennant Creek research and in the RIPIA report indicate that digital literacy and proficiency are the crux of the matter for remote Aboriginal people in responding to cyber-safety. In particular, the privacy problems posed by social media are not well understood: people in remote communities are often unaware that 'anybody in the world can see them' online. A youth worker in a Barkly community said that 'nobody has privacy settings and nobody wants them', even though she'd tried to persuade people of the value of using them on Facebook. She described how 'Someone might post on Facebook at three in the morning saying, "I'm going to have a sniff now" or a drink, and everyone in the community will read it.' A woman at Ali Curung told us that she changed her SIM card in her phone regularly so she would not have to receive and read text messages intended for others. This was because of the high prevalence of phone sharing.

Another privacy concern was young people's lack of awareness of the potential impact of having a digital footprint on their employment prospects: 'Young people don't realize how being on Facebook will impact on them', a senior Aboriginal woman said. 'They have no understanding of the "digital footprint" they're leaving - the fact they'll never lose it and it may even affect their employability. There are enough barriers to Aboriginal employment already.' These privacy-based issues relate in turn to remote Aboriginal people's lower levels of digital and English literacy in contrast with the Australian mainstream, along with the experience of being accelerated into ICT use within a relatively short period.

Middle-aged and older people often expressed concern about the unguarded online activities of Aboriginal children and youth, and a fear that young people might be 'tricking them' with social media.[89] Faced with extensive disadvantage and a large youth population – 25 per cent of people in the Barkly are under 17 – it's understandable that elders, along with schools and the community sector, fear that cyber-bullying may exacerbate existing social problems in Tennant Creek. But many of the anxieties about cyber-safety issues relate to the cultural and digital disconnects between older and younger generations, and to uncertainty about how to navigate the dynamics between these worlds. One community worker said, 'People split it up between their cultural responsibilities and then their Facebook/Divas personality. But when it suits them, they'll be in the other world.' This dichotomy between digital and cultural worlds is often framed in terms of a cyber culture identified with youth, and outside the controls and protocols of traditional culture. This attitude is typically associated with older Aboriginal people.

Similarly, linguistic anthropologist Inge Kral observes from her research into remote Aboriginal youth and digital media in the Ngaanyatjarra lands in Western Australia that the use of digital technologies and new media 'is defining a generational identity distinct from that of their elders, with new media representing a site where youths are exhibiting agency and a technological expertise that exceeds that of the older generation'.[90] Moreover, this notion of a generational digital divide reflects familiar anxieties expressed by mainstream culture within industrialized nations about younger generations' ready embrace of technology. Sonia Livingstone, for example, describes these sentiments as follows: 'It is commonly held that at best, social networking is time-wasting and socially isolating, and at worst it allows paedophiles to groom children in their bedroom or sees teenagers lured into suicide pacts while parents think they are doing their homework'.[91] Cultural anthropologist Mizuko Ito suggests that underlying these anxieties is the implicit intergenerational challenge that the greater ICT facility generally associated with youth cultures presents: 'The discourse of digital generations and digital youth posits that the new media empower youth to challenge the social norms and educational agendas of their elders in unique ways.'[92]

Organizations such as the Tennant Creek Council of Elders and Respected Persons[93] and Barkly Arts devised and implemented cyber-safety strategies targeting the needs

---

89   CLC, 'Divas Chat Causing Social Chaos', pp. 4-6.

90   I. Kral, 'Youth Media as Cultural Practice: Remote Indigenous Youth Speaking out Loud', *Australian Aboriginal Studies* 1 (2011).

91   S. Livingstone, 'Taking Risky Opportunities in Youthful Content Creation: Teenagers' Use of Social Networking Sites for Intimacy, Privacy and Self-Expression', *New Media & Society* 10.3 (2008): 395.

92   M. Ito, J. Antin, M. Finn, A. Law, A. Manion, S. Mitnick, D. Schlossberg, S. Yardi and H.A. Horst, *Hanging Out, Messing Around, and Geeking Out: Kids Living and Learning with New Media*, Cambridge, MA: MIT Press, 2009.

93   The Council was not running in 2015, as its funding had ceased, although informal arrangements were in place.

of different generational groups in the Barkly, such as the lower levels of digital literacy among older generations, and a lack of understanding of Aboriginal cultural protocols amongst youth. These strategies included 'Divas Cops' chat-room monitors, mediation of cyber-bullying incidents by the Tennant Creek Council of Elders and Respected Persons, and the creation of Techno Codey/Culture Codey, an online avatar that explains digital and cultural issues surrounding cyber-safety.[94]

The RIPIA *Cyber Safety Program Report*, which also produced three short film projects and intergenerational artistic activities in response to cyber-safety issues, observes: 'The importance of a family and community managed response to cyber safety issues, with the assistance of police, schools and youth workers [...] depending on the situation, indicates further consultation, study and the creation of appropriate and effective resources.'[95] This includes improving digital literacy and training 'digitally literate mediators [for] when cyber safety concerns arise within remote communities', because: 'Developing digital literacy empowers not only individual users, but extends the capacity of resolve among members within families and the community who may not be social networking services users themselves, but who fulfill important roles as leader and mediators.'[96]

CONCLUSION

Cyber-safety became an issue in the region during the years we visited the outstations. Developing proficiency in using social media and ICTs across different age groups is key to empowering remote community members to manage these issues. At a deeper level, the issue of cyber-safety demonstrates that platforms such as Facebook and Divas Chat are significant elements of the media ecology in remote communities, and are as important as infrastructure. Although corporate platforms can behave in the public interest, whether and how they are able to respond to the particular dynamics of remote communities when problems arise is a more complex question, and one that requires further research.[97]

Overall, the emphasis on personal and family uses of the computers appears to have developed from the location of the ICTs in the home, in conjunction with the smallness and remoteness of the communities, the degree of mobility of some participants, and

---

94   Hogan, 'Behind the Mulga Curtain'; Hogan et al., *Submission to the Inquiry into Issues Surrounding Cyber-Safety for Indigenous Australians*.

95   Iten, *Cyber Safety Program Report*, p. 12.

96   Iten, *Cyber Safety Program Report*, p. 16.

97   M. Ananny, 'From Noxious to Public? Tracing Ethical Dynamics of Social Media Platform Conversions', *Social Media + Society* 1.1 (2015).

the relative newness of ICTs to community members as users. Different community members also displayed different levels of enthusiasm for the ICTs, and used them to varying degrees. In a study of older internet users, Selwyn, Gorard and Furlong found that internet use was generally a means of pursing existing interests rather than creating new interests: 'People who were using the internet on a broad and frequent basis were generally building upon and extending previously developed interests or using the internet as part of a repertoire of IT and non IT-based means.'[98] We observed a similar trend on the outstations.

More complex and more elaborate uses of the computers would possibly require significant training and assistance – issues that will be taken up in Chapter 6. Simple, everyday changes represented by the use of the home computers for administrative activities indicate, however, the potential value that internet access represents for smaller settlements, for example, in connecting to mainstream agencies, in contrast to larger communities with existing access to onsite services (i.e. at the community store and Regional Council office). In this way, ICT access for highly remote people is particularly significant as governments shift as much service delivery as possible from 'over-the-counter' and/ or postal methods to an online-only environment. Without this, there is a real risk that many remote Aboriginal people will simply 'drop offline' and be further disadvantaged.

---

98   Selwyn, Gorard and Furlong, 'Whose Internet Is It Anyway? Exploring Adults' (Non) Use of the Internet in Everyday Life', p. 13.

Chapter 6: Skills and Training

As early as February 2012, Karen described how she'd helped others in the community use the computers, especially to access Centrelink accounts, including her husband and a couple of female relatives, commenting that it was 'more me showing them' than anyone telling her what to do. She may have been saying this to impress on us how ICT proficient she'd become; several months later, she was adamant she hadn't shown anyone else how to do things on the computer, nor had anyone else shown her how to do anything. Other community members, however, reported Karen assisting them in such tasks as using email, setting a computer password and negotiating Centrelink's website. On a later field trip, Karen commented that while 'everyone has different bank accounts', they 'might use [her] computer to check money in their account'. Another young woman at Mungalawurru also observed that other people, both men and women, often asked Karen to help them use the computer, though she herself didn't ask Karen for help.

But towards the end of the project, Karen seemed to have wearied of this ad hoc role as the ICT help person for the community. When we asked her in August 2013 whether she'd been assisting anyone else with Centrelink, she replied, 'I don't really like doing other people's stuff'. By this point, as we'll discuss in Chapter 7, Karen had become more autonomous in her use of the computer, because she'd moved it into a separate room mainly for her own use.

Mary, the senior woman at Imangara from Chapter 5, played a prominent role in liaising with us, and in discussions about distribution of ICT resources within the community. But like most older and some middle-aged people in the three communities, and also those at Papunya and Ali Curung, she had no previous ICT skills or experience of computers. On our first research trip to Imangara, Mary commented that 'only Andrew' from the Centre for Appropriate Technology (CAT) had shown her how to do things on the computer. On subsequent visits, she told us that her granddaughter, who was in her early 20s, had assisted her. When the young woman left the community to live in Alice Springs for a while, Mary said that her grandson was now helping her use Centrelink and online banking sites. The granddaughter later returned and resumed living with her grandmother. Her cousin, another young woman living in a neighboring house, also named Mary's granddaughter as the person who'd taught her how to access YouTube, play games online and print photos. This granddaughter had a high pre-existing level of ICT proficiency: for example, she had a Hotmail email address, as well as Twitter and Facebook accounts, which she accessed on her mobile phone outside the community before it had internet connectivity. While living in the community, she sent emails to CAT, asking them to bring replacement inks and other items on their next visit.

However, we also gained the impression that the granddaughter was monopolizing use of the computers in two houses, without giving as much assistance to her grandmother as she could have done, such as showing her how to use email: Mary continued to request that we help her with basic administrative activities well into 2013. As with the account of Karen's cooling towards her 'ICT help' role, this story suggests that Aboriginal people, even more digitally proficient community members, will not necessarily assist each other to use ICTs by sharing skills, and that younger people will not necessarily help older ones negotiate online services, for reasons that we'll discuss below.

These stories are indicative of digital literacy and skills transfer trends that emerged during the project. Generally, younger residents (18-29 years), like Karen at Mungala-wurru, and Emily and Mary's other granddaughters at Imangara, who had computing experience from school or elsewhere, were more self-sufficient with using ICTs. They usually only asked us for specific assistance with problems or complex tasks, which fell more within the category of technical or application support than training. When we asked participants whether they thought they were getting better at using computers, 18-29-year-olds most often (approximately one-third of self-assessments) said they'd improved during the project.

In our initial meetings with the three communities, we found that rates of computer non-adoption were proportionately highest amongst those aged 45-60 years (88 per cent non-adopters) and 60+ years (83 per cent non-adopters). Physical disability, such as poor eyesight or conditions such as back or leg problems, compounded their reluctance to use computers. One woman, for example, complained that a leg injury prevented her from sitting for any length of time at the computer.

Although elders like Mary often played pivotal roles in discussions about the project, and in decision-making about distributing ICT resources, their level of ICT usage tended to be relatively basic, and they often struggled with learning new skills. Senior women and men maintained roles in managing ICT resource distribution, which younger community members respected during meetings (as in the story about Mary and Emily at Imangara), even when they had plans to make different arrangements about their computer and internet access. Importantly, we would not describe Mary as a non-user, as she regularly asked others to conduct online transactions on her behalf. What has been described as 'use-by-proxy' is important, as it demonstrates that even those who do not have the skills or inclination to use the internet might still be experiencing its benefits.[99]

SCHOOLS

Schools are key providers of computers and internet access in remote Australia; they act as conduits for various ICT programs, and have been teaching digital literacy skills to

---

99   Selwyn, Gorard and Furlong, 'Whose Internet Is It Anyway? Exploring Adults' (Non) Use of the Internet in Everyday Life'.

children, and sometimes to parents and teachers' assistants. Although a full study of ICTs in remote schools was beyond our means, we called in at schools on a number of occasions to talk informally with the teachers, and made contact with the one program that promoted at-home use of devices, One Education (a spin-off of the international NGO, One Laptop per Child). These encounters provided us with some insights into schools as sites of internet access. For example, the Murray Downs school near Imangara was connected to the internet via satellite.[100] The school was using both tablets and desktop computers in the classroom, primarily for drill-and-practice education applications for mathematics and English. One teacher mentioned to us that the children were possessive of the tablets, hiding them in the classroom so they did not have to share with their peers. All teachers we spoke to considered the children to be fast learners when it came to the devices, and saw educational value in their use. Some adults in the community had accessed the internet at the school prior to our arrival through training organized by a teacher who had since left the school, and another teacher assisted parents by purchasing iPads for them when he went to Alice Springs, to save them from paying higher prices nearby.

Our general impression was that school-based internet and computer use could vary significantly depending on the teacher. Only 40 per cent of teachers in very remote schools in the Northern Territory stay teaching at the same school for more than a year. Such high teacher turnover (see Brasche and Harrington, 2012, for reasons why this is the case) means that there is no consistent approach to ICTs. Some teachers had narrow ideas of what is appropriate use in the classroom environment, and even teachers who are optimistic about the use of technology for learning, do not necessarily wish to support activities beyond those which fit within lesson plans.

Does such a limited experience of ICTs at school impact on attitudes and use of ICTs later in life? Small remote Indigenous communities have the (now rare) feature whereby many children are able to access ICTs at school but not at home. Although we were not able to pursue this question fully, we did observe that at the start of our project in 2010, none of those under 30 who had used computers at school had gone on to purchase a computer for use at home. However, these participants were certainly more confident users than those without any prior experience of computers.

---

100 The Murray Downs school had an attendance rate of around 75 per cent in 2013 and 2014 although enrolments had dwindled to twenty-three students in 2014, down from the forty-three in 2010; Northern Territory Department of Education, 'Enrolment and Attendance Statistics', http://www.education.nt.gov.au/students/at-school/enrolment-attendance/enrolment-attendance-statistics/2013-enrolment-and-attendance-statistics.

In 2012, One Education received $11.7 million to deploy 50,000 bespoke laptops in disadvantaged primary schools across Australia.[101] Australian schools that met certain socio-economic criteria – including serving low-income and remote areas, and the percentage of students that identified as Indigenous – were eligible for a subsidy (government derived) that allowed them to access the program and acquire the hardware for $100 per laptop. The laptops were also being used by the Northern Territory Libraries within their Remote Indigenous Public Internet Access (RIPIA) program.

Our primary interest in the One Education program was that it was founded on a custodial philosophy, whereby the students own the devices and use them at home and at school. If students were taking the devices home, then this would be potentially significant for those communities, not just the children. The general strategy of putting the devices directly in the hands of children is thought to 'compensate for unequal access to technologies in the home environment and thus help bridge educational and social gaps'.[102] A US analysis found that, when controlling for income, race and parents' education, those with a home computer were 6–8 per cent more likely to graduate from high school than teens who did not have a home computer.[103] However, even within the One Education program, we found that, in Australia at least, teacher practices varied widely. Teachers in Indigenous schools were not likely to allow children to take the One Education devices home, with some believing the devices would be damaged in overcrowded housing environments. Some permitted free time on a daily basis, others used them only for classroom lessons, and a minority of teachers used them as a reward for good behavior.[104] Over half the schools reported issues with connectivity in 2012, finding it difficult to connect the devices to the education department's IT system (One Education has since been working to rectify this). The program's biggest issue was teacher turnover: as teachers voluntarily participate in the program, if a replacement teacher does not wish

---

101 One Education was known as 'One Laptop per Child Australia' at that time. Co-author Ellie Rennie, together with education technology researcher Sarah Howard, conducted a survey of schools within the One Education system as part of evaluations for the Department of Education (see S. Howard and E. Rennie, 'Free for All: A Case Study Examining Implementation Factors of One-to-One Device Programs', *Computers in the Schools*, 30.4 (2013): 359-377. Prior to the 2012 Department of Education funding, 1 in 3 of the 160 schools participating in the program were Indigenous schools, in that at least 75 per cent of the students were Indigenous. In 2015, despite the program's expansion, a quarter of schools involved in the One Education program were Indigenous schools. One Education provides child-sized, robust laptops (that can be converted into a tablet) to classrooms once the teachers have participated in an online training program.

102 M. Warschauer and T. Matuchniak, 'New Technology and Digital Worlds: Analyzing Evidence of Equity in Access, Use, and Outcomes', *Review of Research in Education* 34.1 (2010): 180.

103 R.W. Fairlie, D.O. Beltran and K.K. Das, 'Home Computers and Educational Outcomes: Evidence from the NLSY97 and CPS*', *Economic Inquiry* 48.3 (2010).

104 Howard and Rennie, 'Free for All'.

to participate, the laptops can go unused. Nonetheless, the program was providing a level of training and a community of practice for teachers, who overwhelmingly believed that the devices were good for learning. Schools and one-to-one laptop programs will remain an important means of ICT skills development in remote communities.

SKILLS TRANSFER AND THE DIGITAL DIVIDE

At the project's outset, we were uncertain how much people would share the computers or teach each other how to use them. So-called 'avoidance relationships' between the genders and within kinship networks exist within Aboriginal society, such as it being considered taboo for a son-in-law to speak with his mother-in-law. There are also continuing protocols concerning the transfer of knowledge between older and younger people. Karen's increasingly personal use of the computer and her disinclination to help others underlines Chapter 3's insight that households, and even individuals, in these remote central Australian Aboriginal communities can be autonomous. This emphasis on personal and household ICT use, together with the limited skills-sharing that took place, have implications for providing training and support, and for facilitating socially-inclusive ICT arrangements in remote Aboriginal communities. They also put notions about an 'Aboriginal preference' for group or communal learning to the test.

While several people said during early meetings that children should be allowed on computers because they can teach others how to use them, there wasn't much evidence of intergenerational sharing of ICT skills on the outstations. The relatively limited amount of skills transfer that occurred runs counter to what a popular understanding of the ethos of Aboriginal culture might suggest: for example, that sharing practices might automatically foster sharing of ICT resources and skills amongst participants. It also challenges early assertions by telecommunications academics and policymakers in mainstream debates that the digital divide will fix itself as network and equipment costs fall and the internet becomes more and more a part of daily life.

While we did not seek to provide any accredited form of training, or to undertake formal assessments, we decided that, when asked, we would help those who wanted to learn. Training in the use of computer and internet applications often occurred on an ad hoc basis on house visits while providing technical support during the CAT team's regular maintenance visits, and sometimes on research trips to the communities. Virtually all of these interactions were face-to-face; very few could have been carried out using remote communication, given that none of the households had a fixed landline telephone or mobile phone access. Residents rarely used email or Skype to ask how to do something or to solve a problem. On the couple of occasions when this happened, the issue almost always required personal follow-up during a community visit.

Community members who maintained an interest in the computers were often those who already had a degree of digital literacy and were more likely to seek help. Some improvements in participants' skill levels were evident during the project. For example, when we asked them six months into the trial whether they had gotten better at using the computer, two-thirds replied positively, listing new or improved skills related to using email; online banking; typing; word processing; folder and desktop management; writing letters, stories and songs; use of spreadsheets; downloading material (movies, music and games); Facebook; and viewing photographs and other pictures.

But a year into the project, it became apparent that without further digital education and skills development of some kind, other remote community members, especially older ones, were likely to find dealing with services, such as banks and government agencies that increasingly rely on internet interfaces, particularly challenging. Consequently, we devoted more attention in the second half of 2012 to investigating what training approaches might provide the most benefits for remote Aboriginal residents, especially given their range of ICT skills and the particular social practices and protocols operating within these communities.

DEVELOPING AN ICT TRAINING APPROACH FOR REMOTE ABORIGINAL PEOPLE

Research during the 1980s and 1990s into Aboriginal adult education and training suggested that Aboriginal people were more comfortable learning in groups than individually.[105] But when we asked residents how they liked to receive training about computers and internet use, most (88 per cent) said they preferred to learn individually or as a couple/pair. Without exception, all of them wanted to learn on their own computers, preferably in their own homes (or Community Development Employment Projects [CDEP] shed or Women's Centre for those who were using shared desktop computers), rather than group training in a shared space in the community or the nearest town.

This response is consistent with Battiste's model, which proposes that Indigenous people prefer independent learning and individual instruction, along with some common characteristics referred to within other research, such as direct learning by seeing and doing,

---

105 S. Harris and J. Kinslow-Harris, *Culture and Learning: Tradition and Education in North-East Arnhem Land,* Canberra: Australian Institute of Aboriginal and Torres Strait Islander Studies, 1980; P. Hughes and A.J. More, *Aboriginal Ways of Learning,* Adelaide: Paul Hughes, 2004; P. Hughes and A.J. More, 'Aboriginal Ways of Learning and Learning Styles', Brisbane: Australian Association for Research in Education, 1997; J.A. Robinson and R.M. Nichol, 'Building Bridges Between Aboriginal and Western Mathematics: Creating an Effective Mathematics Learning Environment', *Education in Rural Australia* 8.2 (1998).

observation, experiential learning, and applying knowledge to real circumstances.[106] More recent research has sought to construct a framework that accommodates both independent learning orientations in Aboriginal students and the importance of community links emphasizing the group.[107] Furthermore, a large body of research indicates that active involvement by adult learners in the design of a learning program is more likely to result in their engagement with, and support for, the program; this is particularly true of Aboriginal learners, where a two-way or multiple-way system that allows for Aboriginal ownership and cross-cultural understanding is crucial to success.[108]

To investigate this further, we discussed with community members, either individually or with their partner or a close relative, matters such as where they preferred to receive training, at what times, whether in groups or one-on-one, what encouraged them to learn, what they were interested in learning to do, and what they already felt confident doing on the computers and internet. We also asked whether they had any specific physical needs, such as glasses or hearing aids, and tried to assess how avoidance relationships might affect training situations. At the time, almost 60 per cent of the residents were available, a situation that was not unusual given that numbers of community members present on field trips varied throughout the project. Those who took part in discussing these training issues were broadly representative of participants, possessing a range of literacy and numeracy skills, and including young men and women aged in their 20s and 30s, as well as older women in their 40s, 50s and 60s.

---

106 M. Battiste, *Indigenous Knowledge and Pedagogy in First Nations Education: A Literature Review with Recommendations*, Ottawa: Apamuwek Institute, 2002, pp. 15, 18.

107 T. Yunkaporta, *Aboriginal Pedagogies at the Cultural Interface*, Professional Doctorate (Research) thesis, James Cook University, Townsville, Qld, 2009.

108 J. Byrnes, 'Aboriginal Learning Styles and Adult Education: Is a Synthesis Possible?', *Australian Journal of Adult and Community Education* 33.3 (1993); M. Donovan, 'Can Information Communication Technological Tools Be Used to Suit Aboriginal Learning Pedagogies', *Information Technology and Indigenous People* (2007), p. 96; M. Eady and S. Woodcock, 'Understanding the Need: Using Collaboratively Created Draft Guiding Principles to Direct Online Synchronous Learning in Indigenous Communities', *International Journal for Educational Integrity* 6.2 (2010); I. Kral and I. Falk, *What Is All That Learning For? Indigenous Adult English Literacy Practices, Training, Community Capacity and Health*, Adelaide: NCVER, 2004, p. 56; M. Malin and D. Maidment, 'Evaluation of Irrkerlantye Learning Centre' (unpublished report), Darwin: Cooperative Research Centre for Aboriginal and Tropical Health, 2003, p. 97; Northern Territory Department of Education, *Learning Lessons: An Independent Review of Indigenous Education in the Northern Territory*, Darwin: Northern Territory Department of Education, 1999, http://www.education.nt.gov.au/__data/assets/pdf_file/0005/7475/learning_lessons_review.pdf; T. Yunkaporta, *Aboriginal Pedagogies at the Cultural Interface*; A. Mahon, *Deadly Dreaming: Bi-Cultural Strategies for Working with Indigenous Adults in Education*, Australian Council for Adult Literacy conference, Surfers Paradise, Australia, 3-4 October, 2008, http://www.acal.edu.au/conference/08/Deadly_Dreaming_Mahon.pdf.

Aside from requesting training individually or in a pair, and in their own homes, they also unanimously opted for training during each monthly visit, mostly for 'a little bit' or 'a bit' of time, although some suggested times from thirty minutes up to half a day. Familiarity with the surroundings, equipment and people appeared to be important, combined with the ease of not having to travel to town, which involves additional costs, as well as organizing transport and accommodation. Research conducted elsewhere in central Australia also indicates a preference for in-community learning rather than at an external location.[109] Learning individually affords privacy, allows learners to focus on their own interests, and provides an atmosphere where they're likely to feel more at ease, more comfortable in asking questions, and away from situations in which they might potentially feel embarrassment (shame) at not understanding instructions or knowing how to do something.[110]

Residents identified various tasks they wanted to learn, ranging from using email; online banking; downloading movies and music; uploading photographs; touch typing; customizing the Windows display; writing stories; using Facebook and Skype; shopping online; taking an online language course; using Excel; online training in literacy and numeracy for both adults and children; making signs, posters and notices; checking weather reports; and internet browsing. Several people named the same tasks as activities that they already felt confident doing, perhaps indicating that they wished to become more proficient at that task, or that they wished to learn additional or more complex tasks within an application. Community members did not always say explicitly why they wanted to learn different activities, although some said they wanted to 'get better' at a certain task, to enhance their existing employment skills, or to contact Centrelink more easily.

Using desktop computers as the focus and the tool for ICT training may also have been more suited to individual rather than group learning. Other researchers have observed that computers themselves fit readily with Aboriginal educational styles because they are interactive, involve learning by doing, and permit trial and error. They also allow people to progress at their own pace, and are real-time oriented as well as being 'endlessly patient, repetitive'.[111]

We also asked about their preferred group composition (age and gender) for training, and whether there were any cultural relationships that might preclude anyone from being

109   For example: I. Kral and I. Falk, *What Is All That Learning For? Indigenous Adult English Literacy Practices, Training, Community Capacity and Health*, p. 41.

110   M. Donovan, 'Is It a Digital Divide Because It's No Good When Talking from an Aboriginal Point? Giving Aboriginal Design to Educational Practices', http://www.persons.org.uk/ci/mm/nmtc/nmtc2/donovan%20paper.pdf; N. Harrison, *Teaching and Learning in Aboriginal Education*, Melbourne: Oxford University Press, 2011, pp. 53-54.

111   O'Donogue 1992 and Steen 1997, as cited in Donovan, 'Can Information Communication Technological Tools Be Used to Suit Aboriginal Learning Pedagogies?'.

in the same room as someone else. No-one expressed any particular preferences about age or gender, apart from one elderly woman who said she'd rather learn with women only. Similarly, only one person, again an older woman, identified cultural avoidance of individuals either from within their community or from another community as a potential issue. Her response, that she could not be in the same room as anyone from another community, concurred with anecdotal evidence suggesting that, in remote central Australian communities, the older generations (elders) continue to uphold traditional cultural practices in relation to interpersonal relationships. None of the younger community members identified avoidance relationships as an issue, which is in keeping with observations that younger generations sometimes place less emphasis on maintaining these traditions.

No-one requested an interpreter to explain things in language, which was not surprising given that all the computer applications are in English. Eady and Woodcock have also noted that many Indigenous learners prefer to receive instruction in English in order to improve their language, literacy and numeracy skills to be able to interact more effectively with Western society or 'whitefellas'.[112]

AN INDIVIDUAL, OPPORTUNISTIC APPROACH TO LEARNING

The findings from the discussions we had with community members about learning preferences suggested that it might be appropriate to reconsider some of the commonly held notions about adult Aboriginal people preferring to learn in groups, particularly in regard to ICT training. This confirmed the ad hoc approach to learning that had already emerged in the project, in which we often spent time with individuals and one or two other family members in their homes, responding to their requests for training and technical support on the computer. During the remainder of the project, we tried to fine-tune this approach, which could best be described as opportunistic and flexible, by providing training tailored to individual adult community members' needs, aspirations and preferences.

Given that the timing, content and location are all largely determined by the learner, the main challenge for the trainer in this approach lies in attempting to predict how much time, individually and collectively, the learning will take.[113] Consequently, the CAT team set aside additional time for training during their technical support trips. In practice, about 70 per cent of their time was spent on providing technical support, and 30 per cent on training during each visit. An average of four learning opportunities per visit to each community occurred, varying from none – for example when participants were

---

112   M. Eady and S. Woodcock, 'Understanding the Need: Using Collaboratively Created Draft Guiding Principles to Direct Online Synchronous Learning in Indigenous Communities', *International Journal for Educational Integrity* 6.2 (2010): 964.

113   A. Crouch, *Home Internet for Remote Indigenous Communities: Technical Report*, p. 39.

absent or researchers' time was taken up entirely with managing technical incidents – to sixteen. The CAT team also occasionally received and responded to support requests from community members by email or phone between visits.

Learners largely determined the session's length, although it was impacted to a lesser extent by competing demands on our time. Sessions ranged from short-task specific learning opportunities of ten to twenty minutes to intensive three-hourly sessions in which community members participated in a range of activities. Almost three-quarters of the learning opportunities occurred as one-on-one sessions between the learner and the researcher, 20 per cent in pairs and 9 per cent in groups, reflecting participants' preferred learning modes.

In most (71 per cent) of these sessions, participants determined what they wished to learn, usually by asking us a question such as: 'Could you show me how to [undertake a certain activity]?' We demonstrated how to do that particular task several times, and then asked the participant to repeat it until they felt confident. Overall, most of the learning opportunities and participants' training revolved around using the internet, despite us urging them to learn maintenance (see Appendix 3, Figure 11). However, on occasions, learning also occurred when researchers were occupied with providing technical support rather than training: community members learned computer maintenance tasks mainly by watching us change ink cartridges, clear ink nozzles, and other troubleshooting activities associated with printers and, to a lesser extent, the computers themselves. Occasionally, we suggested certain tasks we felt participants might be interested in learning, or that they would need to know before the move to self-funded internet plans (see Appendix 3, Figure 11).

Early in the project, usage of the computers and the internet focused mainly on online banking, downloading music and printing photographs. Later, some community members began to ask more complex queries such as how to access internet on ICT devices: for example, there were several requests at Imangara during 2013 for WiFi in order to allow their children to access the internet via iPads.

Other household members and friends were often present, watching and listening, if not otherwise actively participating in one-on-one sessions. Some group discussions took place within community meetings where we discussed administrative matters such as how quotas work, the shift to individual satellite services and billing accounts, and so on. These provided a forum in which common issues could be raised, and information, including hand-outs, was passed on to all residents at the same time.

EXPERIENCES WITH GROUP TRAINING APPROACHES

Towards the end of the trial, we attempted to organize group training for some community members at Imangara who wanted to try this style of learning, and for researchers to compare the individual and group experiences. The proposed activity was a one-day Digital Stories workshop to be delivered by a multimedia trainer from Barkly Arts in a meeting room at Ali Curung, 30 kilometers away. But when a couple of our researchers arrived in Imangara the day before the workshop to remind community members that it was happening (they had sent email messages beforehand), the place was a ghost town. Only one older woman appeared to be there, sitting on her veranda. She told us that the others were 'all gone': some to Tennant Creek for a royalty meeting; the others, including Mary, for a funeral and a sing-a-long at Lake Nash. She had wanted to go with them, but they left without her. She told us they might be back 'tonight [Tuesday] or tomorrow'.

Driving towards Imangara the next morning, we met a car of people from Ali Curung, who told us that everyone was going on to Mount Isa now for a rodeo, and that no-one would be back until Monday at the earliest. A little later, we saw a couple of people on the road who turned out to be Mary's relatives. We offered them a ride and they asked us to go back up the road to get another couple. The four of them had been at the roadhouse bar at Wauchope the night before, but their car had broken down and they'd slept inside with no blankets, which was apparently very cold. When we found them, the couple asked to be dropped in Ali Curung so they could arrange to get the car.

The couple arrived back at Imangara after lunch and retreated into their house, as did Mary's other relatives. We didn't see them for the rest of the day; they'd probably all gone to sleep, although someone told us the granddaughter was on the computer. By this time, we'd cancelled the workshop that was scheduled for the afternoon. A couple of other middle-aged women were in the community, and we later ran into them at the Murray Downs shop. The senior man and the young people arrived back in Imangara the following day.

Two middle-aged women said they'd like to do the Digital Stories training sometime, whereas none of the young people showed any interest. This confirmed our existing impression that there was more interest in ICT learning amongst the middle-aged members of the community than for the young ones, who were already somewhat proficient from having used computers at school.

Overall, this experience indicated that structured training was impractical and not at all efficient in a community of this size. Structured group training is probably more suited to larger communities with a youth or media center and ongoing engagement from youth workers and cultural workers, and as part of a continuing experience of training/activity.

The experience taught us that training needs to be flexible to cater for high levels of mobility and uncertainty. The unpredictable rhythms of people's lives, as well as the more 'everyday', household focus on computer use, made it feel artificial to impose structured training on community members at Imangara. By the time we offered group training, the novelty value of computers and trying to do new things on them had also worn off, although the computers had by then become a valued part of household infrastructure that people seemed to want to maintain.

CONCLUSION

In remote Indigenous communities, age and gender differentials impact on learning opportunities, as do relationships between family groups. We found that individual learning within private households in a way that was responsive to the participant's needs and requests for training was the most equitable and inclusive approach. People were also more likely to be interested in uses of the internet that brought small but noticeable benefits to their everyday lives.

Our experience was thus contrary to the commonly held notion that Aboriginal people like to learn in groups, at least when it comes to computers and associated software. That the subject matter (computers) was the same as the learning mechanism, and that it was delivered in an informal home environment, goes only partway towards explaining the preference for individual learning. The emphasis on everyday uses of the computers and internet within a domestic setting, combined with the trend towards discrete family and household ownership and use of the computers, probably strongly influenced the desire for individual learning within these small communities.

There are clear implications for the delivery of ICT-related training in remote Aboriginal communities, particularly as take-up of individually owned devices such as laptops and iPads is likely to continue.[114] Although logistically challenging and resource intensive, a flexible, opportunistic approach that tailors learning opportunities to the individual's needs and takes place within private, safe spaces rather than as formal, structured training can be effective (although we discuss in Chapter 8 how a different approach can work where there is a long-term shared computer facility). Without more exposure to the capabilities of information and communications technology, including digital education and skills development, remote community members, especially older ones, may fail to grasp its benefits.

---

114 McCallugh cited in D. Featherstone, 'The Aboriginal Invention of Broadband: How Yarnangu
     Are Using ICTs in the Ngaanyatjarra Lands of Western Australia', in L. Ormond-Parker, A. Corn,
     C. Fforde, K. Obata and S. O'Sullivan, *Information Technologies and Indigenous Communities*,
     Canberra: AIATSIS Research Publications, 2013, p. 43.

Chapter 7: Gender

The overall trend in survey-based studies of internet adoption and use is that men, especially younger ones, tend to be early adopters of internet technology and are more strongly represented in ICT usage: boys are 'generally quicker than girls to lay claim to cyberspace and digital media'.[115] The World Internet Project found in 2007 that in 'all twelve WIP countries assessed for this study, men use the Internet somewhat more than women', although over time, 'a slow diminishing of the gender divides' occurs as women's participation generally slightly increases while men's slightly decreases.[116] Some feminist researchers have described a 'gender digital divide', and the male-coding of the information and communications sector.[117] For the three outstations, having desktop computers in the home thus seemed a scenario that might stereotypically appeal to young men.[118] However, we found that this was not necessarily the case. Women appeared to be the dominant users of the computers and internet at home, while men were frequent users of shared computer facilities.

There is considerable discussion within the anthropological literature about the gendering of activities and domains within traditional Aboriginal societies in terms of separate spheres with complementary functional roles.[119] In her landmark review, 'Gender and Aboriginal Society', anthropologist Francesca Merlan observes how remote northern Australian Indigenous social contexts are characterized by 'the frequently found Aboriginal tendency toward dualism - insistence ideologically and practically upon some degree

115   S. Weber and S. Dixon, *Growing Up Online: Young People and Digital Technologies*, New York: Palgrave Macmillan, 2007, p. 256.

116   W.H. Dutton, A. Shepherd and C. Di Gennaro, 'Digital Divides and Choices Reconfiguring Access: National and Cross National Patterns of Internet Diffusion and Use' in B. Anderson, M. Brynin, Y. Raban and J. Gershuny (eds) *Information and Communication Technologies in Society E-Living in a Digital Europe*, London: Routledge, 2007, p. 37.

117   S. Huyer and T. Sikoska, *Overcoming the Gender Digital Divide: Understanding ICTs and Their Potential for the Empowerment of Women*, Santo Domingo, Dominican Republic: UN-INSTRAW, 2003, pp. 2, 12; A. Thas, C. Ramilo and C. Cinoco, 'Gender and ICT', *UNDP Asia-Pacific Development Information Programme E-Primer*, New Delhi: Elsevier, 2007, p. 2.

118   Dutton, Shepherd and Di Gennaro, 'Digital Divides and Choices Reconfiguring Access', p. 42.

119   See for example: D. Bell, *Daughters of the Dreaming*, Melbourne: Allen and Unwin, 1983; G. Cowlishaw, 'Infanticide in Aboriginal Australia', *Oceania* 48.4 (1978): 262-283; G. Cowlishaw, 'Socialisation and Subordination among Australian Aborigines' *Man* 17.3 (September, 1982): 492-507; G. Cowlishaw, *Women's Realm: A Study of Socialization, Sexuality and Reproduction Among Australian Aborigines*, PhD diss., University of Sydney, Australia, 1979; A. Hamilton, 'A Complex Strategical Situation: Gender and Power in Aboriginal Australia' in N. Grieve and P. Grimshaw (eds) *Australian Imjmen: Feminist Perspectives*, Melbourne: Oxford University Press, 1981; P.M. Kaberry, *Aboriginal Women*, London: George Routledge and Sons Pty Ltd, 1939.

of male-female separatism'.[120] Anthropologists and others have described the gendering of activities and domains within traditional Aboriginal societies in terms of separate spheres with complementary functional roles, with perspectives differing as to whether gender inequalities are inherent within this schema or whether they result from, or are exacerbated by, the imposition of European culture.[121] Some (such as Cowlishaw and Hamilton) claim that women occupy a subordinate role within this schema, while others (such as Bell and Kaberry) argue that Aboriginal women exercise and enjoy a degree of autonomy in traditional society.[122]

Merlan urges caution, however, in invoking the notion of autonomy in relation to the gendering of activities and domains, because of its different conceptualization within Aboriginal and European frameworks. She states that Aboriginal selfhood 'is importantly constituted through social relatedness, and thus is not to be confused with western notions of individualism'.[123] She also draws on Annette Hamilton's discussion of how gender autonomy might be confused with labor and cultural division within Aboriginal social life because men's and women's lives appear to be self-contained.[124]

As feminist scholar McClintock has said, 'domesticity is both a *space* and a *relationship of power*'.[125] The impact of the gender division of labor within domestic space in central Australian remote Aboriginal communities is thus worth considering in relation to ICT infrastructures and programs.

---

120   F. Merlan, 'Gender in Aboriginal Society: A Review' in R. M. Berndt and R. Tonkinson (eds) *Social Anthropology and Australian Aboriginal Studies*, Canberra: Aboriginal Studies Press, 1988, p. 20.

121   Merlan, 'Gender in Aboriginal Society', p. 29.

122   Cowlishaw, 'Infanticide in Aboriginal Australia'; Cowlishaw, 'Socialisation and Subordination Among Australian Aborigines'; Cowlishaw, *Women's Realm: A Study of Socialization, Sexuality and Reproduction among Australian Aborigines*; Hamilton, 'A Complex Strategical Situation: Gender and Power in Aboriginal Australia'; D. Bell, *Daughters of the Dreaming*, Melbourne: Allen and Unwin, 1983; Kaberry, *Aboriginal Women*.

123   Merlan, 'Gender in Aboriginal Society' p. 30; cf. Macdonald, 'Economies and Personhood: Demand Sharing Among the Wiradjuri of New South Wales'; N. Peterson, 'Demand Sharing: Reciprocity and the Pressure for Generosity Among Foragers', *American Anthropologist* 95.4 (1993); G. Robinson, 'Families, Generations, and Self: Conflict, Loyalty, and Recognition in an Australian Aboriginal Society', *Ethos* 25.3 (1997): 304.

124   McClintock 1995 as cited in Merlan, 'Gender in Aboriginal Society' p. 30.

125   McClintock 1995 as cited in J. Lydon, '"Our Sense of Beauty": Visuality, Space and Gender on Victoria's Aboriginal Reserves, South-Eastern Australia', *History and Anthropology* 16.2 (2005): 222.

WOMEN'S INTERNET USE

When we commenced, Karen's husband had a laptop, which he had borrowed from a relative. The laptop had been purchased in another state, and he believed the WiFi only connected to the internet there. Karen did not use the laptop. Not long after the communities received computers and internet access, some women began to play a key role in using the computers for household purposes. As discussed in Chapter 5 (Uses), Karen described managing her family's administration by accessing Centrelink every day, paying bills and trying to teach her husband how to pay his Austar account online. Her husband, on the other hand, reported using the computer for work purposes to check emails from his employer on the cattle project. In 2012, Karen said they were equally responsible for the computer, but by 2013, she reported that keeping it safe was 'a bit of [him], most of me; if I'm not around, he makes sure it's closed. Yeah, and kids aren't on it. If something happens – maybe [the kids] throwing the mouse around – he tells me'. She now used the computer the most, whereas he was 'always busy on his PlayStation'. They swapped if they got bored, and, 'If there's something on my computer he wants, he grabs it, puts it on a USB stick, then onto his PlayStation'.

Later when Karen took us to see the computer on the same visit, her husband was sleeping face down on a foam mattress in their living room, exhausted from the day's mustering. Karen led us into the spare bedroom where the computer was kept: there was almost nothing inside apart from the computer in its box on a desk. Karen and her husband were like a couple with their own toys, with him on the PlayStation in the main room and her on the computer in its separate room. Although she said the kids used the computer as well, the pride with which Karen maintained the room suggested that it was her personal space.

In the same community, another woman soon assumed responsibility for her household's computing activities, commenting that while her husband only used the computer for playing card games, he often requested that she perform administrative tasks for him, such as sending emails on his behalf to staff at the Central Land Council (CLC) and the cattle project. When we asked him why he wasn't using the computer so much, he claimed that he didn't know how, and that he was too busy to learn, although he wouldn't mind being able to manage information about the cattle project, such as mustering details, prices and sales, on the computer. Several months later, he had still not made any progress in learning how to use the computer, and was instructing his wife to write reports for the cattle project. She said, 'He tells me what to write, and I write and print it out. I check incoming email every morning.' She also printed out emails for another male relative.

At Kwale Kwale in February 2012, Rhonda, the tertiary-educated, middle-aged woman who worked part-time in Alice Springs, told us that she wanted to teach her husband to use the computer, but he was 'too frightened to go near it'. She was also hoping to set up Skype so he could talk to his daughters, who lived away from the community. Rhonda said she wanted to learn how to access internet banking, shopping and Centrelink so she could teach others in the community how to use them, along with Skype and making Microsoft Word documents. In Chapter 5, we discussed how she had planned to use word processing programs on the computer to make multilingual books about bush tucker with another community member. She had also thought she might order groceries online from supermarkets in Alice Springs, which she could sell, along with home-grown vegetables, at a stall in the community. She reported using the computer mostly to contact friends by email as well as to do contract work; another community member described Rhonda using her home computer as her 'office'.

As these stories suggest, certain young and middle-aged women came to play a key role in taking responsibility for the computers within individual households, often using them for administrative purposes, sometimes on behalf of other family members. The computers became a domestic hub of sorts, an extension of everyday practices associated with a more female-oriented sphere, including banking, online shopping and child-related educational activities. While community members all mentioned using the computers for personal entertainment and administration, women more often listed accessing Centrelink and internet banking than men in their top five activities on the computer (see Appendix 3, Figure 8). They also described shopping online for items such as car parts, cars, garden stuff, music CDs, plates, forks, iPads, kids' games, Bibles, Bible tapes, Christian books and a laptop. Men mainly reported using the computers to play games or to watch movies (see Appendix 3, Figure 9), and often seemed happy to allow women to manage household finances online as well as contacting local organizations on their behalf.

Community members identified women, followed by children, as the computers' most frequent users, with women making up two-thirds of those aged 18–29 years (see Appendix 3, Figure 7). When we asked participants to assess their level of computer skills, women (roughly one-third) and 18–29-year-olds (again, approximately one-third) gave the most positive self-assessments of their computer skills, which supports the observation that women, especially the younger ones, had developed greater digital literacy skills during the project. These trends correlate with those from our original survey of community members' computer experience and skills prior to installation, which found a greater proportion of women (52 per cent) had some ICT proficiency in contrast to men (29 per cent).

We observed that women were more likely to tell us about their social media use. A report by Remote Indigenous Public Internet Access (RIPIA) found that women made up most of the social media users on the three platforms used by remote community members: 59 per cent of Facebook users and 65 per cent of Divas Chat and airG users.[126] When the RIPIA researcher asked community members at Papunya whether they thought people understood how to manage their privacy settings on social media accounts, they responded informally 'that females understood, but males did not', a response that was supported by survey data indicating 'that females comprised 89 per cent of the "yes" response' in this community.[127] The RIPIA researcher suggested that being able to manage privacy settings indicated 'that individuals who spend more time engaging with digital devices and social networking services, in this case being females [...] are able to develop higher levels of digital literacy'.[128]

Participants at Imangara often mentioned children as computer users (45 per cent of responses). This was probably because of the greater numbers of children there than in Mungalawurru who were able to stay in the community while attending the nearby local infants and primary school.[129] The high rates of young women and children who reported using the computers tends to support the 'domestic hub' emphasis of use of the computers. As discussed in the previous chapter, although senior women over 60 years of age at Imangara and Mungalawurru often acted in a 'figurehead' capacity, liaising with researchers and in resource distribution at community meetings, their actual ICT usage was fairly limited (see Chapter 6).

When we asked who in the household looked after the computer during the project, individual women were most often mentioned as being chiefly responsible (around 60 per cent at both Imangara and Mungalawurru); that is, rather than individual men, couples ('we both do') or households ('all of us'). Once again, youth was a significant factor, again suggesting a correlation between this role and higher levels of digital literacy: mainly women (86 per cent) aged 18-29 years at Imangara and only women and men in their 20s and 30s at Mungalawurru were named as responsible for the computers.

Overall, these results reflect a higher rate of engagement with the ICTs amongst young women, in using and taking responsibility for the computers, as well as being willing informants (see Appendix 3, Figures 7 and 8).

---

126 Iten, *Cyber Safety Program Report*, p. 9.

127 Iten, *Cyber Safety Program Report*, p. 16.

128 Iten, *Cyber Safety Program Report*, p. 16.

129 Karen moved from Mungalawurru to Tennant Creek once her oldest child turned five, to support him while he attended school.

MEN'S INTERNET USE

One young man in his early 20s stayed at Mungalawurru for about 12-18 months, sharing a computer with four other young adults and a child in a mutual living space at a house that transitory community members tended to occupy. When we first met him in July 2012, he reported using the computer for fairly basic purposes – to check emails, to browse the internet and to download music – but said that he 'wouldn't pay to keep it; I don't use it enough'. He also mentioned the role that young women played in assisting him to use the computer, saying that he'd been watching others print out letters and photos, and access Centrelink online, which he wanted to learn how to do himself. However, he identified the main obstacle to him in using the computer as being that 'sometimes others using it stops me from using it'.

Four months later, he said that two young women used the computer most in his house, one of whom he identified as being the person who looked after the computer. While he thought he was using the computer the 'same amount' as before, he said that he had improved 'by looking at other people using it', citing checking BasicsCard balances as something he had learned in this way. He named Karen first as someone who had shown him new activities, then Andrew, who 'showed him little bit email'. Karen, who was listening in on the conversation, remarked that the young man 'tells me if I have an important one'. The young man was more positive about the value of ICT access since we'd last spoken to him, saying he thought the computers had been 'great – awesome, eh' for the community, because people could 'download music, videos; look at entertainment'. As a result, he 'stay[ed] in Mungalawurru more. At town, [you] do nothing'. He also said he would be happy to pay $30 per month for an internet plan.

This man's story, as someone who was initially uninterested in ICTs until he saw their benefits, demonstrates how community members with lower degrees of digital literacy may engage more with ICTs if they're exposed to their use. A year or so after we first met him, however, he had left Mungalawurru, which, as we discussed in Chapter 4, was not an uncommon pattern amongst young men in remote communities, who are more likely than young women to need to travel to find work. There are also cultural precedents for young men to live a transitory lifestyle; Myers describes how until they have married (often in middle age amongst the Pintupi) and have passed through further stages of instruction conducted by older men, 'young men cannot settle down, cannot stay in one place'.[130] Traditionally, young unmarried men post-initiation were: 'free and unfettered [...] not yet channeled into reproduction but under the guidance of larger society as embodied by older men'.[131]

---

130   Myers, *Pintupi Country, Pintupi Self*, p. 145.

131   Myers, *Pintupi Country, Pintupi Self*, p. 238.

The man's story indicates how transitory some remote community members' lifestyles can be, particularly young males, with the result that their exposure to ICTs may be limited and their level of digital proficiency lower than that of less-mobile community members. By contrast, the young women he knew, who frequently displayed high levels of computer skills, were often less mobile, and more likely to be found in the community when we visited.

Four men were in prison for periods ranging from six to twelve months during the first two years after the computers were installed, and thus had fewer opportunities to ask questions and learn basic skills from us. At Mungalawurru, men were often involved in a local cattle project and hunting, which meant that they weren't always present when we were visiting, or that they returned in the late afternoon just as we were leaving the community. In households where participants reported men using the computers for entertainment and administrative purposes, they often came to expect that women, especially female partners, would perform administrative tasks for them on the computers, even within a few months after installation.

Research by the Desert Knowledge CRC corroborates the notion of dual systems in relation to technical functions undertaken within remote community life, which tend to be divided along gender lines, but with some tasks shared by both sexes. In their 2008 paper, *Housing for Livelihoods: The Lifecycle of Housing and Infrastructure Through a Whole-of-System Approach in Remote Aboriginal Settlements*, researchers Seeman, Parnell, McFallan and Tucker identify a series of activities (see Figure 4 in Appendix 3) as being predominantly women's technical functions; some – such as washing and repairing clothes – of which relate directly to the domestic sphere, while others – teaching and education, health, administration, arts and crafts – are less strongly linked, possibly because they have been introduced through Western contact.[132] Tasks relating to an external domain of outdoor activities were coded as predominantly men's technical functions, with a 'middle ground' of tasks perceived as gender neutral or equally shared by the sexes.

Seemann and his fellow researchers also observed the impact of government and private technical support funding cycles on gender employment issues in remote communities: 'men's work, seen mostly in the technical fields, was sporadic or opportunist; women's work, seen mostly in the educational and health fields, was steady, institutional, developmental and programmed'.[133] They noted that there was an increased emphasis on providing training for '[s]emi-technical and non-industrial occupational skills, such as

---

132 K.W. Seemann, M. Parnell, S. McFallan and S. Tucker, *Housing for Livelihoods: The Lifecycle of Housing and Infrastructure Through a Whole-of-System Approach in Remote Aboriginal Settlements*, Vol. 29, Alice Springs: Desert Knowledge CRC, 2008, p. 16.

133 Seemann et al., *Housing for Livelihoods*, p. 17.

settlement health and primary school teacher assistant skills' which tends to emphasize organizational and cross-communicational competencies, and attracted more Aboriginal women than men as participants.[134] There was less funding available for training and skills development for 'specialist trade or industrial technology occupations' associated with men, and 'this had more of a social effect on the skills development and educational participation rate for Aboriginal men than for Aboriginal women, particularly for small settlement populations'.[135] As well as the cultural precedent for higher levels of mobility amongst young men, the lack of employment and training opportunities connected with male-associated technical functions may partly explain their infrequent presence at the computers. In addition to the domestic location of the desktop computers, participants may also have perceived the ICT skills and training opportunities (discussed in Chapter 3) we offered during the project to be more aligned with women's technical functions and typical occupations. For example, one husband's comments (above) about wanting his wife to write administrative reports for him about the cattle project suggests that he may have seen this 'home office' use of the computer as more part of her domain of technical activity, but complementary to his cattle work within a male domain of external activity. Merlan observes that: 'Women's productive and especially redistributive role was important in defining Aboriginal domesticity, and the current membership of particular domestic groups.'[136] Women's greater participation in the project – looking after the computers, doing tasks online for family and liaising with researchers – may reflect the correlation of the computers with the more female-oriented domain of the household as an extension of the women's technical and reproductive role in Aboriginal society.

DIFFICULTIES IN OBSERVING GENDER DYNAMICS

There was a gradual attrition of male community members from interview sessions and training. Even in the initial stages, men made up slightly less than half (45 per cent) of the participants in community meetings about the computers. At the time, we observed that young men in particular were often out at work or in town, and therefore more difficult to interview.[137] A couple of years after we installed the computers in the communities, men's rate of participation in surveys and discussions on our research trips had declined to just under one-third (29 per cent). With only a few exceptions, when men interacted with us, it was often as a member of a couple or a family group, and they were generally less forthcoming than the women present. The women occasionally mentioned

---

134   Seemann et al., *Housing for Livelihoods*, pp. 17-18.

135   Seemann et al., *Housing for Livelihoods*, p. 18.

136   Merlan, 'Gender in Aboriginal Society', p. 36.

137   Australian Communications and Media Authority, 'Communications Report 2009-10', http://www.
      acma.gov.au/webwr/_assets/main/lib311995/2009-10_comms_report-complete.pdf, p. 27.

some young men - brothers, nephews, grandsons - using the computers, with a couple of women in their 20s once reporting that their 16-year-old nephew had shown them how to do things on the computer. When we asked Mary on one occasion whether the 'young fellas use the computers', she replied, 'Yeah, they use them. They help me use the computers', which may suggest that young men used the ICTs and helped others with them more than was evident when we were in the communities.

Women's greater rate of participation (71 per cent) was likely to have been influenced by the fact that we were a majority of women, and interacting with us was therefore possibly considered the responsibility of the women. The greater numbers of women mentioned as frequent computer users may also reflect gender peer group dynamics: that is, not only did more women participate in the field research, but they also tended to cite themselves and their female contemporaries more often as users (as in the responses to the question in the previous section about who looked after the computer, where each gender tended to report use by its members more often). Therefore, although our interactions with the outstation residents suggested a gender-coding of spaces, roles and activities associated with computer use, we do not consider these to be conclusive results.

GENDER ACCESS AT A SHARED FACILITY

As discussed in the next chapter, we visited Papunya in May 2012 to examine the Papunya Computer Room (PCR) as an example of ICT usage at a shared facility in a large remote community. During this trip, we spoke to a sample of community members about their use of computers and the internet, not all of whom were regular computer room users. We found that young men rather than young women were the dominant users.

Most of the women we spoke to in the community considered the PCR to be specifically associated with young men, and said they did not feel comfortable there because of the cultural protocols about the need for men and women to maintain separate spaces. Middle-aged and older people of both sexes at Papunya also expressed the view that the computer room was for young people, or they could not use computers because they had not received computer training at school.

There were often only a handful of women using the facility when we visited, whereas the main computer room was usually full of young men and sometimes kids. Young men's greater use of the PCR relates in part to its original purpose as a diversionary outlet: it was established in early 2009 after the second visit to the community by the Senate Inquiry into Petrol Sniffing, to provide an alternative source of educational and creative industry activities for young people, especially males aged 14-25 years, who had missed out on primary education because of substance misuse. It also has overlaps with creative industry activities at the Warumpi studio, catering particularly to young men's interests in making and listening to music (see Chapter 8).

The higher rate of male users we observed in May 2012 was also at odds with results from a survey of the PCR that the Central Australian Youth Link Up Service (CAYLUS) conducted in 2010, when usage according to gender was in the order of 44 per cent females and 56 per cent males.[138] Within the following years, the computer room appears to have become identified as a distinctly young male space. Similarly, when we conducted research into internet use at Ali Curung, we were told that young males tended to dominate the computer room when it was open; young women only used it when a youth worker provided specific programs and activities for them.

THE KUNGKAS' ROOM AND EQUITY OF GENDER ACCESS AT THE PCR

In early 2012, CAYLUS, in conjunction with the Papunya community, set up a Kungkas' (or women's) room alongside the main computer room in response to the perception that the PCR was largely a young male space. The Kungkas' room, a 'lounge'-style space with books and toys, where mothers could bring children while they used the computers, was intended to provide a location where women would feel comfortable about accessing the computers, as well as addressing the overflow of users from the main room. A female community development worker was engaged to undertake self-directed learning with young women in the Kungkas' room.

At the time of our visit to Papunya in May 2012, the Kunkgas' room had only been open for several months, and there weren't any significant increases in female computer users. It did not appear to have gained sufficient momentum yet to change perceptions about who felt comfortable using the computer facility. Some female non-users in the community, most of whom were middle-aged or older, told us they were unaware of the Kungkas' room's existence, which suggests the computing facility continued to be associated more with youth activities.

When we spoke to CAYLUS a year later, they reported that while there were approximately seventy users per day at the PCR, use of the Kungkas' room tended to wax and wane, often according to whether female support workers were present. They also said that some boys had been entering the Kungkas' room and 'getting flirty' with the girls, but that local Papunya female staff members were unable to get the boys to leave, because of inter-family relationships. PCR and CAYLUS staff also observed that certain family relationships, as well as age and gender groups, could influence who felt comfortable using the computer room, similar to how access to the Women's Centre computers at Imangara became largely restricted to one family. CAYLUS suggested that some white support staff would probably always be involved in managing the computer room, because of the need to take into account cultural constraints relating to gender and family affiliations.[139]

---

138   Central Australian Youth Link Up Service, *Annual Attendance Trends Data: July*, 2010.

139   J. McFarland 2013, personal communication.

In September 2013, the PCR underwent a further evolution when it was relocated in the Maku Shed (further discussed in Chapter 9). Originally, a small room in the Maku Shed was set aside for Kungkas only, but it proved difficult for the coordinator to supervise along with the main room, and was closed after two of its computer screens were damaged. The coordinator did not think, however, that gender was as significant an issue in the Maku Shed as in the original PCR building, because it was a larger space and harder for the men to dominate, although she thought that avoidance relationships still needed to be managed.

The Papunya experience indicates that one drawback of a shared facility arrangement such as a computer center or kiosk is its capacity to be patronized by a particular group to the exclusion of other sections of the local community. In the case of the original PCR, the greater presence of young men in the main room discouraged other groups, such as women and older people, from using the computers. Consequently, cultural constraints relating to gender and family affiliations, whereby members of the opposite sex and certain family groupings cannot occupy the same space, shaped the planning of successive versions of the computer room, particularly in regard to space and staffing arrangements.

CONCLUSION

Contrary to the expectations of international literature, and the experience of shared facilities at Papunya and Ali Curung, women engaged more substantially in ICT use in the outstations. This outcome suggests household-based ICT arrangements might preference women as users, given their associations with domestic space and administrative tasks (although this evidence was perhaps distorted by the majority female composition of our research team). It raises the possibility, however, that locating computers and internet access within household space might lead to stronger association of digital technology with a female-coded domain and technical activities, with positive flow-on effects in facilitating greater ICT usage by women and children. This is a significant benefit of providing ICT access on a household basis, extending women's educational and creative opportunities, as well as assisting with the practical aspects of their lives. Overall, the unintentional age and gender biases associated with the location of computers and internet access in both the outstation trial and the PCR indicate the need to consider Aboriginal cultural norms and behavior in regard to gender, age and avoidance relationships in providing ICT infrastructure and arrangements, as well as training and technical support, to facilitate equality of access in remote Aboriginal communities.

PART III

Chapter 8: Alternative Regimes

The outstation residents' encounters with satellite internet, as recounted in previous chapters, was aided and shaped by our efforts. Assistance with software downloads and passwords, the cables, ink and spare parts we provided, our dealings with installers, and myriad other small tasks, impacted on the residents' experience of the internet. The Home Internet Project thus involved what can be considered a unique 'terms of use' - albeit a consultative one - in that those who took part knowingly agreed to our involvement, and were given a set of choices and a level of guidance. In the process we observed, and were brought into, the social dimensions of computing and internet use that emerged.

The question that arises is the extent to which different arrangements for technology, provisioning and support might have resulted in a different level of engagement or experience of the internet. As mentioned in Chapter 1, a number of programs attempting to deliver internet access have been implemented in remote communities since the 1990s. These have produced highly varied levels of infrastructure, facilities and technological approaches across different communities. A small number of larger communities have also received the kinds of infrastructure and telecommunication services widely available in metropolitan and regional areas, such as mobile broadband and ADSL. In this chapter, we discuss the resulting patchwork of internet access, and discuss the pros and cons of the various models.

We also examine how each of these arrangements impacts on issues of affordability, the different retail mechanisms they offer (where relevant), and the ongoing costs of maintaining networks and equipment. As shown in Part II, the spatial and social dimensions of internet access change according to whether the internet is accessed in public or domestic spaces, and whether these arrangements favor certain groups of users, or encourage use of a particular type of device. Some of the programs that have been implemented in remote communities provide free access, whereas others involve particular retail mechanisms (explored further in Chapter 9). An important issue is the sustainability of these various regimes, and whether they encourage reliance on outside agencies and providers through subsidies and maintenance arrangements, or rely primarily on commercial providers.

In this chapter, we focus on two larger communities, one of which has a large shared internet access facility and did not receive mobile coverage until mid-2014 (Papunya, as introduced in the previous chapter), and another which has had mobile broadband for some years (Ali Curung). As we were not able to spend the same level of time engaging with the residents in these larger communities, our account is exploratory rather than being a full comparison with the satellite experience on the outstations. From interviews with residents and others connected to the communities, we were able to understand the various conveniences and difficulties that those living in the two larger communities experienced in accessing the internet, and what they were using the internet for.

During the course of our research, information about various other infrastructures, trials and projects emerged, including WiFi hotspots in communities with satellite pay phones initiated by the Department of Broadband, Communications and the Digital Economy (now the Department of Communications and the Arts). In the final part of the chapter, we consider international models and discuss why they may or may not eventuate in remote Australia.

THE PAPUNYA INTERNET AND COMPUTER ROOM

As mentioned in the previous chapter, the Papunya Computer Room (PCR) was established in early 2009 to provide alternative educative and diversionary activities for young people in the community, especially males aged 14-25 years who had been identified by the Senate Inquiry into Petrol Sniffing.[1] We followed the evolution of the PCR from 2010-2014. Even within this relatively short time frame, the PCR underwent a series of significant transitions in adapting to available ICT, including the introduction of mobile coverage, and in attempting to meet the needs of the community. Those engaged in the development of the computer room at the Papunya community grappled with how to facilitate equitable ICT access for local community members in view of social inclusiveness, available forms of connectivity and ICT equipment, technical and training support, ongoing costs and long-term sustainability.

When we visited in 2012, the PCR comprised two rooms within a Northern Territory Department of Education (DoE NT) building in the community – a main room for community use, with eight donated iMac desktop workstations, and a Kunkgas' room for women and children (as discussed in the previous chapter) with four iMac desktop computers and a lounge area. The computer room relied chiefly on a series of volunteers on short-term contracts to provide administrative and training/mentoring to community members who use its facilities. Use of the computers and equipment was free, so as not to discourage any community members from using the facility. The computer room possessed both an ethernet and wireless network (ADSL) in mid-2012. The community received mobile coverage in late March 2014.

The main use of computers at the PCR was as a form of entertainment, rather than for administrative activities or formal education. Collaborative and creative industries activities featured more significantly at the PCR, but were non-existent in the project

---

1   Central Australian Youth Link Up Service, 'Papunya Computer Room', http://caylus.org.au/
     papunya-computer-room/; The Parliament of Australia Senate Standing Committee on
     Community Affairs, 'Inquiry into Petrol Sniffing and Substance Abuse in Central Australia',
     Commonwealth of Australia, http://www.aph.gov.au/Parliamentary_Business/Committees/Senate/
     Community_Affairs/Completed_inquiries/2008-10/petrol_sniffing_substance_abuse08/index.

communities, which reflects the relative capacity and sophistication of the PCR and the community's connections with creative enterprises, such as the Papunya-Tula and Papunya Tjupi arts movements, and well-known local bands such as the Warumpi Band and the Tjupi Band. Use of the internet for administrative purposes was lower than on the outstations. While some community members used computers for online shopping, relatively few people undertook tasks such as accessing banking and online services and resources on the PCR terminals. However, there was less need to use the internet at Papunya to contact service agencies, given the presence of government services and organizations such as the Central Land Council (CLC) and the Congress Aboriginal Health Service within the community. When we interviewed PCR staff in 2014, they said that the computers were still being used mainly for entertainment, although Facebook had emerged as a new significant usage. While the coordinator had 'set up a lot of online banking and things like that', people generally accessed bank and Centrelink accounts at terminals available for those purposes at the community store, the Centrelink and Shire offices at Papunya.

THE EVOLUTION OF THE MAKU SHED

In September 2013, the PCR transitioned to the Maku Shed, a multi-purpose hub that provides a range of social engagement activities for the community. The Maku Shed is a large Nissen hut at Papunya, which had been re-purposed as a men's social club with pool tables and large screens for watching sport. The computers were moved into the Maku Shed to provide additional activities as part of an overarching exercise in community development that sought to take the computer room to the next level as a self-sufficient enterprise. It was also fuelled by the need to find a larger space for the computer facility, and to support other popular community activities, such as a cooking and nutrition program, and to address the long-term sustainability of the PCR, which had been surviving on a patchwork of philanthropic funds sourced by the Central Australian Youth Link Up Service (CAYLUS).

The Papunya store, which is required to put half its profits into community development, supported the transition to the Maku Shed as its main community development project for 2014. At the time, the Papunya store was paying the PCR coordinator's salary, as well as in the Maku Shed's power and water bills. Internet and computer use at the Maku Shed was made available on a ticketing system, priced from $0.50 to $1, with tickets supplied by the Northern Territory Remote Indigenous Public Internet Access (RIPIA). Soft drinks and evening meals were also sold. While the funds raised by these sales only covered the internet plan, the idea was to give people an understanding of what is involved in running a small business, and to encourage a greater sense of community ownership.

Co-author Eleanor visited Papunya in June 2014 for an update on the transition to the Maku Shed, and on the use of mobile phones after coverage had been extended to the community. The Maku Shed was still using the computers that had been donated to the PCR in 2009 by a youth organization in Melbourne, although some were 'dying a little'. CAYLUS had given Papunya several more computers since the Shed's opening, and in June 2014, there were eleven functional computers at the Maku Shed, with three in for repair.

ACCESS AND PARTICIPATION AT THE MAKU SHED

In the previous chapter, we discussed how, with the move into a larger, multi-purpose space at the Maku Shed, the PCR staff found there were fewer issues involving avoidance relationships and gender segregation. Ensuring that the computer room was open during hours that were suited to different age groups in the community became a key factor in facilitating greater access.

The Maku Shed hours were changed to a later time slot (1-9 pm) to cater for the use of the facility for youth activities, and so that people could avoid the extremes in temperature by visiting later in the day. The computers were popular with primary school-age kids and teenagers after school, with 17-30-year olds being their main users at night. Consequently, older adults, especially those who were working, were less likely to use the computers. The Maku Shed supervisor commented: 'There are so many kids in here, from 3:30 to 6 pm; it's so intense the adults don't want to be in here.' It was rare for anyone over 60 to use the Maku Shed, although middle-aged community members occasionally visited.

CAYLUS and the Papunya store were initially concerned that particular family groups might dominate, as they had at other facilities in the community. We also heard of this occurring in other communities where shared internet facilities were operating. However, the Maku Shed supervisor thought that avoidance relationships had proved to be less of an issue with the move of the shared facility into a larger space, suggesting that it was more likely that particular family members would commandeer the computer in smaller spaces, including households. She gave an example of a family who'd had a computer at home, but had ended up coming to the Maku Shed because one person had monopolized use of the computer. By contrast, the emphasis of the Maku Shed was 'more about sharing with community', rather than being family oriented. People even came to the Maku Shed to 'sit on the couch, using their phones because it's a lot more exciting than being at home'.

SUPERVISION, TRAINING AND MENTORING AT THE MAKU SHED

Staffing arrangements, training and mentoring activities played a further role in increasing social inclusion at the shared facility in both of its versions as the PCR and the Maku Shed. When the computer room was located in the smaller DoE NT building, there really needed to be staff of the same sex as users in each of the main and Kungkas' rooms to ensure that members of both sexes would patronize the facility, and would receive digital literacy training and support.

CAYLUS and PCR staff mooted that whitefella involvement would always be necessary at a remote community computer facility, because of kinship obligations and avoidance relationships ('Family relationships get the better of people, because of the level of humbug from kids and so on'). However, greater engagement of community members of both sexes and from different family groups, including autonomously for short periods of time, occurred with the transition to a larger space at the Maku Shed, along with the development of greater ICT skills amongst community members over time. A team of ten local residents supported the Maku Shed supervisor in overseeing use of the computers, but also in running the facility when she was absent from Papunya. In order to deal with any avoidance relationship issues, a male and a female, usually a member of one of the community's prominent families and someone from another family, were normally left in charge of the Maku Shed.

Scheduling training at appropriate times was mentioned as a significant issue. The Maku Shed supervisor observed external training providers: 'They choose to do it at the wrong time. If you want to engage people, I think it should be done at nighttime, for one. That's when people are most active around here as well, particularly in summer.' She stressed that, in providing training to remote community members, it was necessary 'to be flex-ible with time. And be really opportunistic. Just grab people when you can. Form those relationships with people so they'll want to attend your class, rather than just say when it's on'. The need for flexibility, along with an individual focus and the development of relationships with community members to understand their learning needs, also accords with aspects of our experience of delivering training to communities in the project.

By contrast, when an outside organization had offered a computer skills course at Papu-nya – which was held only for a specific week – attendance rates were low, with the 'usual suspects' participating and receiving certificates. This outcome was not unusual; orga-nized training had poor participation and success rates across the board at Papunya. 'Last time anyone tried to do training on an organized scale, only four people got certificates', the PCR co-ordinator remarked to us in July 2014, 'and they were four people who were pretty much guaranteed to get certificates anyway'. Community members also perceived a lack of purpose to the organized training delivered at Papunya – that it was unlikely to provide a pathway to local employment. 'People have been trained in a thousand things', the PCR co-ordinator observed, 'but there's no capacity to work [for employment – i.e. very few jobs available locally].' Likewise, the trainers delivering courses generally did not canvas what community members wished to learn or how they wished to learn, or build relationships through which they might gain some idea of people's learning needs.[2]

---

2   For a discussion of over-training in Indigenous communities, see H. Hughes and M. Hughes, *Indigenous Education 2012*, Sydney: Centre for Independent Studies, 2012.

SHARED FACILITIES AND LONG-TERM SUSTAINABILITY

Of the ICT access models available, the shared facility approach, of which the PCR/Maku Shed is the most highly developed, offers the lowest implementation costs, because all the facilities are centralized and shared. However, the operational costs can be very high. These may include the cost for renting secure building space (assuming that is available, which is often not the case) or the expensive alternative of constructing a new building, and the cost of providing and accommodating a supervisor for the center.

The access center model will always be constrained by the need for the security of the facility and the availability of a supervisor, and for these reasons most centers only open during business hours, and sometimes for only a few days per week. Supervision brings the obvious benefit that a skilled person is on hand to assist users in using unfamiliar applications, provide ICT training, and solve particular support problems. The access center can also be an effective vehicle for supporting school-based computing activities, provided there is effective collaboration between the schoolteachers and the center supervisor. However, subsidizing the costs associated with engaging a supervisor can be difficult. While these supervisory positions are often staffed by one or more volunteers to reduce costs, that approach introduces a greater than normal administrative overhead to recruit, orientate and manage volunteers who may only stay in the community for one or two months. In the transition from the PCR to the Maku Shed, introducing a fee-for-access model and sales of small items, was insufficient to support a supervisor's salary, and funds had to be sourced from other community development enterprises within Papunya – an arrangement unlikely to be feasible in a minor community.

THE COMMUNITY WIFI MODEL

Since the Home Internet Project commenced, another ICT option has been introduced into the remote Northern Territory Aboriginal context: access to community WiFi points and networks. One of the first versions of this approach accompanied the development of the solar-powered satellite community phone in 2009 by APN (the owners of ISP Activ8) for use at small outstations in remote areas. Approximately 300 of these Commonwealth government-funded phones are now in service at remote locations with a population of less than fifty people, and have all been enhanced to provide WiFi access points. This arrangement operates on a 'BYOD' (Bring Your Own Device) basis in which individual users supply their own WiFi-equipped laptop, tablet or smartphone computing device to connect to the internet. In 2014, one of the women in Imangara told us she had been using one of these WiFi points when visiting a family outstation. She was very pleased that it was available.

Most versions of the community WiFi model implemented in remote communities to date are similar to the enhanced solar-powered satellite community phone one, insofar as they are BYOD and consist of a single WiFi access point, which concentrates all ICT users, and hence traffic, around a single point and internet source in the community. But unless the community is small (for example, a family sized outstation), a single domestic National Broadband Network (NBN) satellite service is unlikely to have the capacity to provide sufficient broadband speed for all the users who may wish to connect simultaneously. WiFi is technically limited to a radius of about 50 meters from the access point, and coverage typically diminishes further with obstacles such as vegetation and building walls (particularly metal-clad walls) in the way, making use within community buildings and houses unreliable. The larger the community, the more access points are needed to provide realistic coverage, particularly if equity of access for all residents is to be ensured.

The potential benefits of WiFi include the ability to install filters and to restrict access when individuals are found to be causing harm online. The spatial consequences of WiFi – how and where individuals access the internet – is an area that requires further investigation. For instance, in April 2015, CAYLUS called for free WiFi to be installed in Alice Springs town camps as a diversionary activity for young people. A news article quoted Nicholas Williams, a youth worker at CAYLUS, observing that before WiFi was available in Hermannsburg, kids were more likely to be 'breaking in areas, hanging around where they're not supposed to'.[3] Since the WiFi became available, kids tended to use that area, knowing it is 'their area', even after hours.

An example of a community WiFi network which seeks to respond to equity of access issues is that at Milyakburra, a remote settlement on Bickerton Island. This arrangement was set up under the Commonwealth government-funded RIPIA scheme, which at the time was mostly supporting ICT access via library facilities in Northern Territory Top End communities; however, RIPIA installed a WiFi network at Milyakburra because it was so small that it lacked a library or other suitable community building. The network consisted of two wireless access points installed on high points (the roof of the business center and a centrally located radio mast) within the community, and in-home wireless repeaters were installed in each dwelling so that internet access could be extended to premises at the edge of the community, thus ensuring equity of access on a household basis. Reports from the Northern Territory RIPIA scheme indicated that WiFi access at hubs such as libraries in Top End communities were likewise well-patronized, day and night, by users with mobile devices inside or outside the buildings.[4]

In order to access WiFi hotspots, residents need mobile devices such as smart phones, tablets or laptops. However, the prices of iPads, laptops and other mobile devices can

---

3   R. Ellen and R. Herrick, 'John Elferink Dismisses Idea for Free Wi-Fi in Alice Springs Town Camps to Reduce Youth Crime', *ABC News*, http://www.abc.net.au/news/2015-04-10/elferink-dismisses-wi-fi-idea-for-alice-springs-town-camps/6384214.

4   A. Gray, personal communication, 3 July 2013.

be prohibitive if bought at community stores rather than at electronics shops in regional centers and cities. We observed a number of people purchasing devices on rent-to-buy plans, spending as much as $1,500 in total on an iPad in 2013. The expense and lack of availability of such devices in some very remote locations could undermine the social inclusiveness of this model.

MOBILE TELEPHONY

By mid 2015, mobile broadband coverage for Indigenous residents of central Australia was limited to about 8,500 people in fourteen discrete locations (another four locations were identified as roadhouses and mines), which constituted approximately half the total Indigenous population of the region. [5] Four of these sites were completed in 2014 as a joint project between Telstra and the Northern Territory government.[6]

A number of studies have noted the high rates of mobile phone adoption in remote communities since 2007. Early studies focused on mobile telephony as a substitute for basic telephony services, and therefore did not cover internet use – unsurprising given that smart phone use was lower in general at that time (30 per cent of mobile telephone services in operation allowed internet connectivity in 2010).[7] Moreover, data rates for pre-paid mobile broadband were high at that time, and iPhone and Android phones, which provided the first easy icon-based access to applications rather than internet web browsers, were released in 2007 and 2008 respectively. However, these studies do provide useful insights into the social aspects of early mobile phone adoptions and use. *Ingerrekenhe Antirrkweme*, a 2007 study of mobile phone use amongst low-income Aboriginal people in Alice Springs and town camps, found that 56 per cent owned mobile phones.[8] Of the respondents, 72 per cent lived in town (including 33 per

---

5   Communities with Telstra mobile coverage in the region as of August 2015: Ali Curung, Ampilawatja, Arlpara, Ti Tree, Yuendumu, Papunya, Hermannsburg, Mutitjulu, Santa Teresa, Lajamanu, Elliot, and Newcastle Waters, as well as the townships of Alice Springs and Tennant Creek, including town camps. The community of Amoonguna had coverage due to its proximity to Alice Springs. Other non-community sites included Granites mine, Barkly homestead/Wayside Inn, Barrow Creek, Urapunja power station, and the Erldunda road house; Australian Bureau of Statistics, 'Macdonnell and Barkly Statistical Area 3, Indigenous Profile, by Household', www.abs. gov.au/websitedbs/censushome.nsf/home.

6   Ampilatwatja, Arlparra, Newcastle Waters, Papunya and Mutijulu. Mutijulu had some coverage prior to this due to its proximity to Yulara (Uluru tourist township).

7   Australian Communications and Media Authority, 'Communications Report 2009-10', http://www. acma.gov.au/webwr/_assets/main/lib311995/2009-10_comms_report-complete.pdf.

8   Tangentyere Council Research Hub and Central Land Council, *Ingerrekenhe Antirrkweme: Mobile Phone Use among Low Income Aboriginal People – a Central Australian Snapshot*, Alice Springs: Tangentyere Council Research Hub and Central Land Council, 2007, p. 6.

cent who lived in town camps where mobile coverage is available), and 25 per cent lived in remote communities. In terms of mobile phone ownership, 69 per cent of those who lived in town had a mobile phone, compared with only 35 per cent of those who lived in remote communities. Participants who were on Centrelink benefits were spending 13.5 per cent of their income on their mobile phone.

Researchers Brady, Dyson and Asela also noted 'the very high rate of mobile adoption' amongst remote-living Indigenous people where there was mobile coverage.[9] Their study of the Indigenous take-up of mobile telephony on an island in the Torres Strait, published in 2008, attributed the mobile phone's popularity amongst the Aboriginal population to its relative cheapness and portability, especially in remote contexts where people frequently travel long distances. Mobile phones are also valuable for remote-living people in maintaining family and social contacts, especially given the significance of kinship networks in Aboriginal culture.[10] The near-ubiquity of mobile phone ownership amongst Aboriginal people in remote Australia, in contrast to the relatively low uptake of other communications arrangements in these communities, led Brady, Dyson and Asela to conclude that mobile telephony is the most appropriate 'fit' for this population. They state: 'Contrasting the enthusiasm for mobile phones and other ICT deemed valuable by the community [...] versus technologies which have been used only with reluctance or for the limited life of one-off projects convinces us that the Indigenous people are making informed choices about their ICT adoption.'[11]

They attribute the preference for mobile telephony to its compatibility with the 'inherent strengths of the culture' – communicating by text and calls meshes with the orality of Indigenous tradition – and the degree of 'motivation' that this form of communication elicits: that is, 'motivation is created by fulfilling obligations to family and friends, such as by communication and keeping in contact'.[12]

However, the availability of mobile telephones also caused financial problems for some, particularly in relation to data usage. In September 2009, Johnny Namayiwa of Goulburn Island, 300 kilometers northeast of Darwin, went to the media to expose what he saw as an unfair economic issue facing Indigenous people living in remote Australia.[13]

9   F.R. Brady, L.E. Dyson and T. Asela, 'Indigenous Adoption of Mobile Phones and Oral Culture',
     Cultural Attitutes Towards Technology and Communications Conference, Murdoch University,
     Perth, 2008, p. 393.

10   Brady, Dyson and Asela, 'Indigenous Adoption of Mobile Phones and Oral Culture', pp. 393-4.

11   Brady, Dyson and Asela, 'Indigenous Adoption of Mobile Phones and Oral Culture', p. 396.

12   Brady, Dyson and Asela, 'Indigenous Adoption of Mobile Phones and Oral Culture', p. 396.

13   I. Razak, 'Telstra Accused of Ripping Off Aborigines', ABC News, http://www.abc.net.au/news/
     stories/2009/09/09/2680645.

Mr Namayiwa was alarmed that residents had been phoned by the telecommunications provider, Telstra, and sold $49 mobile plans, but were now facing bills in excess of $1,000. A few days later, having investigated the issue, Telstra stated publicly that it was aware of two such cases, and that much of the cost for the capped plans related to internet use through the mobile phones. In this instance, Telstra eventually waived the bills.

ACCESS TO MOBILE BROADBAND IN ALI CURUNG

Towards the end of 2013, we undertook two trips to Ali Curung, a town of approximately 500 people near Imangara, to interview residents on their internet use, assisted by two local women and one local man (see description of method in Chapter 2). We spoke to eighty-five people from forty-five households, representing 58 per cent of Ali Curung's total Indigenous households.

When asked, 'Do you use the internet?' only twenty-three (27 per cent) were *not* using the internet when we spoke to them, and ten of those had used it at some point in the past. Therefore, almost 1 in 7 people who had used the internet at some time were *not* using it at the time of the interview, demonstrating that some will fall in and out of internet connectivity. Only thirteen people had either never used the internet or were not sure if they had.

Age was not a significant factor in non-use. However, younger people were engaging with more applications and online tasks than older people, and those with mobile broadband were doing more online than those who accessed it only once a week or once a month. The latter group's uses were confined to Centrelink and checking bank balances.

As Ali Curung is only a twenty-minute drive from Imangara, we were struck by the comparatively high rates of internet use in this larger town, given that Imangara had such low rates when we commenced our research. There were two possible explanations: either Ali Curung, and possibly other communities, had experienced a sudden rise in internet use since 2010, or factors particular to Ali Curung were influencing people's decision to use the internet. If most people in Ali Curung had started using the internet in recent years, is it possible that Imangara would have done so without our involvement? Both communities have a similar socio-economic profile, suggesting that affordability was not the reason for the difference, even though Imangara residents had indicated that 'money' was a reason they did not have internet connections at the start of the project. Some Imangara residents appeared to spend time in Ali Curung on occasion (one Imangara resident relocated to Ali Curung during the course of our research), suggesting that some level of knowledge transfer between the communities was likely.

We asked the residents of Ali Curung how long they had been using the internet or had owned particular devices, and found that 65 per cent of users had first started using the internet three years ago or less. Ali Curung received mobile phone reception prior to 2009, and mobile phones were the most common means of accessing the internet: 67.4 per cent of those interviewed owned a mobile phone (or possibly had easy access to a family member's), and 57 per cent of those were using their mobile phone to access the internet. However, when asked, 'How long have you had a mobile phone for?', 60 per cent told us that they had possessed a mobile phone for three years or less, suggesting that smart phone adoption and internet use through the mobile phone had occurred in recent years in Ali Curung, and somewhat rapidly. Only 32 per cent of people had owned a mobile for between five and ten years, while just over 5 per cent had owned a mobile phone for more than ten years. Tablet devices were reasonably popular with just over 30 per cent of people in possession of one. However, 70 per cent of those who had a tablet device had owned it for six months or less. Of the forty-five houses, seven had a desktop computer, only one of which was connected to the internet by a USB 3G mobile broadband stick modem. No households had a satellite internet connection. In addition, thirteen people were using the desktop computer at the Shire office, but only for Centrelink and internet banking. Nineteen people (22 per cent) told us that they had a laptop computer, although some of these may have been shared.

Importantly, none of those who were using the internet at the time were paying for the internet through post-paid billing. All who were paying for the internet (forty-five in total) were purchasing pre-paid mobile broadband credit, which was available for purchase at the store. The decision to choose pre-paid over post-paid plans enables people to avoid the bill shock experienced by Mr Namayiwa in the above example. One consequence that we observed in the Ali Curung study is that people are regularly without internet when their pre-paid credit expires, and some were topping up credit frequently. Sharing of devices, and hence sharing of credit, appeared to be common. One-third of those with an internet connection stated that they sometimes shared the cost with others.

So as it turns out, internet use in Ali Curung was probably much lower in 2010 when our first interviews in Imangara were occurring. However, when we analyzed the evidence from the Ali Curung study in relation to the broader findings of the Home Internet project, we concluded that Imangara might not have experienced the sudden rise in internet adoption in the absence of an assistance program. Without deliberate substitutes (including initiatives such as community WiFi or the assistance offered by us in the outstations), the way in which mobile broadband is sold, as well as the simplicity of connectivity through mobile broadband devices, circumvents some of the obstacles we observed in relation to satellite internet on the outstations. In Chapter 9, we discuss further the 'digital choices' being made in remote communities, and provide a theoretical framework for thinking through the unevenness of internet access between communities and regions.

THE DISH

In 2014, co-author Andrew developed a low-cost means of extending mobile coverage to locations within 40 kilometers of mobile reception. The invention was to become the Centre for Appropriate Technology's (CAT's) mobile hotspots project. Each hotspot consists of a re-purposed domestic satellite dish, which is used to amplify a nearby mobile signal. The structure uses no power or software to operate, and needs no maintenance, requiring only to be placed at a suitable height within the (extended) range. The first hotspot was placed in Boggy Hole, established in conjunction with the CLC, and allows tourists and locals who have become stuck on the notoriously bad road to the Finke National Park to call for help.[14] The hotspot is now also being used in communities just outside of mobile range, and at other highway spots where people can be stranded waiting for a lift or bus. In 2015, the Northern Territory government and the Aboriginals Benefit Account funded a total of thirty dishes in the central Australia region. Among the first sites to get a dish were Imangara, which receives a signal from Ali Curung; Tara, which now benefits from the Barrow Creek mobile phone tower (Chapter 1); and the bus stop on the Stuart Highway at the turnoff to Ali Curung.

INTERNATIONAL DEVELOPMENTS: MICROTELCOS

In 2013, an independent ISP in Papua, Indonesia, turned its existing network into mobile broadband using a low-cost, open-source base station technology created by US start-up company Endaga, created by PhD student Kurtis Heimerl at the University of California, Berkeley. The ability to access voice, SMS and data over mobile phones meant that those living in the village could easily reach people who were gathering supplies in town, a two-day trip by road.[15] Endaga provides a retail mechanism, including SIM cards and internationally recognizable phone numbers which enable entrepreneurs to establish their own 'microtelco' and charge users for calls. The technology is robust, does not require expensive protection from the elements and air-conditioning, and can be mounted in trees or on water towers as long as there is a power source.

A number of remote Indigenous communities in Mexico have also installed low-cost mobile base stations, and are transmitting using spectrum that is made available for Indigenous community radio in places where that spectrum is neglected by national

---

14   E. Sleath and N. Maloney, 'Mobile Phone Hotspots Trialled in the Outback', *ABC News*, http://www.abc.net.au/local/stories/2015/03/16/4198439.htm.

15   Endaga sales material, www.endaga.com.

spectrum licensees (under Mexico's constitution).[16] The Mexican network was established through Rhizomatica, an NGO with a mission to 'increase access to mobile telecommunications to the over 2 billion people without affordable coverage and the 700 million with none at all'.[17] Previously, residents were using landlines that charged a per-minute fee, which required standing in line, and using runners to inform each other of incoming calls. Following years of unsuccessful lobbying to get telecommunications companies to provide mobile broadband services, the communities decided to use their municipal money to establish their own community-owned and operated micro-telecommunications enterprises in rural Oaxaca, Mexico, with each base station costing approximately US$7,500.[18] In January 2015, Mexico assigned radiospectrum 'cellular' bands for 'social use', and created fifteen-year not-for-profit licenses.

Mobile telephony has become a significant enabler in the developing world, used for financial transactions such as remittance payments from migrant workers to their home families, or assisting small-scale farmers and traders to share information. Often the 'everyday' means of being informed and communicating, write Goggin and Clark, can result in economic and social opportunities, 'activating important dimensions of human rights in development, building upon and extending the well-recognised contribution of telecommunications'.[19]

In *The Great Indian Phone Book: How Cheap Mobile Phones Change Business, Politics and Daily Life*, Robin Jeffrey and Assa Doron describe how telecommunications companies competed with each other during the early 2000s to capture the large population base of poor and illiterate people in India as a market in order to ensure the viability of the roll-out of mobile telephone infrastructure. Thus: '[T]ens of millions of people had to acquire telephones if mobile telephony was to reward the huge investment required to build and maintain vast networks of mobile cell-towers.'[20] The competition between companies resulted in dramatic cuts to the cost of calls and phones in an effort to make pre-paid mobile phone plans affordable 'even [for] those who could make only a small

16   'DIY Telecoms', *The Economist* (March 7 2015), http://www.economist.com/news/technology-quarterly/21645498-fed-up-failings-big-operators-remote-mexican-communities-are-acting.

17   Rhizomatica, 'About', http://rhizomatica.org/about-2/.

18   T. Hatt, K. Okeleke and M. Meloan, 'Closing the Coverage Gap: A View from Asia', *GSMA Intelligence* (June 2015), https://gsmaintelligence.com/research/?file=e245c423854fcfd38eeae0a918cc91c8&download.

19   G. Goggin and J. Clark. 'Mobile Phones and Community Development: A Contact Zone between Media and Citizenship', *Development in Practice* 19:4-5 (2009): 595.

20   Doron and Jeffrey, *The Great Indian Phone Book: How the Cheap Cell Phone Changes Business, Politics, and Daily Life*, p. 72.

investment'.[21] However, a further aspect of courting this low socio-economic status market base involved tailoring their customer service experience so that it was 'cheap, easy and fast'.[22] One company, Bharti Airtel, tried to incorporate a range of retail outlets into their sales chain, and to demystify the processes around obtaining and using mobile phones by training a network of dealers to sell and install SIM cards on new customers' phones: 'To the uninitiated, the procedure seemed difficult, though it took only a few experiments with phones to learn how to change SIM cards confidently.'[23] This simple process, however, involved a significant outlay of financial and training resources, as 'it took thousands of hours of training to bring tens of thousands of hours of training to bring tens of thousands of distributors, travelling salespersons and small shopkeepers to a basic level of confidence'.[24] While that scale of operation would not be required to train an ISP's customer service representatives to broker satellite broadband access and plan payment for remote Indigenous consumers, the market drivers stimulating competition between the Indian telecommunications companies to create cheaper phone packages and more user-friendly processes for a low socio-economic status group do not exist to the same degree in remote Indigenous Australia.

Galperin and Bar see potential in microtelcos, defined by Galperin as 'small-scale telecom operators that combine local entrepreneurship, innovative business models, and low-cost technologies to offer an array of ICT services in areas of little interest to traditional operators'.[25] Microtelcos promise to overcome inequities in mobile broadband access due to their creative approaches to capital, labor and technology that 'maximize returns based on their knowledge of local conditions and demand preferences'. Microtelcos are thus capable of 'finding business models (including payment collection mechanisms) appropriate to local conditions' where large operators are reluctant to go.[26]

What are the prospects for microtelcos in Australia's remote Indigenous communities? Australian telecommunications spectrum regulation does not allow for 'use it or lose it' style spectrum access that Indigenous communities in Mexico exploited. However, in Australia, individuals and organizations can apply to the ACMA for a public telecommunications service license using various paired frequency ranges.

---

21   Doron and Jeffrey, *The Great Indian Phone Book*, p. 72.

22   Doron and Jeffrey, *The Great Indian Phone Book*, p. 72.

23   Doron and Jeffrey, *The Great Indian Phone Book*, p. 72.

24   Doron and Jeffrey, *The Great Indian Phone Book*, p. 74.

25   H. Galperin, and F. Bar, 'The Microtelco Opportunity: Evidence from Latin America', *Information Technologies & International Development* 3.2 (2006): 73.

26   H. Galperin and J. Mariscal, 'Digital Poverty: Latin American and Caribbean Perspectives', *Practical Publishing* (2007), http://www.idrc.ca/EN/Resources/Publications/openebooks/342-3/index.html, p. 96.

The cost of a microcell itself is perhaps affordable for small communities that have access to mining royalties and the like (within the range of USD$3,000-6,000, although electricity and maintenance costs would also need to be factored in). Microtelcos can operate to a reasonable standard using non-geostationary satellite backhaul.[27] However, the costs of backhaul can be high in Australia. It is also worth noting that although companies such as Endaga provide phone numbers and interconnection to service providers, in 2015 the wholesale price of a single phone number (purchased by the service provider and presumably factored into call charges) is currently six times that of a phone number in the United States, and incurs incoming call costs. Therefore, although microtelcos could emerge in remote Australia, providing a competitive call charge rate to consumers could be a challenge.

As discussed in Chapter 1, Australia's Universal Service Obligation (USO) provides subsidies to the provider (Telstra) for standard telephone services and payphones only. As Stuart Corner writes, when the Labor government made changes to the USO in 2012 (in order to accommodate the NBN), many believed that an opportunity for radical reform was missed, including the possibility of a USO that would take account of the 'popularity and reliance on mobile telephony'.[28] If the USO was adapted to encompass mobile voice services, then subsidies could be directed towards the most socially desirable infrastructure, perhaps paving the way for greater penetration of mobile coverage in remote Australia.

CONCLUSION

In Chapter 1, we discussed the history of telecommunications in remote Australia as being defined by the consequences of low population density, where metropolitan areas have subsidized infrastructure to regional and rural areas.[29] The various scenarios outlined above, including computer centers and public WiFi, are attempts to provide some means of access in conditions of market failure. Public WiFi, which in other contexts is a transi-

---

27   Such as the O3B non-geostationary satellites (backed by Google and other investors), which orbit close to earth and therefore offer low latency speeds – making voice connections acceptable – and fast loading for data services. O3B was designed to serve the 'Other 3 Billion' who do not have internet connections, and is providing satellite backhaul for mobile broadband in countries such as the Solomon Islands.

28   S. Corner, 'Universal Telecommunications Services: A Brief History and Analysis of the Issues Surrounding the New Australian Legislation on the Universal Service Obligation', *Telecommunications Journal of Australia* 62.2 (2012): 22.

29   Corner, 'Universal Telecommunications Services: A Brief History and Analysis of the Issues Surrounding the New Australian Legislation on the Universal Service Obligation'; S. Davies, *Urban Based Support for Rural and Remote Australian Telecommunications*, Broadband for the Bush Alliance, 2014.

tory solution for people when away from home and work, is intended as a first level of service in some remote communities, making up for the lack of fiber optic and mobile broadband infrastructure. Remote communities, such as in the Maku Shed in Papunya, have been experimenting with how to make public WiFi sustainable. However, there is no clear path to ensuring that WiFi or mobile broadband are possible in communities of all sizes, or how these might tie in with existing infrastructure and legislative technologies such as the NBN and the USO.

Chapter 9: Digital Choices

In 2010 we presented the outstation residents with a list of reasons that might explain why they had not already purchased internet subscriptions, based on what they had told us in earlier consultations. We then asked them to rank the reasons in order of significance. The greatest barrier to internet adoption turned out to be what we, for the sake of language simplicity, had called 'no cash/too costly/$'. Other reasons included 'Not important'; 'No-one to help fix them'; 'Don't know how to use it'; 'English too hard to read' (we verbally explained the list for those for whom English was indeed too hard to read). By the end of the project when residents were given the option to maintain the internet at their own expense, 'no cash' emerged again as the major factor. However, 'no cash' was not necessarily just a matter of affordability, but also as a result of a more complex and intertwined set of issues to do with the flow of money within and out of the community, time-specific spending priorities, and – most importantly – the difficulties of paying for internet and navigating payment systems. Some of the other barriers identified at the start of the project were also likely to have related to the broad category of money, such as poor English language preventing people from understanding the various contracts on offer.

Thus the problem of money was not necessarily a matter of what one was prepared to pay, but of how things were paid for. As discussed in the previous chapter, satellite broadband was available at cheaper rates than mobile broadband in Ali Curung, and yet none of the households we spoke to (half of all houses in that community) had a satellite internet subscription at the time, while around 70 per cent of people had mobile broadband. Not everyone managed to maintain a pre-paid mobile broadband all the time, which indicates that affordability was indeed an issue. However, it was clear that people were willing to pay for the internet when they could, but only under circumstances that suited them.

The concept of the digital divide is based on the idea that consumer choice alone will not create an equitable society (see Chapter 2). However, what if the choices on offer – including the retail mechanism and devices – were to change or expand? Some of these offerings might meet the needs of those who were formerly not able, or not inclined, to adopt. Moreover, once some people acquire the internet, they may influence others to do the same. In this chapter, we explore the social dimensions of 'digital choices' in relation to the digital divide in remote Australia. In the final part of the chapter, we provide a theory to explain the digital divide in remote Australia, which we call 'the demic dealbreaker', expanding on economic choice theory to take into account how the sociality of place and network effects can lead entire communities and groups to adopt or not to adopt. The theory provides a means for thinking through different arrangements and policy approaches that may help to resolve the digital divide in remote Australia.

THE DIGITAL DIVIDE AND DISADVANTAGE

Two decades of digital divide studies tell us that internet adoption falls along socio-economic lines, relating variation in the use of digital and online resources to differential social advantage.[30] Early studies revealed that those who were quick to adopt the internet were earning more, and had higher levels of schooling, than those who were not. The trend continued, with those least likely to use the internet also the most socially exclud-ed.[31] For instance, Helsper's analysis of three major data sets in the UK revealed that three out of four of those who suffer 'deep' social exclusion have only limited engagement with internet-based services, and are seven times more likely to be disengaged from the internet than those who are socially advantaged.[32] The 'stratification hypothesis' is also supported in the World Internet Project, which revealed that the internet is used more by the highest-income quartiles in twelve participating countries. [33]

In the case of Indigenous Australia, it is possible to draw a correlation between the digi-tal divide and disadvantage. A series of studies by the Centre for Aboriginal Economic Policy Research has found that, overall, Indigenous people living in urban and town locations are better off than those living in remote areas. In all parts of the country (remote and non-remote, with a significant Indigenous population), Indigenous people were also found to be worse off than non-Indigenous Australians living nearby across a range of socio-economic measures, including educational attainment, income, labor force participation and housing.[34] They are also the least likely to have an internet con-nection at home, seemingly supporting the hypothesis that social exclusion and digital exclusion influence each other.[35] In an analysis of the 2006 census data, the Australian Bureau of Statistics suggested that 'the lower rate of connectivity for Indigenous people

---

30   K.R. Wilson, J.S. Wallin and C. Reiser, 'Social Stratification and the Digital Divide', *Social Science Computer Review* 21.2 (2003); J. Van Dijk and K. Hacker, 'The Digital Divide as a Complex and Dynamic Phenomenon', *The Information Society* 19.4 (2003); P. Norris. 'The Worldwide Digital Divide', Annual Meeting of the Political Studies Association of the UK, London School of Economics and Political Science, 2000; N. Selwyn, 'Reconsidering Political and Popular Understandings of the Digital Divide', *New Media & Society* 6.3 (2004).

31   Dutton, Shepherd and Di Gennaro, 'Digital Divides and Choices Reconfiguring Access'.

32   Helsper, *Digital Inclusion*, p. 9.

33   Dutton, Shepherd and Di Gennaro, 'Digital Divides and Choices Reconfiguring Access', p. 33.

34   N. Biddle, *CAEPR Indigenous Population Project 2011 Census Papers*, Canberra: ANU Centre for Aboriginal Economic Policy Research, 2013.

35   Australian Bureau of Statistics, 'Patterns of Internet Access in Australia', http://www.abs.gov.au/ausstats/abs@.nsf/mf/8146.0.55.001/.

might be attributed to a range of several socio-economic factors'.[36] The statistics reflect significant hardships experienced by many living in remote communities, hardships that many of households in this book experienced to varying degrees, from subtle to extreme.

However, as discussed in Chapter 8, by 2013, broadband adoption was high in Ali Curung, where there were different choices on offer through mobile broadband retail. We confirmed this observation through a close analysis of 2011 census data. The result aligned with our own observations of differences between Ali Curung and outstations where satellite was the only option: where there was mobile broadband, people were far more willing or able to have an internet connection.

In 2011, only eleven locations in the southern half of the Northern Territory (south of 19 degrees South) had mobile phone coverage. These were the townships of Alice Springs and Tennant Creek (including town camps), the tourist resort of Yulara (near Uluru), three highway stops, and five remote Indigenous communities (Yuendumu, Hermannsburg, Ti Tree, Santa Teresa and Ali Curung). The towns, their town camps (Indigenous housing estates), and the five remote communities can be identified in the census data using the Indigenous Structure of the Australian Statistical Geography Standard, which enables analysis of discrete communities, or of a group of small communities in a given area.[37] Where the boundaries correspond to a particular community or town with mobile reception, it can be assumed that most of the houses in that Indigenous Location (ILOC) have coverage, or are in close enough proximity to mobile reception for it to be a viable option for broadband consumers. This is not the case with three ILOCs that cover large areas, and where there were likely only to be pockets of reception: 'Julalikari – Outstations' (forty Indigenous households, some of which may be in close proximity to Tennant Creek), 'South MacDonnell Ranges' (seventy-two Indigenous households, some of which may be in close proximity to Alice Springs), and 'Tjuwanpa Outstations' (thirty-eight Indigenous households, some of which may be within range of Hermannsburg mobile reception).

We found that across all ILOCs known to have mobile reception in 2011, at least 40 per cent of households had an internet connection of some kind (13 percent were not stated and 47 per cent reported they had no internet connection). This compares with only 4 per cent of households with an internet connection in areas that did not have mobile reception. (The number increases to 7 per cent when the Julalikari, South MacDonnell Ranges and Twanpa Outstations are included – nonetheless a striking difference).

---

36   Australian Bureau of Statistics, 'Patterns of Internet Access in Australia'.

37   It is possible to do this analysis by aggregating populations at a more nuanced level by mobile reception coordinates rather than ILOCs. However, Telstra was unable to provide accurate coordinates for mobile coverage in 2011.

It is worth noting that although it should be possible to tell from the census data what kind of connection people were using, we decided that this particular information was unreliable, and therefore used only the 'internet/no internet' figures.[38] As Indigenous households in many of these communities share a similar socio-economic profile, we can conclude that social exclusion is not necessarily the cause of digital exclusion. Even when money is tight, we found that many people are prepared to pay for the internet when they have experienced it on an ongoing basis. Internet adoption is not 'determined' by one's socio-economic status, but can be a choice that is made when various factors of convenience and motivation are weighed up. The reasons underpinning the decision to purchase internet services, and the circumstances that inform that choice, are intricately tied up in contemporary and traditional obligations and patterns, and the pressures and preoccupations of daily life. We return to this point at the end of the chapter, discussing how the decisions of some can, through network effects, slow down internet adoption for the community or group. First, however, it is necessary to examine the 'digital choices' informing internet adoption in remote communities.

'WORRY ABOUT THE INTERNET'

We returned to the communities four months after the transition to self-funded internet access arrangements to see how they'd fared. We planned to drive from Alice to Tennant Creek, visiting Mungalawurru first, but we stopped off at Imangara en route to remind them we'd be visiting later in the week.

When we drove into the community, Mary hurried out onto her verandah and said there'd been 'worry about the internet'. She was particularly concerned about not being able to access her bank account. We then talked to another woman, Louise, who told us that her internet connection was still working – she'd been checking Westpac and Gumtree but she hadn't been able to use her email account. She produced a letter she'd received from the internet service provider (ISP), which she didn't understand, and showed it to

---

38   Peculiarities in the data relating to the type of internet connection are likely to have been the result of the way in which the survey was administered. The census is completed in remote communities with the assistance of ABS staff, who administer the survey door-to-door, whereas elsewhere it is completed by household members either online or on paper. The census asked residents what type of internet connection was available at the dwelling. The options included 'broadband', 'dial-up' and 'other', with an explanatory note that 'other' includes 'internet access through mobile phones etc'. However, in Santa Teresa, a community with mobile coverage, no dwellings were identified as having an 'other' internet connection, while thirty houses chose 'not stated'. In Yuendumu, twenty-seven houses stated that they had an 'other' connection and only three were not stated. There are a number of possible explanations for these inconsistencies, including whether the question was adequately explained to the participant, as well as confusion as to whether individual access to the internet via a mobile device is considered to belong to a dwelling or not. Despite these discrepancies, when grouped into ILOCs with mobile coverage and those without, the differences in internet adoption appear to be statistically significant.

us. The letter was dated four months previously, and it said that the ISP had changed her password to protect her privacy, and that she would have to ring them to get the new one. She also told us that Emily's WiFi wasn't working; she wasn't sure why, but she thought Emily mightn't have paid the bill.

We weren't totally surprised by these developments, because co-author Andrew had noticed problems with payment of some accounts before we'd left Alice Springs. Mary had also rung him a couple of times, wanting to know what had happened to her internet access. When we stopped off at the store near Imangara, the storekeeper told us she thought some community members' accounts had lapsed after three months because they hadn't paid their bills. She observed that most people in the community seemed to spend their money quickly, on or just after 'payday', when they received either wages or social security payments. The older people in particular tended to swipe through as many purchases as possible, often for younger family members, until their available credit was exhausted. The absence of money in their accounts so soon after payday would also explain why so many of the ISP's direct debits bounced, because the monthly billing date would not necessarily coincide with the fortnightly wage and social security payments community members received.

We encountered a similar situation at Mungalawurru the next morning. One family had been using their computer to lodge their Centrelink forms until one day in February, when the internet had stopped working. The husband had intended to submit his form that day, but lodged it in town instead because 'the internet was closed'. They'd tried a neighbour's house but the internet was not working there either. 'Everyone's using the phone now' to lodge their Centrelink forms, the wife told us. When we rang the ISP later, they confirmed that they would give customers three months' grace to pay bills before cutting them off. Payments had been going through to their account for a time, but when the payments stopped, the ISP eventually cut them off.

When we saw the neighbour the next day in Tennant Creek, she told us that although she was having problems accessing the internet on her home computer, payment wasn't the issue: she was up to date with her account. Andrew checked online on their behalf, and made a list of who was not up to date with payments, and the neighbour wasn't one of them.

The following morning, we visited Karen, who'd been living in a town camp in Tennant Creek (since moving from Mungalawurru) to be with her eldest son when he started school. She was using a pre-paid mobile phone plan ($40) to access the internet on her computer, which she topped up regularly: 'I'd never want it to run out because I like the internet.' She was still the main computer user in the house, and downloaded music onto USB keys for other family members. Although she kept the computer in a 'special place', she preferred using it in Mungalawurru where it was 'okay' – that is, safer because she had more control over it.

In the afternoon, we drove back to Imangara and organized a meeting at the Women's Centre the next day, so people could ring the ISP and sort out their billing situation. It had been raining heavily in the Barkly the week before our visit, and people were more comfortable sitting outside the Centre on plastic chairs rather than clustering around a telephone booth in the mud. A group of people joined us, and Andrew rang the ISP. He told the support person that we were ringing from a remote community in the Northern Territory, then put one of the residents on the phone. She had had problems reading the original letter from the ISP; it wasn't clear whether this was because of sight or literacy issues, or a combination of both. The ISP representative gave the woman an email ID and a new password, which Andrew recorded for her. Another woman spoke to the ISP about her billing situation and the debt on her account. When we'd spoken to her the previous day, it wasn't clear whether she realized her internet connection had stopped working because she hadn't paid, or thought it was for some other other technical reason. The ISP was prepared to waive her bill if she paid $40 in the next couple of days.

After the meeting outside the Women's Centre, we visited Mary to discuss her billing situation. We suggested to her that she ask some of her grandsons to contribute to the bill, which by then had accrued to $140, because it wasn't fair that she should pay the whole thing when they were using the internet too. We weren't sure whether Mary would run with this idea, but she said, 'No, it's not fair', and, nodding at her grandson, 'Don't worry, I'll deal with this'. She addressed him in language; he looked uncomfortable, but agreed that he would make a contribution to the bill. Mary wanted to alternate the direct debit payments between herself and the grandson on a monthly basis, but we told her this wouldn't be possible, and that he'd have to organize a transfer from his account or pay her $20 in cash per month. The man's wife agreed; she'd been quietly following the conversation, in deference to Mary as a senior woman perhaps, but she seemed to be on top of the detail.

We saw Mary later that day. She'd been down to check her account at the store, but discovered she didn't have enough money to pay the outstanding amount. We said it was possible the ISP might waive her bill with a part payment, as they'd done with others'. In any case, she seemed keen to maintain internet access so she could check her Centrelink and bank balances, but also for her adult children's and grandchildren's use.

As mentioned at the start of the chapter, we expected that 'billing and household economics [would] play a role', and speculated that the interplay of factors such as low incomes, high unemployment rates, and higher-than-average numbers of dependents living in remote community households would have some impact on affordability, though we did not know which factors would prove most significant.[39] While cost did not impact greatly on community members' choices to continue internet access during the transition

---

39   Rennie et al., 'At Home on the Outstation', p. 590.

period, billing and management of payment of plans emerged within several months of the introduction of self-funded internet arrangements as a decisive factor affecting their capacity to maintain internet access on the home computers.

In particular, the incapacity of the ISP's billing mechanisms to accommodate aspects of the remote community members' circumstances proved problematic, such as their style of social organization, along with the level of English literacy and whitefella administrative facility required to negotiate interactions with the ISP's processes and customer service representatives.

FACILITATING EQUITABLE ICT ACCESS IN REMOTE INDIGENOUS COMMUNITIES

The immediate change for householders after the transition was the need to pay for their own individual internet accounts. However, since the services and facilities were already in place in the communities, affordability was not such a major factor, because the actual amounts people chose to pay for internet plans were fairly modest ($3540 per month). Generally, those households who prioritized ICT access were likely to be able to find the resources to keep an individual internet service operational, even though it was not subsidized. Residents were also aware of the costs associated with appliances and energy consumption, and knew that computer usage could increase their power bills (already averaging around $50 a month). This awareness of the need to manage increased household service costs was also reflected by some residents' attempts to limit other community members' and visitors' computer and internet access through the use of passwords, and thus control their power bills.

Despite the willingness of some community members to allocate a portion of household budgets to internet services, navigating and managing the ISP's billing mechanisms proved problematic for them. About half the householders struggled over the first six months to maintain sufficient balances in their nominated bank accounts to support the monthly payments when they became due, resulting in temporary loss of internet access in some cases, and much larger withdrawals when the accrued fee was eventually debited. While in theory the ISP offers a pre-paid account option that might relieve this situation, it requires payment for six months' usage in advance, which is too high a lump sum payment for remote community residents operating on very low incomes. One obvious improvement would be a 'pay by the Gigabyte' pre-paid satellite broadband option, analogous to the well-established pre-paid SIM option for mobile phones, which would overcome the need to involve the customer's financial institution in both the application process and monthly billing. However, in our conversations with retail service providers, we learnt that such arrangements are thwarted by the way in which they are required to purchase satellite capacity from the wholesaler, the National Broadband Network (NBNCo).

The Central Australian Youth Link Up Service (CAYLUS) has documented similar situations that have emerged in other central Australian communities without mobile coverage, in which local families applied with the assistance of the local regional council for satellite accounts under the NBN so that they could have internet access on a household basis.[40] These internet services have since fallen into disuse after families defaulted on payment for broadband plans. Households were unable to pay the bills because their resources were spread too thinly amongst a large number of highly mobile residents, making regular payment almost impossible. As in the post-transition phase at the communities, these residents struggled with the administrative processes required to terminate the direct debit arrangements, because of the level of 'English legalese' needed to negotiate with service providers. Some people who signed up for direct debit for internet plan charges were still being billed, even though they no longer received a service. There was no onsite or external expertise available to repair or replace any computer equipment that was damaged. Essentially, this household computing arrangement languished because of a lack of ongoing IT technical support to assist community members with maintenance and administrative issues. The only conclusion to draw from these experiences is that subsidies for satellite broadband connection in remote areas are not sufficient to support ongoing home computer and internet access for remote Aboriginal communities without external assistance for the installation process, and for more complex technical and maintenance support issues.

At the start of the project, we speculated that provision of broadband on a household basis might be incompatible with remote Indigenous people's social and economic modes of organization, because in 'smaller communities, the extra-household economy may be more important than the individual household, whereby linked households share resources', and thus '[r]esidents might seek contributions to bills quickly from a number of people who are not necessarily residents of that household'.[41]

However, as discussed in Chapter 3, households tended to be fairly autonomous in their ownership and usage of the home computers and internet access. Instead, the trend was towards discrete family/household, even highly personalized use of the PCs, even those situated in shared, public spaces. Additionally, as the trial progressed, there was increasing recognition of personal ownership, particularly as people became more aware that the financial costs of maintaining the ICT and internet access were being borne by the owners. This in turn seems to have impacted on the extent to which, and circumstances in which, owners were prepared to allow others to use their computers, with people becoming less inclined to share their PCs and internet access with individuals outside of their immediate family/household.

---

40   Central Australian Youth Link Up Service, *Proposal Re: Better Way of Providing Broadband in Remote Communities*, Alice Springs: Tangentyere Council, 2014.

41   Rennie et al., 'At Home on the Outstation', pp. 591; Hogan et al., *Submission to the Inquiry into Issues Surrounding Cyber-Safety for Indigenous Australians*.

As they transitioned to self-maintained services, the majority of households opted for individual internet services and accounts (as in the story in Chapter 3 recounted about Mary's family's negotiation of ICT arrangements), with most householders being unenthusiastic about paying for their neighbours' use. We saw a similar trend across households, whereby usage was confined to immediate family members rather than shared with the community. Consequently, participants opted to pay for internet use on a household basis, with payments made from the account of the resident within the house who was generally the most active in the project.

In their research into the social and economic composition of Aboriginal households at Kuranda in north Queensland, Finlayson and Auld found similar trends within household financial management to those discovered by Smith:

> Economic units within households do not necessarily share resources and do not all contribute to the common financial costs of managing the dwelling itself. Even amongst core residents, joint contributions to household finances are not regularly given. Most household members take the attitude that their incomes (welfare in large part) belong exclusively to themselves [...] People without cash incomes may be financially supported to a certain extent by others, but such support cannot be relied upon for long periods.[42]

We observed that the burden of payment for household internet access often fell heavily on the individual whose account was used, as in the case of a participant like Mary, who paid for her household's internet and computer use without receiving financial contributions from them, or without having any straightforward way of doing so through online billing. Ultimately, her internet plan was suspended, because the demands from family on her finances were such that her bank account was empty soon after payday, which meant that funds were unavailable on the internet plan's monthly payment date.

However, those with responsibility for the computers did come up with some quite innovative solutions, such as those mentioned above (monthly payments to alternate between different people's accounts, or setting up a separate account solely for internet plan payments). A facility to synchronize internet plan direct debits with payment of wages or social security benefits, potentially as a BasicsCard essential service deduction, could also be an arrangement more suited to remote community members. However, at the time when these particular houses were attempting self-funded arrangements, only limited payment options were available, and the ISP was not flexible enough to accom-

---

42   J. Finlayson and A.J. Auld, 'Shoe or Stew?: Balancing Wants and Needs in Indigenous Households:
     A Study of Appropriate Income Support Payments and Policies for Families', ANU Centre
     for Aboriginal Economic Policy Research Discussion Paper No. 182, 1999; D.E. Smith, *Toward
     an Aboriginal Household Expenditure Survey: Conceptual, Methodological and Cultural
     Considerations*, Canberra: ANU Centre for Aboriginal Economic Policy Research, 1991, p. 13.

modate arrangements that would be more amenable to remote community members' financial and social circumstances.

Additionally, in Chapter 3, we noted that although the computers and internet access were valued at a broad level by the residents, the extent to which they were valued varied among individuals and changed over time, and fluctuated according to circumstances. For example, there may be instances whereby people prioritize expenditure on other items, such as fixing a car or paying for a funeral. Billing and payment methods not only need to be more flexible not only to accommodate greater residential mobility than is the case in the mainstream, but also in order to recognize the financial circumstances that surround many individuals living in remote communities.

COMMUNICATION CHALLENGES: NEGOTIATING WHITEFELLA SYSTEMS

The difficulties the residents encountered with the administrative aspects of managing their internet plan and email accounts after the transition to self-funded arrangements were not surprising. As discussed in Chapter 2, we experienced some arduous processes when setting up the accounts ourselves. The technical team's facilitation of the application for NBNCo Interim Satellite Service (ISS) services, and their implementation on behalf of twelve households, was also a resource-intensive experience. Each instance required a mixture of online, postal, text message, email, and phone transactions, including obtaining the householder's signatures for the registration, service application and payment forms. While the majority of such transactions proceeded smoothly, they required regular liaison between the facilitator, the customer and the provider to ensure that the customer would be at home when signatures were needed, or when the installer was due to arrive onsite. It is unlikely that the residents would have been successful in carrying out the various steps required for the transition to occur with their limited telecommunications options and knowledge of the processes, combined with the NBNCo and ISP staff's relatively uninformed perceptions of remote community realities.

A further example of the communication issues that can emerge between ISPs and remote community residents was the confusion caused by the password changes the ISP made to the residents' email accounts after the transition. The residents' applications for their new internet services during the transition included the technical team's contact details for coordinating the installation process; the technical team members then informed the residents of their new email addresses and passwords. However, a couple of months after the transition occurred, the ISP decided that the provision of these passwords to the technical team was a security breach, because the team members were 'not authorised contacts for the residents'. Consequently, the ISP unilaterally changed most of the passwords, cutting the technical team, and therefore the residents, most of whom could not be contacted except by post, out of the dialogue. Despite now having their new internet service, the residents could not use email, and could not access their online account details to make contact with the ISP. A letter arrived in the post from the ISP some time later advising them to phone in for their new password, but this left most residents in a state of confusion. Even Louise, who had more facility and confidence in relating to whitefellas and their forms of administration than most other participants, struggled to understand the letter, because of the level of 'legalese' used.

The fact that even the more ICT- and financially adept residents had not made any attempts to contact the ISP to resolve their respective internet and email account problems indicates how incomprehensible and daunting the residents found aspects of the ISP's administrative processes to negotiate without the assistance of an intermediary. The series of actions that ISPs require customers to go through to obtain satellite broadband service and manage payment of an internet plan is reasonably straightforward if the customer is readily contactable by phone, has a good grasp of English, and has sufficient knowledge about broadband services to be able to make an informed choice of service plan. However, the process is much less straightforward when the customer does not meet all of these criteria, as is often the case for remote community residents where the only external communications option is a single payphone.

These challenges can be further compounded by the prevalence of hearing and eyesight issues in remote communities. For example, a woman in Mungalawurru made the quite reasonable suggestion of dealing with potential internet plan payment issues by setting up a separate bank account; however, this option would not have been easy for her to manage without the assistance formerly provided by the technical team. As well as having to negotiate barriers such a lower level of English literacy and the ISP's convoluted administrative procedures, she would probably struggle to understand a conversation with a customer service representative because of her degree of hearing loss.

The communication issues surrounding remote community members' self-management of internet and email accounts that emerged after the transition to self-managed services highlighted clear issues: Their limited knowledge of, and facility with, these administrative processes; the ISP's lack of knowledge of the remote community context; the limited availability of telecommunications as avenues for contact; and low English literacy. All of these factors are likely to impact on their services.

An analogous situation existed at the Papunya Computer Room (PCR), where CAYLUS managed the physical and financial aspects of the community's access to the internet via a shared facility, along with the provision of technical and training support. Notably, such cultural brokerage is facilitated within the remote Indigenous context by Aboriginal community-controlled organizations, which frequently draw on piecemeal funding support from available government programs and voluntary organizations for capital, connectivity and human resources. Without this support, the relative smallness of remote Indigenous communities, along with their geographical isolation and differences in language and culture, would likely render these populations largely invisible to government policymakers and service providers. In the case of telecommunications providers, the invisibility of remote Indigenous populations, and the limited demand they represent as a consumer base, means they are unlikely to address even relatively simple communication and administrative barriers to ICT take-up. In other words, there is little incentive for telecommunications providers to develop financial and administrative services and processes tailored to capturing this market, except without invoking goodwill platforms such as 'equity of access', 'global citizenship' and 'social inclusion'.

DIGITAL CHOICES AND DEMIC DEAL-BREAKERS

The digital divide, at the most basic level, fits within broader theories of innovation diffusion, in that it describes how technologies are communicated through networks, resulting in particular patterns of distribution. As Hilbert writes, the digital divide is an inevitable fact when seen as the diffusion of innovation:

> Independent of the kind of network, the diffusion through a social network is never immediate. While the innovation spreads through the network and the diffusion curve unfolds, some are included and others excluded from the benefits of the new innovation. The result is an unavoidable divide. This divide is inevitable. It is the inescapable result of the fact that it takes a certain amount of time for innovations to spread through social networks with particular shapes and characteristics.[43]

The inevitability of the divide exists in relation to the presence or absence of information, in that those without information about the technology are unable to acquire or use it. Once that information becomes available, then presumably the divide begins to diminish. However, even with information, some will choose not to adopt. In their study of mobile phone adoption (discussed in Chapter 8), Brady and Dyson write:

> Contrasting the enthusiasm for mobile phones and other ICT deemed valuable by the community [...] versus technologies which have been used only with reluctance or for the limited life of one-off projects convinces us that the Indigenous people are making informed choices about their ICT adoption. Recognition of the factors behind these choices may well lead to better ICT investment and implementation decisions in the future.[44]

M. Hilbert, 'The End Justifies the Definition: The Manifold Outlooks on the Digital Divide and Their Practical Usefulness for Policy-Making', *Telecommunications Policy* 35.8 (2011): 718.

F. Brady, L.E. Dyson and Wujal Wujal Aboriginal Shire Council, *Report to Wujal Wujal Aboriginal Shire Council on Mobile Technology in the Bloomfield River Valley*, 2009, p. 396.

In this final section of the chapter, we consider the importance of 'digital choices' as they occur in relation to community norms and social networks. We posit a theory of why and how the digital divide is occurring in remote Australia, which we call the 'demic deal-breaker'.

In her study of UK data sets, Helsper noticed that particular groups were unexpectedly connected, defying predictors such as low socio-economic status: 'Some individuals within socially disadvantaged groups are capable of overcoming barriers to digital engagement.'[45] For instance, disadvantaged people from Afro-Caribbean origins tended to be more highly engaged than expected given their social disadvantages. Helsper's conclusion was that digital choices can be 'driven by cultural factors and the social context of individuals, which influence the development of positive or negative attitudes towards technologies', and that 'innovative and creative approaches' might be required to tackle attitudinal and cultural barriers'.[46] The high rates of internet adoption in Ali Curung also fit within this category of the 'unexpectedly connected'.

Our qualitative work, as well as our analysis of the 2011 census data for the region, suggests that it is not necessarily attitudes to technologies that are influencing digital choices in remote Indigenous communities, but the conditions under which technologies are made accessible. When remote Indigenous sociality is taken into account, the choice to purchase mobile broadband or nothing (i.e. the absence of substitution at the margin) makes sense. Factors such as difficulties with billing systems, inconvenience in dealing with retail providers (related to language barriers, or lack of other infrastructures such as home phones) are significant reasons to stay offline.

The economic choice theory of characteristic filtering (also known as behavioural lexicographical choice theory) describes instances where choosers set targets for particular characteristics, and eliminate products that don't meet those targets completely. In other words, the chooser decides: 'If x does not do y then I will not have anything at all', deciding that the missing characteristic is too important to substitute for something else; for the chooser the missing piece is the deal-breaker. The theory is useful for explaining some instances where choosers do not appear to be maximizing their outcomes – choosing to discount seemingly adequate options.[47] However, the economic theory of characteristic filtering only considers individuals' decision-making; it does not explain how the cultural norms of a group might play a role in why some technologies are adopted and others are not.

---

45   Helsper, *Digital Inclusion*.

46   Helsper, *Digital Inclusion*, p. 10-11.

47   P.E. Earl, 'Economics and Psychology: A Survey', *The Economic Journal* 100.402 (1990).

Two further concepts are useful for expanding on choice theory to explain how the 'deal-breaker' all-or-nothing decision can result in exclusion of an entire group or community. Firstly, in the broadest sense, Indigenous communities, like all communities, are a knowledge group, whereby the group shares its information, stories and culture, forming a particular set of social norms and influencing knowledge flows. Hartley and Potts call these 'we' groups demes (stemming from the Greek 'demos', meaning polity). The 'demic' aspect of the 'deal-breaker' scenario describes the way in which the decision only makes sense when seen in relation to group actions, norms and knowledge-sharing systems. We, the authors, had lengthy discussions as to the extent to which cultural norms are a significant factor in internet adoption, or whether practical issues (such as ability to call the ISP) are the main reason for the choices being made. While we did not reach an agreement on the specifics, as previous chapters have highlighted, life in Indigenous communities involves particular dynamics and ways of doing that influence ICT adoption and use generally.

Secondly, at the individual level, the decision not to adopt can be based on the decision-maker's circumstances, or attributable to a range of factors, including whether others in the group are using digital technologies. For some, no obvious decision is made, but they might accept the status quo based upon what others are doing or not doing. Those who might have few or no digital skills (for instance, those residents who went to school prior to the introduction of computers in classrooms) are unlikely to receive the information required to consider internet adoption unless those they know share it with them. Therefore, if those who might be considered (comparatively) early adopters choose not to purchase the internet – or choose only to use it in town, for instance – then other potential users do not get exposed to the technology.

Social networks thus affect the quality and flow of information, and create community norms (shared ideas about the proper way to behave). Granovetter's influential work on the 'strength of weak ties' is useful for considering how tightly knit communities can come to be without internet.[48] Granovetter argues that our acquaintances – weak social ties – are more likely to give us new information than our close friends and family, as those who we know already share similar knowledge. For Indigenous communities, it is entirely possible that adoption doesn't begin to occur and spread until an outsider (for instance, a youth worker) assists some people within the community with the means to acquire internet. This might also apply to those who understand that satellite internet is available, but have decided that it is too difficult to acquire, so those who have no knowledge of it will remain in the dark. Dense community ties can therefore restrict information, and be an obstacle to technology diffusion and development more generally.[49] Even if

---

48   M.S. Granovetter, 'The Strength of Weak Ties', *American Journal of Sociology* 78.6 (1973).

49   M. Woolcock and D. Narayan, 'Social Capital: Implications for Development Theory, Research, and Policy', *The World Bank Research Observer* 15.2 (2000).

some level of adoption occurs, places such as Imangara and Mungalawurru, which do not have a permanent youth worker or media center, are likely to have fewer of the 'weak ties' that might provide particular digital literacies and skills, such as GarageBand, which have become popular elsewhere.[50] Uses, and not just adoption, can thus be defined by the absence of weak ties.

Shifting the discussion of digital exclusion to 'digital choices' restores some agency for those for whom the decision not to adopt is a practical choice, weighed up against a host of trade-offs and inconveniences. When group dynamics are taken into account, broadband adoption is not only a matter of individual choice, but a socially situated understanding of what will work and what will not, where the parameters are understood within that group in ways that might not be obvious to outsiders.

CONCLUSION: THE CONSEQUENCES OF DIGITAL CHOICES

As discussed in Chapter 2, digital exclusion – like social exclusion – needs to be understood in terms of the causal process. During our time on the outstations, it also became apparent that digital exclusion is not a clear-cut case of 'haves' and 'have nots'. Some residents were not using the internet as the result of a considered choice. For instance, the man who ran the youth project in Kwale Kwale was disinclined to use a computer, but he took up our offer to have one at his place, as other people who assisted him on the project were able to use it. He still experienced the benefits, and it is likely that the computer enabled other capacities (for him and others) flowing from a more efficient management of the records of the youth service. Such instances show there are gradations of use, including those, known as proxy users, who choose to access online services with the help of others.[51]

When the digital divide is seen as a matter of digital choice rather than social exclusion, policies and programs can emerge that provide acceptable systems or incentives for participation. Although the statistics show that internet adoption is higher where there is mobile coverage, unfortunately universal mobile coverage has been deemed too costly by telecommunications companies, and does not fall within current government policy and funding (the Universal Service Obligations [USO], as discussed in Chapter 1). However, alternative billing options for satellite services may increase adoption in areas where mobile is not available. Another response can be the provision of public WiFi in communities (free or through a token system), as discussed in the previous chapter. Understanding digital choices can also help to anticipate what responses are unlikely

50   Kral, 'Youth Media as Cultural Practice: Remote Indigenous Youth Speaking Out Loud'.

51   B. Crump, and A. McIlroy, 'The Digital Divide: Why the "Don't-Want-Tos" Won't Compute: Lessons from a New Zealand ICT Project', *First Monday* 8.12 (2003).

to succeed, particularly where they do not align with the socially embedded decision-making that is occurring. For instance, the experience of the outstations in this book suggests that government investment in faster satellite speeds - as has been the focus thus far of the NBN in remote areas - is unlikely in itself to make sufficient difference for Indigenous families living in small, traditional communities, as it does not address the 'deal-breaker' problem of account set-up and billing. These policy options are discussed further in the final chapter.

The digital choices being made in remote communities should also give us pause to consider the relationship of digital exclusion to social exclusion. If social exclusion is not the determinant of digital exclusion, then digital exclusion is less intractable than we might otherwise believe. In other words, overcoming digital exclusion does not require resolving Indigenous disadvantage more generally. In an article on Indigenous social exclusion, Boyd Hunter makes the point that when Indigenous social issues are seen through the lens of social exclusion, they appear so interlinked as to seem insolvable: 'There is a risk that the notions of social inclusion, and to a lesser extent cumulative causation, can lead to a sort of policy nihilism where the magnitude of the task seems too complex and too hard. Unfortunately, there is not much one can do about this if the dimensions of disadvantage are inextricably linked.'[52]

Digital exclusion in remote Indigenous communities has been too often left in the 'too hard' basket, alongside tasks that seem both more urgent and incredibly complex. However, we think that there are solutions to digital exclusion, and that, with time, the broader benefits may begin to take the burden off other services attempting to improve health and education. Our conclusion is therefore ultimately a positive one: the digital divide in remote Australia can be gradually closed, and there are clear strategies for addressing it. We now turn our attention to some concrete policy approaches emerging from this book.

---

52   B. Hunter, 'Indigenous Social Exclusion: Insights and Challenges for the Concept of Social
     Inclusion', *Family Matters*, 82 (2009): 52.

CONCLUSION: WHAT NEEDS TO HAPPEN NEXT

The digital divide that we have described in this book is not uniform or easily quantifiable. At the risk of simplifying the situation, in this final chapter we offer a plain-language summary of what we discovered, and offer considerations for policy and programs.

As we have seen, vastly different rates of adoption are observable at the regional and local levels: some communities have high rates of adoption, while nearby communities are completely excluded. As Indigenous households in many of these communities share a similar socio-economic profile, we caution against drawing a direct causal link between social exclusion and digital exclusion.

The strikingly uneven patterns of internet adoption between remote communities correspond to the availability of mobile broadband and other government programs. Public-private partnerships in some regions have extended mobile coverage to larger remote communities. In addition, various publicly funded initiatives have provided a level of internet access, including computer rooms and training provided through the Northern Territory Libraries network and remote media organizations. Such programs have been designed to assist Aboriginal people to discover and learn about communications technology within community settings. Community payphones, provided through the former Indigenous Communications Program, are delivering internet to over 300 small communities (with populations under fifty people). The expectation underpinning such programs is that once people are given basic levels of internet skills and experience, they will eventually acquire internet services of their own accord. An unstated assumption is that those living in nearby communities will eventually learn about and adopt internet services through social network effects. However, this is not necessarily the case.

For many in remote communities, internet adoption is not a linear trajectory from non-use to use, but something that people will fall in and out of when coverage and pre-paid credit permit. Affordability is an issue, in that the relative value of internet ICTs is likely to fluctuate depending on an individual's life circumstances; for example, when money is short, basics such as food, power and transport may take priority over fixing a computer/device or paying for subscriptions/data. Particular groups, including older people and those living in small communities, can remain completely excluded, or only experience the benefits of internet use through others (making them users by proxy). Factors such as an individual's mobility and avoidance relationships can play a role in internet adoption, use and skills transferal.

DIGITAL CHOICES AND THE NATIONAL BROADBAND NETWORK (NBN)

We set out to understand why digital exclusion is occurring in remote Australia despite government efforts to equalize the cost of broadband for all Australians regardless of where they live. We found that Indigenous households are generally only acquiring broadband services under certain conditions. Identifiable 'digital choices' are informed by the practicalities and capacities of remote communities, and may be compounded by social norms.

Households in remote communities are choosing not to acquire satellite broadband services, preferring pre-paid mobile broadband in areas where there is mobile coverage. The consumer preference for pre-paid billing, as well as practical difficulties associated with satellite internet connections, means that households are more likely to go without internet than enter into satellite internet contracts. Our findings suggest that policy objectives aimed at improving internet quality (such as faster speeds), although desirable for services and businesses in remote Australia, will not encourage residents of remote communities to adopt broadband. In this book we have questioned whether satellite internet – the Australian government's response to internet access in very remote areas – can meet the needs of remote communities under current arrangements. However, changes to the way that satellite internet is sold and supported could make a significant difference, including enabling WiFi programs that provide residents with the payment flexibility they require.

THE TANGIBLE OUTCOMES OF INTERNET USE

Many of the outstation residents believed there are benefits to being online. Everyday uses such as online banking and shopping can provide a significant level of agency and autonomy for individuals. Checking bank balances and welfare payments emerged as one of the most popular uses of the internet. Internet shopping, entertainment and staying in touch with family via social networking were also common – made more significant when we consider how difficult it can be for those living in remote communities to undertake these activities through other means, given their limited transport and telecommunications options. As very few organizations or agencies attempted to use online communication to reach the residents over the four-year period, we were unable to determine whether internet access can reduce the costs of service provision to outstations.[1]

During the course of our research, cyber-bullying was reported within some central Australian communities and towns. Older generations found cyber-bullying and cyber-safety issues particularly challenging to understand and address. Network-level filtering and terms of use that reflect the specific concerns of elders and residents could be implemented in conjunction with the installation of community WiFi networks in remote communities and settlements (filtering is already occurring where the APN's satellite phones and WiFi are operating).

---

1   With the exception of the Central Land Council (CLC).

Developing digital proficiency in using social media and ICTs across different age groups is also crucial to empowering remote community members to manage these issues. Implementing policies that prevent or discourage internet provision and access, as has occurred under the Northern Territory Emergency Response in relation to the surveillance and supervision of publicly provided computers (2007–2012), is not a viable or equitable solution to cyber-safety issues.

FACTORS INFLUENCING THE ADOPTION OF PAID INTERNET SERVICES

If this particular divide is to be resolved, internet service providers will need to investigate and implement more flexible and user-friendly arrangements and administrative processes for satellite internet, particularly in regard to installation and billing.

As discussed in Chapter 9, facilitating the application process for NBNCo Interim Satellite Services (ISS) proved to be time intensive for us. In our view, without such assistance, very few households in remote Indigenous communities would manage to arrange NBN satellite services. It is unrealistic to expect households to carry out the various steps independently, given their limited access to telephones and knowledge of the processes, combined with the NBNCo and (some) ISP staff's relatively uninformed perceptions of remote community circumstances.

In particular, billing proved to be one of the biggest obstacles to satellite internet services. Despite the willingness of some community members to allocate a portion of household budgets to internet services, navigating and managing the ISP's billing mechanisms was difficult. About half the computer owners struggled over the first six months to maintain sufficient balances in their nominated bank accounts to support the monthly payments when they became due, resulting in temporary or permanent loss of internet access in some cases. For others, direct debits of large, unexpected amounts occurred if bills had been unpaid in previous months.

Our research in Ali Curung,[2] a community with mobile coverage, confirmed that people are prepared to pay for the internet if it suits them. All interviewees who were paying for internet access were paying for pre-paid mobile broadband, even though satellite internet was available at cheaper rates.

---

2   The research involved interviews with approximately one hundred people in Ali Curung in late 2013, with representation from half of all households.

SHARED FACILITIES VERSUS HOME INTERNET

When we commenced the project, there was an assumption in policy and academic analysis that shared facilities were the most appropriate form of internet access for remote communities. In the intervening years, government-funded and NGO programs – including Remote Indigenous Public Internet Access (RIPIA), the community phones project, and work by organizations such as the Central Australian Youth Link Up Service (CAYLUS) – have moved increasingly towards public WiFi.

A core focus of our work was whether home internet (the norm for mainstream Australia) was viable, particularly for communities too small to justify community internet centers. We also tested shared, community-managed WiFi by placing some computers in communal spaces (at the residents' request), and monitoring how they were shared and maintained. We considered practical matters to do with housing, including living arrangements, the condition of the houses and whether residents were home often enough to want a permanent connection to the internet; documented how long PCs and related electronics could withstand the heat, dust and vermin; and assessed ownership patterns (both Western ownership and traditional systems of demand sharing).

Although non-Indigenous people often associate a 'caring and sharing' ethic with Aboriginal culture, and therefore assume that shared or communal internet facilities are most appropriate, we found that individuals wanted to identify as the 'owners' of the computers. Access, and by extension usage, was largely restricted to the household/immediate family members, with the owner determining who could use the PC. Avoidance relationships between families, and the emphasis on discrete family ownership and use of ICT, resulted in certain family groups often dominating access to computers in shared spaces and excluding others, a finding that was corroborated at the computer room at Papunya. Location, access and usage are therefore important considerations for remote Aboriginal owners.

These findings have implications in considering models for the provision of ICT and internet access in remote communities. Specifically, computer room or 'internet café'-type arrangements which are run by Indigenous community members may not be the most suitable mechanism for providing equitable access to the broader community, owing to family and other cultural obligations (kinship). For example, in one of the larger communities we visited, the death of a young man who had been supervising a computer center meant that some others in that kinship network were unwilling to use it.

While in theory the home computing model provided ICT access for the whole family, ranging from grandparents to young, preschool children, the dynamics of inter-familial, gender and age relationships influenced community members' access to and use of the ICTs. The higher profile and level of participation of women in the home computing model suggests that locating computers and internet access within household spaces might lead to a stronger association of digital technology with a female-coded domains and technical activities, with positive flow-on effects in facilitating greater ICT usage by women and children. By contrast, at the Papunya computer center, the main room became so closely identified with young men that a separate space was created for women to access computers and the internet. To ensure equitable ICT access, the ways that different age, gender and family groups became aligned with particular social spaces within remote Aboriginal contexts needs to be considered in ICT planning.

Residents' degree of mobility, both within and outside the community, has implications for ICT provision in relation to access, ownership, management of billing, and sustainability. ICT arrangements need to be flexible in response to residential mobility, and some devices and equipment may be more suitable than others depending on community members' degree of mobility. For instance, residents moved houses within the community for a range of reasons, including available housing stock, maintenance issues in some houses, the cost of power, and cultural customs surrounding death. Such inter-community mobility has consequences for fixed infrastructure costs such as satellite dishes.

The high level of mobility does not necessarily equate to a preference or requirement for mobile devices. PCs can be easier to manage in the domestic setting. In contrast, there is a high degree of sharing of mobile devices.

EQUITABLE IT MAINTENANCE AND TRAINING SUPPORT

Much less sharing and helping occurred between households than we anticipated, not only in relation to access and use, but also in overcoming ICT issues and sharing skills and knowledge. A critical mass of ICT users and hardware is not sufficient to ameliorate the digital divide without providing ICT support and training. The tendency towards discrete family/household and even highly personalized use, together with the social and cultural relationships between different groups, needs to be considered in providing ICT education and training to ensure equity of access in remote communities.

Contrary to views that Aboriginal people prefer group learning because they are communally oriented, we found that community members generally preferred learning opportunities that were flexible enough to accommodate their lifestyle and priorities, and were provided within their homes, often on an individual basis. Individual or home-based learning is possibly also preferred as a way to avoid situations in which their lack of skill is on display, leading to feelings of embarrassment (shame). Although logistically challenging and resource intensive, a flexible, opportunistic approach that tailors learning opportunities to the individual's needs and takes place within private, safe spaces rather than formal, structured group learning is more likely to be effective. These observations were supported by the experience of the Papunya Computer Room (PCR), which mostly offered one-on-one training in response to the failure of attempts at group program delivery.

OVERCOMING THE DIGITAL DIVIDE

Digital exclusion in remote Australia should not be seen as an intractable problem. In communities where satellite internet is the only available internet, innovative solutions are still possible.

For instance, externally maintained WiFi services that provide satellite-delivered internet within communities are possible under current regulatory and retail arrangements. Such services overcome the need for a fixed connection to the home, resolving access for those who may not reside in the community on a permanent basis, and addressing situations where post-paid billing is not feasible for households. Such services would need to be managed by an intermediary organization or commercial enterprise with experience working in remote communities. Sustainable models might involve payment systems that enable people to pre-pay for data allowances in advance (similar to hotel WiFi systems), covering service, download and power costs.

KNOWING THE DIGITAL DIVIDE

On a final note, our understanding of what we have called 'internet on the outstation' developed over a long-term engagement with the residents. It would not have been possible without an existing level of trust between the Aboriginal organizations involved in the study (the Centre for Appropriate Technology [CAT] and the Central Land Council [CLC]), and the outstation elders and residents. Although there is perhaps much we would do differently if we had the chance again, we hope that other organizations may learn from our efforts as they continue to develop programs with Indigenous communities.

At a more fundamental level, issues such as internet infrastructure, affordability and programs are important, not just for the daily communication activities of those who access these services, but also for the services, shires, schools and organizations that interact with communities on an ongoing basis. Nurturing connections between these groups and the organizations that are working at solving communication barriers (such as the Australian Communications Consumer Action Network and the Indigenous Remote Communications Association) is important, and yet there are few resources to enable such collaboration and knowledge exchange.[3] As for research, on-the-ground experience is necessary when it comes to understanding the digital divide. There is a serious need for ongoing collection of data on remote community ICT infrastructures, as well as basic consumer information including expenditure, device preferences and sharing

---

3   The Broadband for the Bush network is the one forum where this occurs (www. broadbandforthebush.com.au). All four partners in the Home Internet Project were involved in Broadband for the Bush during the life of the project, for the purposes of knowledge sharing and capacity building.

behaviors. However, internet adoption and use is inherently tied to everyday practices, priorities, needs and capacities. Only by understanding the social and cultural aspects of life in remote communities can we begin to know the nature of the divide and the tangible benefits of being online.

Postscript

By early 2016, very few of the desktop computers were still being used in the communities. The residents had not rushed to replace broken machines, although the women we met with all continued to see value in having the internet.

At Imangara, both Emily's and Mary's computers needed repairs. They were paying for the internet, even though they could not use it, and were planning on calling the internet service provider to get it suspended. Louise was using her internet connection with her iPad, as her PC had also died.

Many of the computers had been moved out of Mungalawurru. Only the middle-aged couple at Mungalawurru had kept the internet, which we were told had become slow, either because of the NBN satellite connection, or because their machine was getting old. The woman was paying her ISP bills by check now, an arrangement that suited her much better than direct debit. Karen was still living in Tennant Creek, and was using the internet on her husband's phone and on her daughter's iPad, as the computer had finally stopped working.

The senior woman from Mungalawurru, who had been living and working in town during the years we visited, told us that she plans to retire and move back to the outstation. She was planning to get a computer for herself at that time, and wanted more computers for the community. In her opinion, the real value of having the internet is that her family can look up histories and places, and document culture for young people to learn. Although she described activities such as internet banking as useful, she said they were just everyday needs, not 'our way'.

Rhonda's time was taken up with working in Alice Springs, but her plans to create stories for bilingual education for small children had developed rather than diminished. She said she also hopes to produce books on the wildlife at Tjoritja. She still had her computer and was planning on getting an internet connection in the near future. Rhonda's family were now making their own plans for enterprise at Kwale Kwale, and her mother had recently purchased nine baby peacocks.

BIBLIOGRAPHY

Aboriginal and Torres Strait Islander Committee. 'Everybody's Business: Remote Aboriginal and Torres Strait Community Stores', Canberra: Commonwealth of Australia, 2009.

Altman, J.C., M.C. Dillon and K. Jordan. 'Submission to the House of Representatives Standing Committee on Aboriginal and Torres Strait Islander Affairs Inquiry into Community Stores in Remote Aboriginal and Torres Strait Islander Communities', *CAEPR Topical Issue No. 04/2009*, Canberra: ANU Centre for Aboriginal Economic Policy Research, 2009.

Altman, J. 'Development Options on Aboriginal Land: Sustainable Indigenous Hybrid Economies in the Twenty-First Century', in L. Taylor, G. Ward, G. Henderson, R. Davis and L. Wallis (eds) *The Power of Knowledge, the Resonance of Tradition*, Canberra: Aboriginal Studies Press, 2005.

——. 'A Genealogy of "Demand Sharing": From Pure Anthropology to Public Policy', in Y. Musharbash and M. Barber (eds) *Ethnography and the Production of Anthropological Knowledge: Essays in Honour of Nicolas Peterson*, ANU E Press, 2011, pp. 187-200.

——. *In Search of an Outstations Policy for Indigenous Australians*, Canberra: Centre for Aboriginal Economic Policy Research, 2006.

Amnesty International. *The Land Holds Us: Aboriginal Peoples' Right to Traditional Homelands in the Northern Territory*, Broadway, NSW: Amnesty International, 2011.

Ananny, M. 'From Noxious to Public? Tracing Ethical Dynamics of Social Media Platform Conversions', *Social Media + Society* 1.1 (2015): 1-3.

Anderson, B. and K. Tracey. 'Digital Living: The Impact (or Otherwise) of the Internet on Everday British Life' in C. Haythornthwaite and B. Wellman (eds) *The Internet in Everyday Life*, Malden, MA, USA: Blackwell Publishers Ltd, 2002, pp. 139-163.

ARC Centre of Excellence for Creative Industries and Innovation. 'World Internet Project (Australia)', *http://www.cci.edu.au/projects/world-internet-project-australia*.

Austin-Broos, D. *A Different Inequality: The Politics of Debate About Remote Aboriginal Australia* [Kindle Dx Version], Sydney: Allen & Unwin, 2011.

Australian Bureau of Statistics. 'Australia, Remote and Very Remote (Remoteness Factor), Indigenous Profile, by Household', *www.abs.gov.au/websitedbs/censushome.nsf/home*.

——. 'Census of Population and Housing - Counts of Aboriginal and Torres Strait Islander Peoples', *http://www.abs.gov.au/ausstats/abs@.nsf/Lookup/2075.0main+features32011*.

——. 'Housing and Infrastructure in Aboriginal and Torres Strait Islander Communities', *http://www.abs.gov.au/Ausstats/abs@.nsf/Latestproducts/4710.0Main%20Features420 06?opendocument&tabname=Summary&prodno=4710.0&issue=2006&num=&view.*

——. 'Macdonnel and Barkly Statistical Area 3, Indigenous Profile, by Houshold', http:// abs.gov.au/websitedbs/censushome.nsf/home.

——. 'Patterns of Internet Access in Australia', *http://www.abs.gov.au/ausstats/abs@.nsf/ mf/8146.0.55.001/.*

Australian Communications and Media Authority. 'Communications Report 2009-10', *http://www.acma.gov.au/webwr/_assets/main/lib311995/2009-10_comms_report-com- plete.pdf.*

——. 'Communications Report 2012-13'. Canberra: Commonwealth of Australia, 2013.

——. 'Cybersmart Parents: Connecting Parents to Cyber-Safety Resources', Canberra: Australian Media and Communications Authority, 2010.

——. 'The Internet Service Market and Australians in the Online Environment', Canberra, 2011.

——. 'Telecommunications in Remote Indigenous Communications', *http://www.acma.gov. au/theACMA/telecommunications-in-remote-indigenous-communities.*

Australian Financial Counselling and Credit Reform Association. 'ATM Fees in Indig- enous Communities', *AFCCRA, http://www.afccra.org/media%20releases%20documents/ ATM%20Fees%20in%20Remote%20Indigenous%20Communities.pdf.*

Australian Human Rights Commission. *Social Justice Report 2011,* Sydney: Common- wealth of Australia, 2011.

Australian Private Networks. *Indigenous Communications Program: Final Report,* 2014.

Balogh, M. 'Indigenous Australia Addicted to Facebook', news release, 26 August 2014.

Banerjee, A. and E. Duflo. 'Poor Economics: A Radical Rethinking of the Way to Fight Global Poverty', *Population and Development Review* 374 (2011): 796-797.

Bath, J. and N. Biddle. 'Measures of Indigenous Wellbeing and Their Determinants Across the Lifecourse', CAEPR Lecture Series, ANU Centre for Aboriginal Economic Policy Research, 2011.

Battiste, M. *Indigenous Knowledge and Pedagogy in First Nations Education: A Literature Review with Recommendations*, Ottawa: Apamuwek Institute, 2002.

Batty, P. *Governing Cultural Difference: The Incorporation of the Aboriginal Subject into the Mechanisms of Government with Reference to the Development of Aboriginal Radio and Television in Central Australia*, PhD diss., University of South Australia, Adelaide, 2003.

Beadman, B. '"A Tortuous Trail": Bob Beadman's Short History of Outstations', *Alice Online: Australia from the Inside Out..., http://aliceonline.com.au/2011/10/17/a-tortuous-trail-bob-beadmans-short-history-of-outstations/*.

Bell, D. *Daughters of the Dreaming*, Melbourne: Allen and Unwin, 1983.

Best, M.L. and C.M. Maclay. 'Community Internet Access in Rural Areas: Solving the Economic Sustainability Puzzle' in G.S. Kirkman, P.K. Cornelius, J.D. Sachs and K. Schwab (eds) *The Global Information Technology Report: Readiness for the Networked World*, Oxford: Oxford University Press, 2002, pp. 76-89.

Biddle, N. 'Income', Paper 11: *CAEPR Indigenous Population Project 2011 Census Papers*, Canberra: ANU Centre for Aboriginal Economic Policy Research, 2013.

Blanchard, C.A. *Return to Country: The Aboriginal Homelands Movement in Australia*, Canberra: The House of Representatives Standing Committee on Aboriginal Affairs, 1987.

Brady, F.R., L.E. Dyson and T. Asela. *Indigenous Adoption of Mobile Phones and Oral Culture*, Cultural Attitudes Towards Communication and Technology, Perth: Murdoch University, 2008.

Brady, F., L.E. Dyson and Wujal Wujal Aboriginal Shire Council. *Report to Wujal Wujal Aboriginal Shire Council on Mobile Technology in the Bloomfield River Valley*, 2009.

Brasche, I. and I. Harrington. 'Promoting Teacher Quality and Continuity: Tackling the Disadvantages of Remote Indigenous Schools in the Northern Territory', *Australian Journal of Education* 56.2 (2012): 110-125.

Broadband for the Bush Alliance. *Rethinking the Indigenous Communications Program*, policy paper, 2013.

Brown, S. A., V. Venkatesh and H. Bala. 'Household Technology Use: Integrating Household Life Cycle and the Model of Adoption of Technology in Households', *The Information Society* 22.4 (2006): 205-218.

Byrnes, J. 'Aboriginal Learning Styles and Adult Education: Is a Synthesis Possible?', *Australian Journal of Adult and Community Education* 33.3 (1993): 157-171.

Carlson, B. 'The "New Frontier": Emergent Indigenous Identities and Social Media' in M. Harris, M. Nakata and B. Carlson (eds) *The Politics of Identity: Emerging Indigeneity*, Sydney: University of Technology Sydney E-Press, 2013, pp. 147-168.

Central Australian Youth Link Up Service. 'Annual Attendance Trends Data: July', 2010.

——. 'Papunya Computer Room', *http://caylus.org.au/papunya-computer-room/*.

——. 'Proposal Re: Better Way of Providing Broadband in Remote Communities', Alice Springs: Tangentyere Council, 2014.

Central Land Council (CLC). 'Divas Chat Causing Social Chaos', *Land Rights News,* Alice Springs: Central Land Council, 2012, pp. 4-6

Chakravartty, P. 'Rebranding Development Communications in Emergent India', *Nordicom Review* 33 (Special Issue) (2012): 65-76.

Coalition. 'The Coalition's Policy for E-Government and the Digital Economy', Canberra, 2013.

Commonwealth of Australia. 'Budget Paper No. 2: Expense Measures: A New Remote Indigenous Housing Strategy', *http://www.budget.gov.au/2015-16/content/bp2/html/bp2_expense-19.htm*.

——. 'Budget: Indigenous Partnerships', *http://www.budget.gov.au/2005-06/ministerial/html/dotars-12.htm*.

Corner, S. 'Universal Telecommunications Services: A Brief History and Analysis of the Issues Surrounding the New Australian Legislation on the Universal Service Obligation', *Telecommunications Journal of Australia* 62.2 (2012).

Correa, T. and I. Pavez. *Digital Inclusion in Rural Areas: A Qualitative Exploration of Challenges Faced by People from Isolated Communities*, International Communications Association Conference, San Juan, 2015.

Cowlishaw, G. 'Infanticide in Aboriginal Australia', *Oceania* (1978): 262-283.

——. 'A New Protection Policy?', *Inside Story*, 2013, *http://insidestory.org.au/a-new-protection-policy/*.

——. 'Socialization and Subordination Among Australian Aborigines', *Man* (1982): 492-507.

——. *Women's Realm: A Study of Socialization, Sexuality and Reproduction Among Australian Aborigines*, PhD diss., University of Sydney, Sydney, 1979.

Crouch, A. 'The Community Phone Project: An Overview', *DKCRC Working Paper 46*, Alice Springs: Desert Knowledge CRC, 2009.

—— *Home Internet for Remote Indigenous Communities: Technical Report*, Alice Springs: Centre for Appropriate Technology, 2014.

Crump, B. and A. McIlroy. 'The Digital Divide: Why the "Don't-Want-Tos" Won't Compute: Lessons from a New Zealand ICT Project', *First Monday* 8.12 (2003).

Daly, A.E. 'Bridging the Digital Divide: The Role of Community Online Access Centres in Indigenous Communities', Canberra: ANU Centre for Aboriginal Economic Policy Research, 2005.

Davenport, W.H. 'Two Kinds of Value in the Eastern Solomon Islands', in A. Appadurai (ed.) *The Social Life of Things: Commodities in Cultural Perspective*, Cambridge, Cambridge University Press, 1986, pp. 95-109.

Davies, S. *Urban Based Support for Rural and Remote Australian Telecommunications*, Broadband for the Bush Alliance, 2014.

DiMaggio, P. and E. Hargittai. 'From the "Digital Divide" to "Digital Inequality": Studying Internet Use as Penetration Increases', Working Paper 15, Center for Arts and Cultural Policy Studies, Princeton University, 2001.

'DIY Telecoms'. *The Economist*, *http://www.economist.com/news/technology-quarterly/21645498-fed-up-failings-big-operators-remote-mexican-communities-are-acting*.

Donovan, M. 'Is It a Digital Divide Because It's No Good When Talking from an Aboriginal Point? Giving Aboriginal Design to Educational Practices', *http://www.persons.org.uk/ci/mm/nmtc/nmtc2/donovan%20paper.pdf*.

——. 'Can Information Communication Technological Tools Be Used to Suit Aboriginal Learning Pedagogies', *Information Technology and Indigenous People* (2007): 93-104.

Doron, A. and R. Jeffrey. *The Great Indian Phone Book: How the Cheap Cell Phone Changes Business, Politics, and Daily Life*, Cambridge: Harvard University Press, 2013.

Dutton, W.H., A. Shepherd and C. Di Gennaro. 'Digital Divides and Choices Reconfiguring Access: National and Cross National Patterns of Internet Diffusion and Use', in B. Anderson, M. Brynin, Y. Raban and J. Gershuny (eds) *Information and Communication Technologies in Society E-Living in a Digital Europe*, London: Routledge, 2007, pp. 31-45.

Dyson, L.E. 'Design for a Culturally Affirming Indigenous Computer Literacy Course', 2002.

Eady, M. and S. Woodcock. 'Understanding the Need: Using Collaboratively Created Draft Guiding Principles to Direct Online Synchronous Learning in Indigenous Communities', *International Journal for Educational Integrity* 6.2 (2010): 24-40.

Earl, P.E. 'Economics and Psychology: A Survey', *The Economic Journal* 100.402 (1990): 718-755.

Ellen, R. and R. Herrick. 'John Elferink Dismisses Idea for Free Wi-Fi in Alice Springs Town Camps to Reduce Youth Crime', *ABC News, http://www.abc.net.au/news/2015-04-10/ elferink-dismisses-wi-fi-idea-for-alice-springs-town-camps/6384214*.

Elliot, C. 'Social Death and Disenfranchised Grief: An Alyawarr Case Study' in K. Glaskin (ed.) *Mortality, Mourning and Mortuary Practices in Indigenous Australia*, London: Ashgate Publishing, 2008, pp. 103-120.

Enghel, F. and K. Wilkins. 'Communication, Media and Development: Problems and Perspectives', *Nordicom Review* 33 (Special Issue) (2012).

Ewing, S. and J. Thomas. *The Internet in Australia*, Brisbane: ARC Centre of Excellence for Creative Industries and Innovation, Queensland University of Technology, 2010.

Fairlie, R.W., D.O. Beltran and K.K. Das. 'Home Computers and Educational Outcomes: Evidence from the NLSY97 and CPS', Economic Inquiry* 48.3 (2010).

Featherstone, D. 'The Aboriginal Invention of Broadband: How Yarnangu Are Using ICTs in the Ngaanyatjarra Lands of Western Australia' in L. Ormond-Parker, A. Corn, C. Fforde, K. Obata and S. O'sullivan (eds) *Information Technologies and Indigenous Communities*, Canberra: AIATSIS Research Publications, 2013, pp. 27-52.

J. Finlayson, and A.J. Auld. 'Shoe or Stew?: Balancing Wants and Needs in Indigenous Households: A Study of Appropriate Income Support Payments and Policies for Families', *CAEPR Discussion Paper No. 182*, Canberra: ANU Centre for Aboriginal Economic Policy Research, 1999.

Fitzgerald, L. 'New 3G Network Falls Short for Stations and Communities Near Barrow Creek, Northern Territory', *http://www.abc.net.au/news/2014-08-25/barrow-creek-3g-network-lacking/5693386*.

Fletcher, P. 'Speech to the ACCAN USO Forum', *http://paulfletcher.com.au/speeches/portfolio-speeches/item/1316-speech-to-the-accan-uso-forum.html*.

Fogarty, W. *'You Got Any Truck?' Vehicles and Decentralised Mobile Service-Provision in Remote Indigenous Australia,* Canberra: ANU Centre for Aboriginal Economic Policy Research, 2005.

'Free Wi-Fi in Town Camps Could Solve Anti-Social Youth Problem in Alice Springs, Says CAYLUS', *http://www.abc.net.au/news/2015-04-08/free-wifi-in-alice-springs-town-camps-could-solve-youth-problems/6378914*.

Galperin, H. and J. Mariscal. 'Digital Poverty: Latin American and Caribbean Perspectives', *Practical Publishing, http://www.idrc.ca/EN/Resources/Publications/openebooks/342-3/index.html*.

Galperin, H. and F. Bar. 'The Microtelco Opportunity: Evidence from Latin America', *Information Technologies & International Development* 3.2 (2006): 73-86.

Ginsburg, F. 'Rethinking the Digital Age' in D. Hesmondhalgh and J. Toynbee (eds) *The Media and Social Theory*, New York: Routledge, 2008: 127-144.

Godinho, *V. Money, Financial Capability and Well-Being in Indigenous Australia,* PhD diss., Graduate School of Business and Law, RMIT University, Melbourne, 2014.

Goggin, G. and J. Clark. 'Mobile Phones and Community Development: A Contact Zone between Media and Citizenship', *Development in Practice* 19.4-5 (2009): 585-597.

Goolsbee, A. and P.J. Klenow. 'Evidence on Learning and Network Externalities in the Diffusion of Home Computers', *Journal of Law and Economics* 45.2 (2002): 317-343.

Granovetter, M.S. 'The Strength of Weak Ties', *American Journal of Sociology* (1973): 1360-1380.

Green, L., Brady, D., Olafsson, K., Hartley J. and C. Lumby. 'Risks and Safety for Australian Children on the Internet: Full Findings from the AU Kids Online Survey of 9-16 Year Olds and Their Parents', *Cultural Science Journal* 4.1 (2011): 1-73.

Grey-Gardner, R. and M. Young. *Utopia Homelands Project: Lessons from Experience,* Centre for Appropriate Technology, Urapuntja Aboriginal Corporation and the Australian Government Department of Prime Minister and Cabinet, 2014.

Grissmer, D.W., R.F. Subotnik and M. Orland. *A Guide to Incorporating Multiple Methods in Randomized Controlled Trials to Assess Intervention Effects,* Washington, DC: American Psychological Association, 2009.

Hamilton, A. 'A Complex Strategical Situation: Gender and Power in Aboriginal Australia' in N. Grieve and P. Grimshaw (eds) *Australian Imjmen: Feminist Perspectives*, Melbourne: Oxford University Press, 1981, pp. 69-85.

Harris, S. and J. Kinslow-Harris. *Culture and Learning: Tradition and Education in North-East Arnhem Land*, Canberra: Australian Institute of Aboriginal and Torres Strait Islander Studies, 1980.

Harrison, N. *Teaching and Learning in Aboriginal Education*, Melbourne: Oxford University Press, 2011.

Hartley, J. and J. Potts. *Cultural Science: A Natural History of Stories, Demes, Knowledge and Innovation*, London: Bloomsbury Publishing, 2014.

Hartley, J. and E. Rennie. 'Show Business for Ugly People? Media Politics and E-Democracy', Australian Electronic Governance Conference, Melbourne, 14-15 April 2004.

Hatt, T., K. Okeleke and M. Meloan. 'Closing the Coverage Gap: A View from Asia', *GSMA Intelligence*, https://gsmaintelligence.com/research/?file=e245c423854fcfd38eeae0a9 18cc91c8&download.

Helsper, E. *Digital Inclusion: An Analysis of Social Disadvantage and the Information Society*, Department for Communities and Local Government, 2008.

——. 'A Corresponding Fields Model for the Links Between Social and Digital Exclusion', *Communication Theory* 22.4 (2012): 403-426.

Helsper, E., A. V'san Deursen and R. Eynon. *Tangible Outcomes of Internet Use: From Digital Skills to Tangible Outcomes Project Report*, Oxford Internet Institute, University of Twente and London School of Economics and Political Science, 2015.

Hems, L., C. Connolly, and M. Georgouras. 'Measuring Financial Exclusion in Australia', Centre for Social Impact (CSI), University of New South Wales, for National Australia Bank, 2012.

Hiatt, L. 'Traditional Attitudes to Land Resources' in R. M. Berndt (ed.) *Aboriginal Sites: Rites and Resource Development*, Perth: University of Western Australia Press, 1982, pp. 47-53.

Hilbert, M. 'The End Justifies the Definition: The Manifold Outlooks on the Digital Divide and Their Practical Usefulness for Policy-Making', *Telecommunications Policy* 35.8 (2011): 715-736.

Hinkson, M. 'What's in a Dedication? On Being a Warlpiri DJ', *The Australian Journal of Anthropology* 15.2 (2004): 143-162.

Hogan, E. 'Behind the Mulga Curtain', *Inside Story*, 11 July 2014, http://insidestory.org.au/behind-the-mulga-curtain.

——. 'Gender and ICT access in remote central Australian Aboriginal contexts', *Australian Aboriginal Studies*, 2016.1 (2016).

Hogan, E., E. Rennie, A. Crouch, A. Wright, R. Gregory and J. Thomas. 'Submission to the Inquiry into Issues Surrounding Cyber-Safety for Indigenous Australians', Brisbane: ARC Centre of Excellence for Creative Industries and Innovation, Queensland University of Technology, 2013.

Howard, S. and E. Rennie. 'Free for All: A Case Study Examining Implementation Factors of One-to-One Device Programs', *Computers in the Schools* 30.4 (2013): 359-377.

Hughes, H. *Lands of Shame: Aboriginal and Torres Strait Islander 'Homelands' in Transition*, Sydney: Centre for Independent Studies, 2007.

Hughes, H. and M. Hughes. *Indigenous Education 2012*, Sydney: Centre for Independent Studies, 2012.

Hughes, P. and A.J. More. *Aboriginal Ways of Learning*, Adelaide: Paul Hughes, 2004.

——. 'Aboriginal Ways of Learning and Learning Styles', Brisbane: *Australian Association for Research in Education*, 1997.

Hunter, B. 'Indigenous Social Exclusion: Insights and Challenges for the Concept of Social Inclusion', *Family Matters*, 82 (2009): 52.

Huyer, S. and T. Sikoska. 'Overcoming the Gender Digital Divide: Understanding ICTs and Their Potential for the Empowerment of Women', INSTRAW Research Paper Series No. 1, 2003.

Indigenous Housing and Infrastructure Branch of the Department of Family and Community Services. *Review of the National Homelands Policy: Stage One*, Alice Springs: Centre for Appropriate Technology, 2004.

Introna, L.D., and H. Nissenbaum. 'Shaping the Web: Why the Politics of Search Engines Matters', *The Information Society* 16.3 (2000): 169-185.

Iten, L. *Cyber Safety Program Report*, Alice Springs: Northern Territory Library and Central Australian Youth Link Up Service, 2014.

Ito, M., J. Antin, M. Finn, A. Law, A. Manion, S. Mitnick, D. Schlossberg, S. Yardi and H. A. Horst, *Hanging Out, Messing Around, and Geeking Out: Kids Living and Learning with New Media*, Cambridge, MA: MIT Press, 2009.

Johns, G. *No Job No House: An Economically Strategic Approach to Remote Aboriginal Housing*, Canberra: The Menzies Research Centre, 2009.

Joint Select Committee on Cyber-Safety. 'High-Wire Act: Cyber-Safety and the Young', *Interim Report*, Canberra, 2011.

Kaberry, P.M. *Aboriginal Women*, London: George Routledge and Sons Pty Ltd, 1939.

Keen, I. 'The Interpretation of Aboriginal "Property" on the Australian Colonial Frontier' in I. Keen (ed.) *Aboriginal Participation in Australian Economies: Historical and Anthropological Perspectives*, Canberra:: ANU Press, 2010.

Kerins, S. 'The First-Ever Northern Territory Homelands/Outstations Policy', *CAEPR Topical Issue No. 09/2009*, Canberra: ANU Centre for Aboriginal Economic Policy Research, 2009.

Kowal, E. 'Is Culture the Problem or the Solution? Outstation Health and the Politics of Remoteness' in J. Altman and M. Hinkson (eds) *Culture Crisis: Anthropology and Politics in Aboriginal Australia*, Sydney: University of New South Wales Press, 2010, pp. 253-276.

Kraemer, K. L., J. Dedrick and P. Sharma, 'One Laptop Per Child: Vision Vs. Reality', *Communications of the ACM* 52.6 (2009): 66-73.

Kral, I. *Plugged In: Remote Australian Indigenous Youth and Digital Culture*, Canberra: ANU Centre for Aboriginal Economic Policy Research, 2010.

——. 'Youth Media as Cultural Practice: Remote Indigenous Youth Speaking Out Loud', *Australian Aboriginal Studies*, 1 (2011): 4-16.

Kral, I. and I. Falk. *What Is All That Learning For? Indigenous Adult English Literacy Practices, Training, Community Capacity and Health*, Adelaide: NCVER, 2004.

Lattas, A. and B. Morris. 'The Politics of Suffering and the Politics of Anthropology' in J. Altman and M. Hinkson (eds) *Culture Crisis: Anthropology and Politics in Aboriginal Australia*, Sydney: University of New South Wales Press, 2010, pp. 97-133.

Lenovo. 'TBR Quality Project', *http://www.partnerinfo.lenovo.com/partners/us/products/downloads/thinkcentre-mseries/TBR-Quality-Study-ExecSummary.pdf*.

Liston, G. 'Remote Community Hopes to Erect Giant Neon Crucifix', *ABC News, http://www.abc.net.au/news/2008-09-25/fiery-debate-over-dpp-decision/521100*.

Livingstone, S. and L. Haddon. *EU Kids Online: Final Report*, London: EU Kids Online, 2009.

Livingstone, S. 'Taking Risky Opportunities in Youthful Content Creation: Teenagers' Use of Social Networking Sites for Intimacy, Privacy and Self-Expression', *New Media & Society* 10.3 (2008): 393-411.

Livingstone, S. and E. Helsper. 'Gradations in Digital Inclusion: Children, Young People and the Digital Divide', *New Media & Society* 9.4 (2007): 671-696.

Loewenstein, G. and S. Issacharoff. 'Source Dependence in the Valuation of Objects', *Journal of Behavioral Decision Making* 7.3 (1994): 157-168.

Lydon, J. '"Our Sense of Beauty": Visuality, Space and Gender on Victoria's Aboriginal Reserves, South-Eastern Australia', *History and Anthropology* 16.2 (2005): 211-233.

Macdonald, G. 'Economies and Personhood: Demand Sharing among the Wiradjuri of New South Wales' in G. Wenzel, G. Hovelsrud-Broda and N. Kishigami (eds) *The Social Economy of Sharing: Resource Allocation and Modern Hunter-Gatherers*, Osaka: National Museum of Ethnology, 2000, pp. 87-111.

Mahon, A. 'Deadly Dreaming: Bi-Cultural Strategies for Working with Indigenous Adults in Education', Australian Council for Adult Literacy conference, Surfers Paradise, Australia, 3-4 October, 2008, *http://www.acal.edu.au/conference/08/Deadly_Dreaming_Mahon.pdf*.

Malin, M. and D. Maidment. 'Evaluation of Irrkerlantye Learning Centre', unpublished report, Darwin: Cooperative Research Centre for Aboriginal and Tropical Health, 2003.

Mares, P. 'Homeland Security: NT Indigenous Affairs Minister Outlines Policy', *ABC News, http://www.abc.net.au/radionational/programs/nationalinterest/homeland-security-nt-indigenous-affairs-minister/3147812#transcript*.

Mayne, A. *Alternative Interventions. Aboriginal Homelands, Outback Australia and the Centre for Appropriate Technology*, Adelaide: Wakefield Press, 2014.

Mazzarella, W. 'Beautiful Balloon: The Digital Divide and the Charisma of New Media in India', *American Ethnologist* 374 (2010): 783-804.

McCallum, K. and F. Papandrea. 'Community Business: The Internet in Remote Australian Indigenous Communities', *New Media & Society* (2009): 1230-1251.

McElhinney, S. 'Telecommunications Liberalisation and the Quest for Universal Service in Australia', *Telecommunications Policy* 25.4 (2001): 233-248.

McGregor, R. *Indifferent Inclusion: Aboriginal People and the Australian Nation,* Canberra: Canberra Aboriginal Studies Press, 2011.

Merlan, F. 'Gender in Aboriginal Society: A Review', in R.M. Berndt and R. Tonkinson (eds) *Social Anthropology and Australian Aboriginal Studies,* Canberra: Aboriginal Studies Press, 1988, pp. 15-76.

Michaels, E. *The Aboriginal Invention of Television in Central Australia, 1982-1986: Report of the Fellowship to Assess the Impact of Television in Remote Aboriginal Communities,* Canberra: Australian Institute of Aboriginal Studies, 1986.

———. *Bad Aboriginal Art and Other Essays: Tradition, Media, and Technological Horizons,* Vol. 3, Minneapolis: University of Minnesota Press, 1994.

Miller, D. and H.A. Horst. 'The Digital and the Human: A Prospectus for Digital Anthropology' in H. A. Horst and D. Miller (eds) *Digital Anthropology,* London: Bloomsbury Publishing, 2013, pp. 3-35.

Moran, M. 'The Viability of "Hub" Settlements', *Dialogue* 29.1 (2010): 38-51.

Morsillo, R. 'Affordable Broadband for All Australians', *Telecommunications Journal of Australia* 62.5 (2012): 78.1-78.16.

Musharbash, Y. '"Only Whitefella Take That Road": Culture Seen Through the Intervention at Yuendumu', in Hinkson (eds) *Culture Crisis: Anthropology and Politics in Aboriginal Australia,* Sydney: University of New South Wales Press, 2010, pp. 302-318.

———. *Yuendumu Everyday: Contemporary Life in Remote Aboriginal Australia,* Canberra: Aboriginal Studies Press, 2009.

Myers, F. 'Burning the Truck and Holding the Country: Pintupi Forms of Property and Identity', in E.N. Wilmsen (eds) *We Are Here: Politics of Aboriginal Land Tenure,* Los Angeles: University of California Press, 1989, pp. 15-42.

———. 'Introduction: The Empire of Things', in F. Myers (ed.) *The Empire of Things: Regimes of Value and Material Culture,* Santa Fe: School of American Research Press, 2001, pp. 3-64.

———. *Pintupi Country, Pintupi Self: Sentiment, Place and Politics Among Western Desert Aborigines*, Berkeley, Los Angeles: University of California Press, 1986.

———. *Pintupi Country, Pintupi Self: Sentiment, Place, and Politics Among Western Desert Aborigines*, Washington DC: Smithsonian Institute, 1986.

———. 'Place, Identity and Exchange in a Totemic System: Nurturance and the Process of Social Reproduction in Pintupi Society', in J. Fajans (ed.) *Exchanging Products: Producing Exchange*, Sydney: University of Sydney, 1993, pp. 3-57.

———. 'Some Properties of Culture and Persons', in R.A. Ghosh (ed.) *CODE: Collaborative Ownership and the Digital Economy*, Cambridge MA London: MIT Press, 2005, pp. 45-60.

Nafus, D. and J. Sherman. 'Big Data, Big Questions: This One Does Not Go Up to 11: The Quantified Self Movement as an Alternative Big Data Practice', *International Journal of Communication* 8 (2014): 11.

Nicholls, A.V. *The Social Life of the Computer in Ramingining*, Darwin: Charles Darwin University, 2009.

Nobbs, C. 'Ara Irititja: Protecting the Past, Accessing the Future: Indigenous Memories in a Digital Age', *Artlink* 24.1 (2004): 50-51.

Norris, P. *The Worldwide Digital Divide*, Annual Meeting of the Political Studies Association of the UK, London School of Economics and Political Science, 10-13 April 2000.

Northern Territory Department of Education. *Learning Lessons: An Independent Review of Indigenous Education in the Northern Territory*, Darwin: Northern Territory Department of Education, 1999, *http://www.education.nt.gov.au/__data/assets/pdf_file/0005/7475/ learning_lessons_review.pdf*.

———. 'Enrolment and Attendance Statistics', *http://www.education.nt.gov.au/students/ at-school/enrolment-attendance/enrolment-attendance-statistics/2013-enrolment-and- attendance-statistics*.

Northern Territory Government Department of Corporate and Information Services, Submission to the Regional Telecommunications Independent Review Committee, 2015, *https://www.communications.gov.au/sites/g/files/net301/f/Northern%20Territory%20 Government%20-%20Public%20Submission%20RTIRC%202015.pdf*.

Nussbaum, M. 'Capabilities as Fundamental Entitlements: Sen and Social Justice', *Feminist Economics* 9.2-3 (2003): 33-59.

O'Connell, J.F. 'Room to Move: Contemporary Alyawara Settlement Patterns and Their Implications for Aboriginal Housing Policy' in M. Heppell (ed.) *A Black Reality: Aboriginal Camps and Housing in Remote Australia*, Canberra: Australian Institute of Aboriginal Studies, 1979, pp. 97-120.

Olsen, P. 'Teenagers Say Goodbye to Facebook and Hello to Messenger Apps', *The Guardian*, 10 November 2013.

Ormond-Parker, L., A. Corn, K. Obata and S. O'Sullivan, (eds). *Information Technology and Indigenous Communities*, AIATSIS National Indigenous Studies Conference, 2009 and Information Technologies and Indigenous Communities Symposium, 2010, Canberra: AIATSIS, 2013.

Parliament of Australia Senate Standing Committee on Community Affairs. *Inquiry into Issues Surrounding Cyber-Safety for Indigenous Australians*, Canberra: Joint Select Committee on Cyber-Safety, 2013.

Pearce, K.E. and R.E. Rice. 'Digital Divides from Access to Activities: Comparing Mobile and Personal Computer Internet Users', *Journal of Communication* 63.4 (2013): 721-744.

Pearson, N. *Radical Hope: Education and Equality in Australia.* Melbourne: Schwartz Publishing, 2011.

Peter Farr Consultants Australasia. *Connecting Our Communities: Sustainable Networking Strategies for Australian Remote Indigenous Communities*, Canberra: Department of Communications, Information Technology and the Arts, 2003.

Peterson, N. 'Demand Sharing: Reciprocity and the Pressure for Generosity Among Foragers', *American Anthropologist* 95.4 (1993): 860-874.

Pierce, J.L., T. Kostova and K.T. Dirks. 'The State of Psychological Ownership: Integrating and Extending a Century of Research', *Review of General Psychology* 7.1 (2003): 84.

Raiche, H. *Universal Communications in a Broadband World: Working Paper*, Inaugural Australian Communications Consumer Action Network (ACCAN) Conference, Melbourne, 2010.

Razak, I. 'Telstra Accused of Ripping Off Aborigines', *ABC News*, http://www.abc.net.au/news/stories/2009/09/09/2680645.

Regional Telecommunications Independent Review Committee. *Regional Telecommunications Review 2015: Unlocking the Potential in Regional Australia*, Canberra: Commonwealth of Australia, 2015.

Regional Telecommunications Inquiry. *Connecting Regional Australia*, Canberra: Department of Communications, Information Technology and the Arts, 2002.

Renfrew, C. 'Varna and the Emergence of Wealth in Prehistoric Europe' in A. Appadurai (ed.) *The Social Life of Things: Commodities in Cultural Perspective*, Cambridge: Cambridge University Press, 1988, pp. 141-168.

Rennie, E. 'Internet on the Outstation', *Inside Story*, 9 May 2011, *http://insidestory.org.au/internet-on-the-outstation*.

Rennie, E., A. Crouch, J. Thomas and P. Taylor. 'Beyond Public Access? Reconsidering Broadband for Remote Indigenous Communities', *Communication, Politics & Culture* 43.1 (2010): 48-69.

Rennie, E., A. Crouch, A. Wright and J. Thomas. *Home Internet for Remote Indigenous Communities*, Australian Communications Consumer Action Network, 2011.

——. 'At Home on the Outstation: Barriers to Home Internet in Remote Indigenous Communities', *Telecommunications Policy* 37.6 (2013): 583–593.

Rennie, E. and J. Potts. 'Auction Subsidies and the Universal Service Obligation: The Case for Remote Indigenous Communities', Submission to the Regional Telecommunications Independent Review (RTIRC), 2015.

Rennie, E. and J. Hartley. *The Story So Far: Digital Storytelling, Narrative and the New Literacy*, Image, Text and Sound Conference, School of Creative Media, RMIT, Melbourne 2004.

Rhizomatica. 'About', *http://rhizomatica.org/about-2/*.

Robinson, G. 'Families, Generations, and Self: Conflict, Loyalty, and Recognition in an Australian Aboriginal Society', *Ethos* 25.3 (1997): 303-332.

Robinson, J.A., and R.M. Nichol. 'Building Bridges Between Aboriginal and Western Mathematics: Creating an Effective Mathematics Learning Environment', *Education in Rural Australia* 8.2 (1998): 9-17.

Rogers, E.M. *Diffusion of Innovations*, 5th ed, New York: Free Press, 2003.

Rowse, T, 'Re-figuring "Indigenous culture"' in J. Altman and M. Hinkson (eds) *Culture Crisis: Anthropology and Politics in Aboriginal Australia*, Kensington: UNSW Press, 2010, pp. 153-178.

Sanders, W. *Working Future: A Critique of Policy by Numbers*, Canberra: Centre for Aboriginal Economic Policy Research, 2010.

Sandvig, C. 'The Internet as an Infrastructure', *The Oxford Handbook of Internet Studies*, 2013, 86-108.

Sansom, B. *The Camp at Wallaby Cross: Aboriginal Fringe Dwellers in Darwin*, Canberra: Australian Institute of Aboriginal Studies, 1980.

Schwab, R.G. *The Calculus of Reciprocity: Principles and Implications of Aboriginal Sharing*, Canberra: Centre for Aboriginal Economic Policy Research, 1995.

Seemann, K.W., M. Parnell, S. McFallan and S. Tucker. *Housing for Livelihoods: The Lifecycle of Housing and Infrastructure Through a Whole-of-System Approach in Remote Aboriginal Settlements*, Vol. 29, Alice Springs: Desert Knowledge CRC, 2008.

Selwyn, N. 'Reconsidering Political and Popular Understandings of the Digital Divide', *New Media & Society* 6.3 (2004): 341-362.

Selwyn, N., S. Gorard and J. Furlong. 'Whose Internet Is It Anyway? Exploring Adults' (Non) Use of the Internet in Everyday Life', *European Journal of Communication* 20.1 (2005): 5-26.

Sen, A. *Social Exclusion: Concept, Application, and Scrutiny*, Asian Development Bank, 2000.

Servaes, J. 'Introduction' in J. Servaes (ed.) *Communication for Development and Social Change*, New Delhi: Sage, 2008, pp. 14-30.

Shaw, G., and P. D'Abbs. *Community Safety and Wellbeing Research Study: Consolidated Report*, Canberra: Department of Families, Housing, Community Services and Indigenous Affairs, 2011.

Sleath, E. and N. Maloney. 'Mobile Phone Hotspots Trialled in the Outback', *ABC News*, *http://www.abc.net.au/local/stories/2015/03/16/4198439.htm*.

Smith, D.E. *Toward an Aboriginal Household Expenditure Survey: Conceptual, Methodological and Cultural Considerations*, Canberra: ANU Centre for Aboriginal Economic Policy Research, 1991.

Sreekumar, T.T., and M. Rivera-Sánchez. 'ICTs and Development: Revisiting the Asian Experience', *Science Technology & Society* 13.2 (2008): 159-174.

Sutton, P. *The Politics of Suffering: Indigenous Australia and the End of the Liberal Consensus*, Carlton: Melbourne University Publishing, 2009.

Tangentyere Council Research Hub and Central Land Council. *Ingerrekenhe Antirrkweme: Mobile Phone Use Among Low Income Aboriginal People: A Central Australian Snapshot*, Alice Springs: Tangentyere Council Research Hub and Central Land Council, 2007.

Tanner, S. *Measuring the Impact of Digital Resources: The Balanced Value Impact Model*, London: King's College, 2012.

Taylor, J. 'Housing Programs at Edward River and Mitchell River Aboriginal Reserves' in M. Heppell (ed.) *A Black Reality: Aboriginal Camps and Housing in Remote Australia*, Canberra: Australian Institute of Aboriginal Studies, 1979, pp. 207-228.

———. *Population and Diversity: Policy Implications of Emerging Indigenous Demographic Trends*, Canberra: Centre for Aboriginal Economic Policy Research, 2006.

Telecommunications Action Plan for Remote Indigenous Communities, Report on the Strategic Study for Improving Telecommunications in Remote Indigenous Communities, Canberra: Department of Communications, Information Technology and the Arts, 2002.

Telstra. 'Universal Service Obligation Standard Marketing Plan', *https://www.telstra.com.au/content/dam/tcom/personal/consumer-advice/doc/consumer/uso-standard-marketing-plan.doc*.

Tenhunen, S. 'Mobile Technology in the Village: ICTs, Culture, and Social Logistics in India', *Journal of the Royal Anthropological Institute* 14.3 (2008): 515-534.

Thas, A., C. Ramilo and C. Cinoco. 'Gender and ICT', *UNDP Asia-Pacific Development Information Programme E-Primer*, New Delhi: Elsevier, 2007.

———. 'Inquiry into Petrol Sniffing and Substance Abuse in Central Australia', Commonwealth of Australia, *http://www.aph.gov.au/Parliamentary_Business/Committees/Senate/Community_Affairs/Completed_inquiries/2008-10/petrol_sniffing_substance_abuse08/index*.

Thomson, D. F. *Bindibu Country*, Melbourne: Thomas Nelson, 1975.

Thorner, S. 'Imagining an Indigital Interface: Ara Irititja Indigenizes the Technologies of Knowledge Management', *Collections* 6.3 (2010): 125-146.

Tingle, L. *Political Amnesia: How We Forgot How to Govern*, Quarterly Essay, Melbourne: Black Inc., 2015.

Tonkinson, R. *The Jigalong Mob: Aboriginal Victors of the Desert Crusade*, Menlo Park, Calif: Cummings Publishing Company, 1974.

US Department of Commerce. *A Nation Online: How Americans Are Expanding Their Use of the Internet*, Economics and Statistics Administration and National Telecommunications and Information Administration, 2002.

Van Deursen, A., J. Van Dijk. 'Increasing Inequalities in What We Do Online: A Longitudinal Cross Sectional Analysis of Internet Activities Among the Dutch Population (2010 to 2013) over Gender, Age, Education, and Income', *Telematics and Informatics* 32.2 (2015): 259-272.

Van Dijk, J. and K. Hacker. 'The Digital Divide as a Complex and Dynamic Phenomenon', *The Information Society* 19.4 (2003): 315-326.

Vanstone, A. *Beyond Conspicuous Compassion: Indigenous Australians Deserve More Than Good Intentions*, Address to the Australia and New Zealand School of Government, Australian National University, Canberra, 7 December 2005.

Verran, H. and M. Christie. 'Postcolonial Databasing? Subverting Old Appropriations, Developing New Associations' in J. Leach and L. Wilson (eds) *Subversion, Conversion, Development: Diversity and the Adoption and Use of Information and Communication Technologies*, Cambridge: MIT Press, 2014, pp. 57-76.

Vodafone Hutchison Australia. *Regional Telecommunications Review 2015: Submission by Vodafone Hutchison Australia*, 2015.

Warschauer, M. 'Dissecting the "Digital Divide": A Case Study in Egypt', *The Information Society* 19.4 (2003): 297-304.

Warschauer, M. and T. Matuchniak, 'New Technology and Digital Worlds: Analyzing Evidence of Equity in Access, Use, and Outcomes', *Review of Research in Education* 34.1 (2010): 180.

Weber, S. and S. Dixon. *Growing Up Online: Young People and Digital Technologies*, New York: Palgrave Macmillan, 2007.

Weiner, A.B. 'Cultural Difference and the Density of Objects', *American Ethnologist* 21.2 (1994): 391-403.

Wilson, K.R., J.S. Wallin and C. Reiser. 'Social Stratification and the Digital Divide', *Social Science Computer Review* 21.2 (2003): 133-143.

Woolcock, M. and D. Narayan. 'Social Capital: Implications for Development Theory, Research, and Policy', *The World Bank Research Observer* 15, no. 2 (2000): 225-249.

Yunkaporta, T. *Aboriginal Pedagogies at the Cultural Interface,* Professional Doctorate (Research) thesis, James Cook University, Townsville, Qld, 2009.

LIST OF ACRONYMS

ABS   Australian Bureau of Statistics

ACCAN   Australian Communications Consumer Action Network

ATSIC   Aboriginal and Torres Strait Islander Commission

CAT   Centre for Appropriate Technology

CDEP   Community Development Employment Projects

CLA   Community Living Area

CLC   Central Land Council

ICP   Indigenous Communications Program

ICT   Information and Communications Technology

ISS   Interim Satellite Service

LTSS   Long Term Satellite Service

NBN   National Broadband Network

NTER   Northern Territory Emergency Response

NTIA   National Telecommunications and Information Administration

RIPIA   Remote Indigenous Public Internet Access

RTIRC   Regional Telecommunications Independent Review Committee

STS   Standard Telephone Services

TAPRIC Telecommunications Action Plan for Remote Indigenous Communities

USO   Universal Service Obligation

APPENDIXES

Appendix 1: Transition to the National Broadband Network (NBN) Interim Satellite Service (ISS)

Take-up of ISS services for the majority of householders was consistent with their intentions in September 2013. In total, ten households (compared with seventeen households or community buildings originally connected in the project) ultimately retained the use of the internet. There has been considerable change in the total composition of households engaged in the project since the original implementation in mid-2011: a number of households were added and/or changed resident members, and most of the shared building computers were re-distributed to individual households along the way. The table below summarizes these changes.

Table 1: Changes of status of buildings and houses

Community	Building	Original status mid-2011	Post transition status early 2014		
				Internet connections?	Original occupants/ users?
Kwale Kwale	Community shed	2 shared computers	1 shared computer	No	Yes
	Residence 1	1 computer	1 computer	No	Yes
	Residence 2	1 computer	1 computer	No	Yes
			1 computer	No	
Mun-galawurru	Community shed	2 shared computers	Nil		No
	Residence 1	Nil	1 computer	Yes	No
	Residence 2 (note 1)	1 computer	1 computer	No (note 1)	No

Community	Building	Original status mid-2011	Post transition status early 2014		
	Residence 3	1 computer	1 computer	Yes	Yes
	Residence 4	1 computer	1 computer	No	No
Imangara	Women's Centre	2 shared computers	Nil		No
	Residence 1	1 computer	1 computer	Yes	No
	Residence 2	1 computer	1 computer	Yes	Yes
	Residence 3	1 computer	1 computer	Yes	Yes
	Residence 4	1 computer	1 computer	No	No
	Residence 5	1 computer	1 computer	Yes	No
	Residence 6	Nil	1 computer	No	No (note 2)
	Residence 7	1 computer with internet	1 computer	Yes	Yes (note 2)
	Residence 8	1 computer with internet	1 computer	No	No
	Residence 9	1 computer with internet	1 computer	Yes	No (note 2)
	Residence 10	Nil	1 computer	Yes	Yes (note 2)
	Residence 11	Nil	1 computer (note 3)	No	No
	Residence 12	Nil	1 computer	No (note 4)	Yes

Community	Building	Original status mid-2011	Post transition status early 2014		
	Residence 13				
Total		20 computers with internet	21 computers	10 of 21	10 of 22

Note 1: Computer is now located in Tennant Creek township. Resident obtains internet connection via a smartphone.

Note 2: These houses were demolished and rebuilt during 2013.

Note 3: Computer is not installed in this house at the time of writing.

Note 4: This house had internet connection from January 2013 until end October 2013 i.e. prior to the transition.

Appendix 2: Location and Movement of the Computers in the Communities

Eleven computers were installed in Imangara from late July to early August 2011; two were located in the Women's Centre for use by the general community and by the couple running the Centre, while the remainder were installed in individual houses. Later in the project, an additional three computers were installed in individual houses not originally included in the study (Figure 1). Although this community building is called the Women's Centre, this space is not the exclusive domain of women. Some men regularly visited the Women's Centre, and at least two men were frequent users of its computers during the project.

Figure 1: Location of households in Imangara that participated in the study in July 2011 with later additions up to the end of September 2013 noted

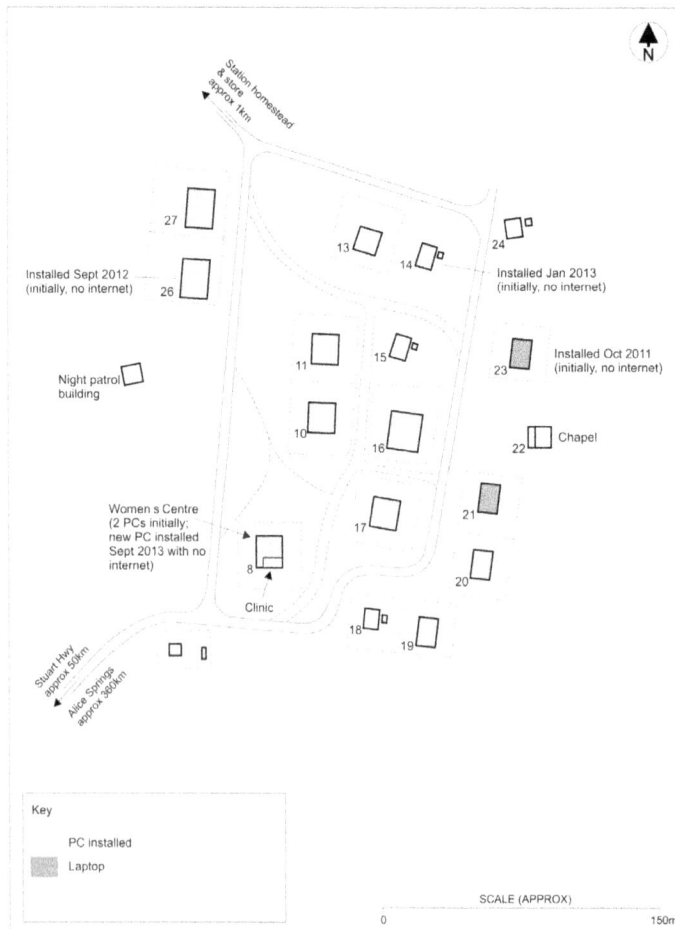

In Mungalawurru, five computers were installed in June 2011, three in individual houses and two in what was referred to as the 'CDEP shed', which was considered to be a public space accessible by all community members (Figure 2). One of these was notionally allocated to a female resident, while the other was understood to be a computer for shared use by those community members who did not receive household computers.

Figure 2: Location of households in Mungalawurru participating in the study in July 2011

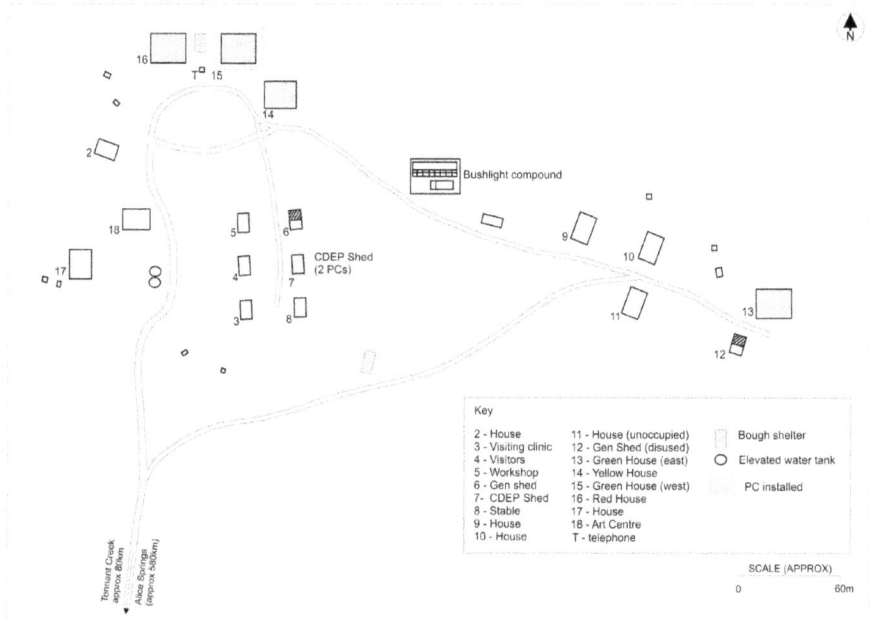

Within the first twelve months of the project's longitudinal phase, 45 per cent of participants at Imangara and 80 per cent of participants at Mungalawurru had signed formal ownership agreements. Additional formal take-up occurred between September 2012 and September 2013: one participant at Mungalawurru, and two residents at Imangara – one of whom was not initially involved in the Home Internet Project study – signed formal ownership agreements. By the end of September 2013, 69 per cent of computers at Imangara and 100 per cent of those at Mungalawurru were subject to formal ownership agreements.

Despite equipment failure, loss or damage, an average of seventeen of the twenty computers installed by early August 2011 were operational during the nine months through to the end of April 2014. (Two computers failed but could be repaired, another was taken out of the community and returned with components missing, and the only laptop was irreparably damaged by a small child.)

Table 2: Failures or losses of core equipment August 2011 to September 2013 inclusive

Item	Total installed population	Qty lost/ removed by resident (A)	Qty failed/ damaged beyond repair (B)	Qty non-functioning and repaired (C)	Mean time between failures (months) (B & C)
Computer	22	2	8	14	26
Monitor	21	2	7	1	68
Computer/ Monitor	22	2	15	15	19
Printer	18	2	22	19	11
UPS	20		8		65
Network	19	2	2	9	45

By comparison with this total of twenty-two computer failures over the twenty-five-month project period, a large survey of failure rates in corporate desktop computers referenced at *http://www.partnerinfo.lenovo.com/partners/us/products/downloads/thinkcentre-mseries/TBR-Quality-Study-ExecSummary.pdf* recorded an average 15.29 per cent failure rate, requiring warranty repair over the first two years of service, or 3.5 failures for an equivalent population of twenty-two computers over twenty-five months.

Table 3: Number of inter- and intra-community computer relocations and removals from the community according to ownership status at the time of relocation/removal, post-installation phase, August 2014, Imangara and Mungalawurru

Incident type and ownership status at time of incident		Imangara	Mungalawurru	Total
Intra-community relocation	Number shared*	2	1	3
	Number nominally owned	2	3	5
	Number Western legal ownership	0	1	1
Removals to Alice Springs by researchers owing to technical failures	Number shared	0	1	1
	Number nominally owned	6	1	7
	Number Western legal ownership	3	3	6
Removals to locations outside of the community by participants	Number shared	0	0	0
	Number nominally owned	2		2
	Number Western legal ownership	1	1	2

Figure 3: Inter- and intra-community computer movements by residents and type of ownership at the time movement occurred, between July 2011 and August 2014, Imangara

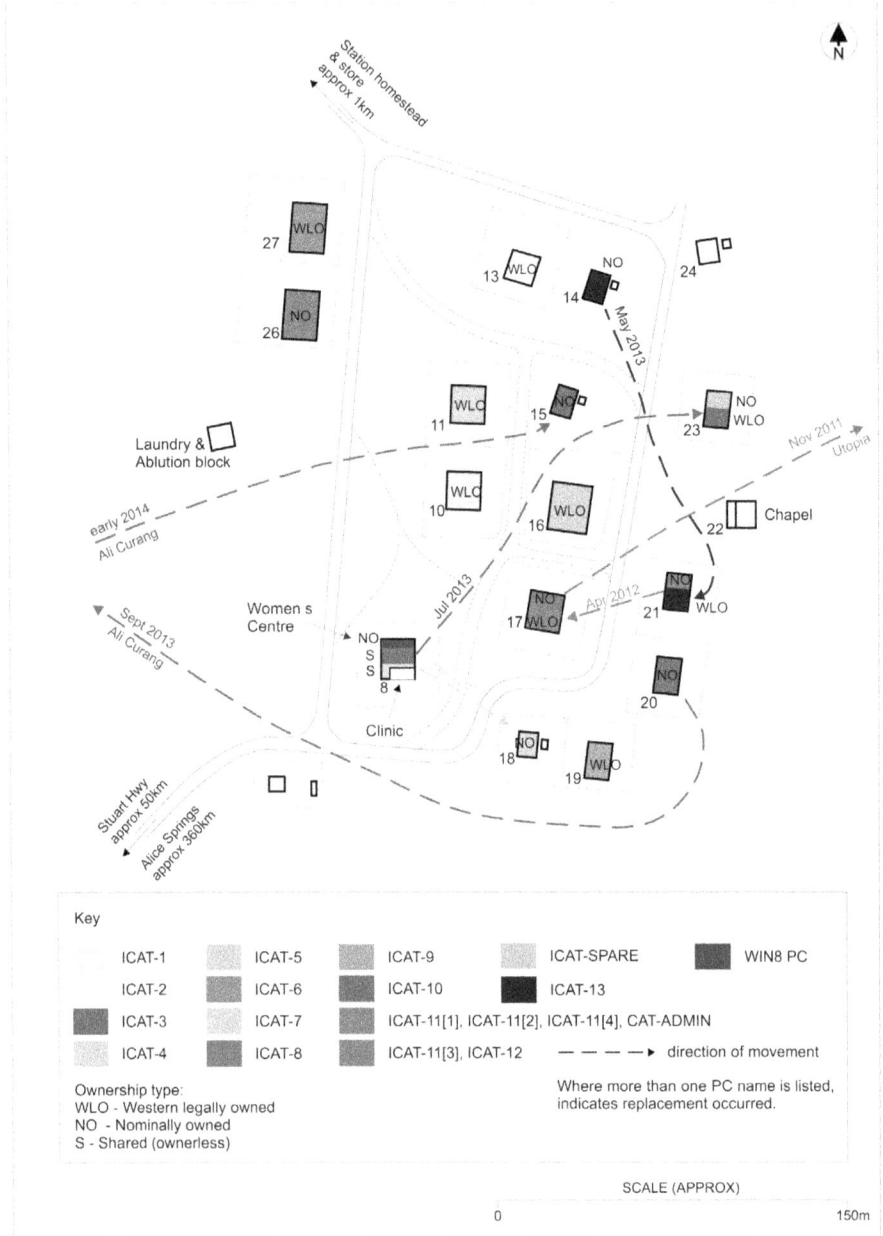

Appendix 3: Gender and Uses

Figure 4: Gender and technical function. Source: Kurt W. Seemann, Matthew Parnell, Stephen McFallan, and Selwyn Tucker. *Housing for Livelihoods: The Lifecycle of Housing and Infrastructure Through a Whole-of-System Approach in Remote Aboriginal Settlements*. Vol. 29, Alice Springs: Desert Knowledge CRC, 2008 (Reproduced with permission of the author).

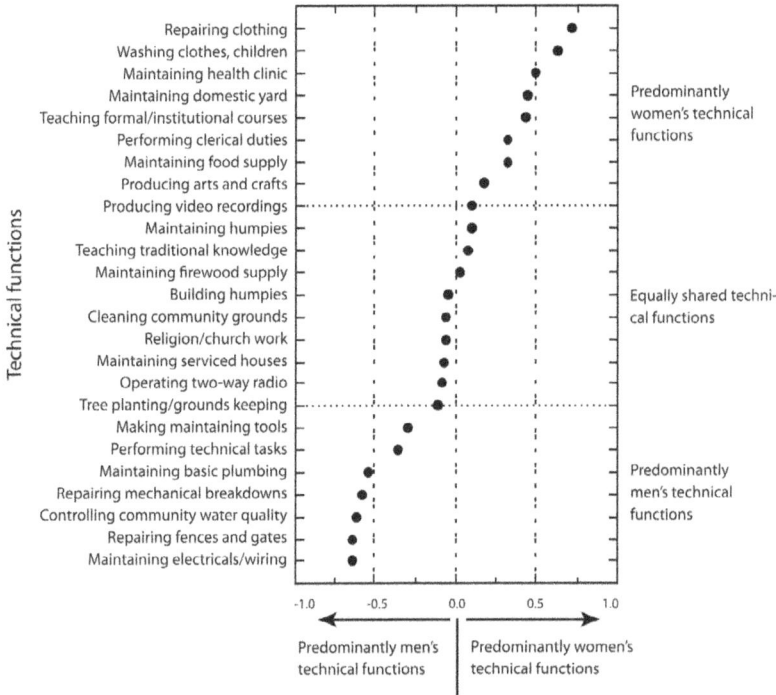

Figure 5: Computer uses (number of users), November 2012

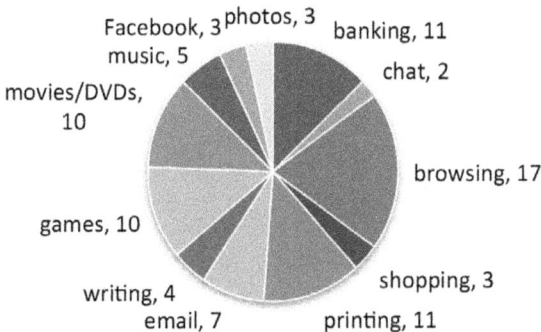

Figure 6: Computer uses (minutes per day), November 2012

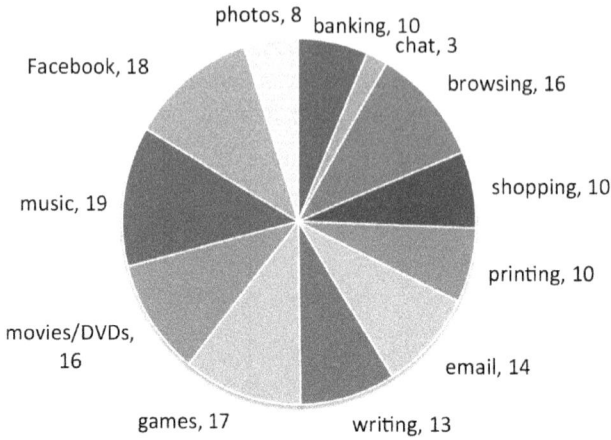

Figure 7: Who uses the computer most often?

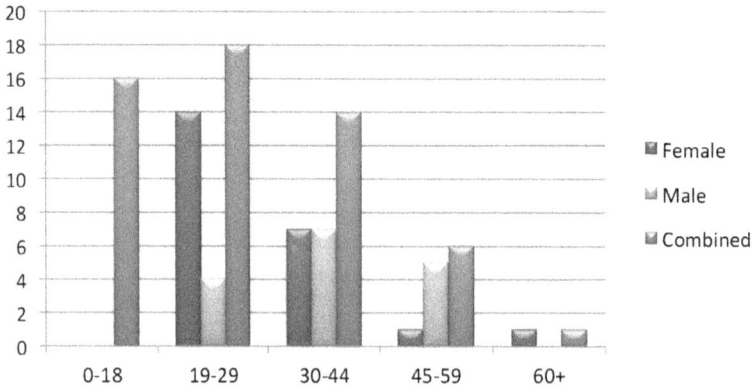

Figure 8: Women's top five ICT activities

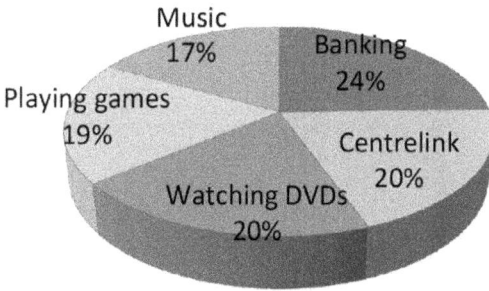

Figure 9: Men's top five ICT activities

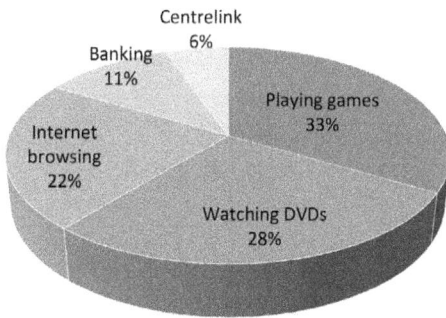

Figure 10: How participants learned new tasks

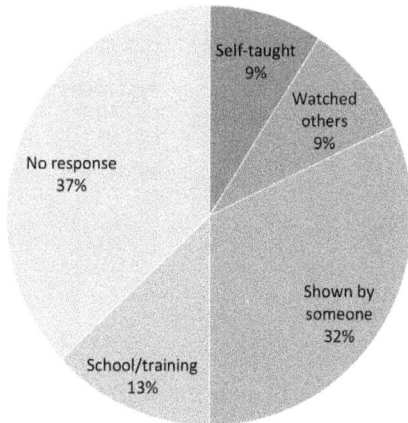

Figure 11: Percentage of each task type requested by learners or suggested by researchers

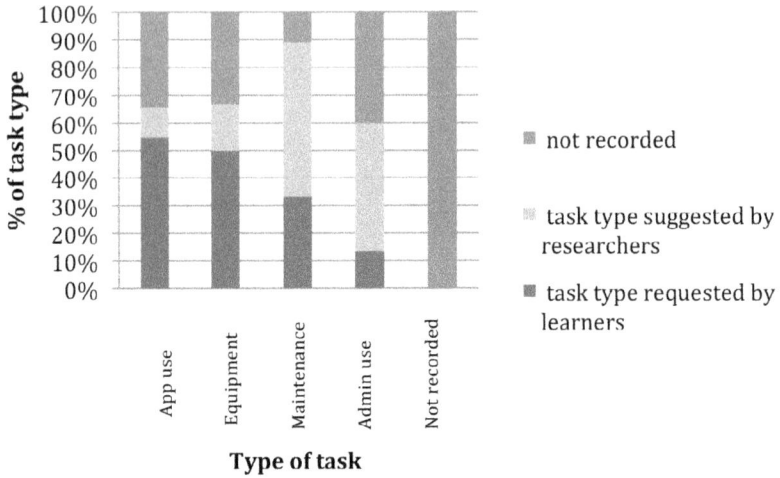

Figure 12: Frequency of the different types of learning tasks
illustrated as a percentage of all learning opportunities during field trips

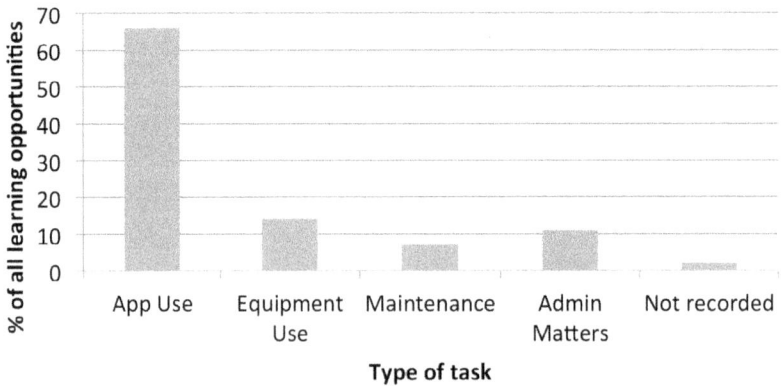

Appendix 4: ICT Program Models and their Features

Table 4: Three community computing program models and their features

Feature	'Home Computing' model (distributed internet facilities and computer in each household)	'Community WiFi', model (centralized internet facilities with users connecting to those using WiFi capable computing devices)	'Community Internet Access Center' model (centralized internet facilities and computers in a supervised room within a community building)
Typical funding model	External funder pays for individual internet connections and computing devices; households pay own internet access fees	External funder pays for internet access and WiFi facilities; users supply their own computing devices	External funder pays for all facilities and supervision
Capital costs	High aggregate cost for individual satellite internet connections and computer hardware at all households	– Medium cost for shared local area network hardware and satellite internet connection at community level – High costs to users for computer hardware	– Medium cost for centralized shared satellite internet access and PC hardware in single building – High building cost (either capital cost for new building or ongoing rental cost for existing building)
Operational costs	– High aggregate internet access charges – High maintenance costs for computing devices (borne by user)	– Medium internet access charges – Low network maintenance costs – High maintenance costs for computing devices (borne by user)	– Medium internet access charges – Low network maintenance costs – Low maintenance costs for computing devices – Very high supervision cost, including supervisor accommodation – Variable building maintenance costs
Overall costs	High	Medium	High
Focus	Family centered	Individual user	Individual user or small groups

Feature	'Home Computing' model (distributed internet facilities and computer in each household)	'Community WiFi', model (centralized internet facilities with users connecting to those using WiFi capable computing devices)	'Community Internet Access Center' model (centralized internet facilities and computers in a supervised room within a community building)
Suitability for mixed gender use	Yes, but the model may encourage use along gender lines, i.e. that the women are responsible for managing and paying for it	Yes, but care needed with placement	Group(s) of one gender may dominate use, making the other reluctant to use the facility
Suitability for young children	Yes	No – access to portable devices unlikely	Yes, with parental supervision
Facilitating school learning	School student friendly with parental support	Limited	Collateral support for schooling with teacher and supervisor collaboration
Suitability for older residents	Yes	Limited – familiarity with mobile computing devices less likely	Group(s) of younger users may dominate use, making older people reluctant to use the facility. Physical access (walking distance) may also be an issue.
Compatibility with capacity offered by NBN satellite consumer services?	High	Medium – multiple satellite services may be needed	Medium – multiple satellite services may be needed
Reliability of network services and equipment	High	High	High
Reliability of computing devices	Low – exposed to home environment	Low – exposed to out-door environment	High – assisted by physical environment and supervision

Feature	'Home Computing' model (distributed internet facilities and computer in each household)	'Community WiFi', model (centralized internet facilities with users connecting to those using WiFi capable computing devices)	'Community Internet Access Center' model (centralized internet facilities and computers in a supervised room within a community building)
Suitability for high level of resident mobility between households?	Low	High – supports portable devices	Varies depending on where residents move to
Limitations	Home environment often not suitable for care of computing hardware (PC, printer)	– Multiple WiFi Access Points required for larger communities – Limited or no coverage within buildings	– Suitable community building may not be available – Only accessible during staffed hours – No option for the resident to own their own computer, so may be seen as 'second choice'